Aim High

Student's Book 2

Tim Falla   Paul A Davies

Paul Kelly

OXFORD

UNIVERSITY PRESS

CONTENTS

1 The real you

Judging by appearances

BEFORE READING

1 What jobs do you think the people in the pictures do? How do you know?

2 What do you think a person's clothes can tell us about them?

READ

What to wear

☐ We shouldn't judge a person by their appearance but we do. In fact, the experts say that when we meet someone for the first time we make a decision about what that person is like in three seconds. But what do we look at? One of the most important things is clothes, but it isn't the brand of clothes that people wear that is important. The important thing is to wear the right clothes for the occasion.

☐ Schools have always understood this and a lot of them ask their students to wear a uniform. Schools where uniforms are not compulsory often give their students a dress code to follow. Why? A lot of teachers think a uniform makes students feel that they are part of their school and that their uniform helps them to be serious about their studies. Teachers say that uniforms can help in other ways too. If all the students wear one, they can't judge each other because of their clothes. They don't know if other students are from rich or poor families. It also avoids arguments about who, or what, is fashionable.

☐ However, it is not only schools that want people to dress in a certain way. We all have ideas that are really stereotypes about what the people in certain professions should wear. If we visit a doctor, we expect to see respectable clothes under the doctor's white coat. When we go into a bank we expect the staff to wear suits or dresses. In fact, a lot of companies have dress codes for their staff because they know that when their customers visit them, they expect to see people dressed in certain types of clothes. Even university students, who often wear a casual 'uniform' of jeans and T-shirts, invest in a suit or dress to attend job interviews in their final year. They know a smart appearance can help them get a job.

☐ But can our clothes really tell people what we are like? Maybe not, but they can show our attitude to what we're doing at that moment. When people see us in the 'right' clothes they think we are serious about what we are doing. Furthermore, if we are clean, smart and polite, people will have confidence in us. But if a person is good at their job, are the clothes they wear really important? Well, would you feel happy visiting a doctor who is wearing a dirty old T-shirt and torn jeans?

1 Read the *Reading tip*. Read the text and match the headings (A–D) with the paragraphs.

A United by clothes
B Are you serious about your job?
C First impressions are important
D Uniforms for everyone

2 🎧 (1.02) Read the text again. Choose the best answers.

1 People
   a decide very quickly what the people they meet are like.
   b only need three seconds to ask about the clothes brands you wear.
   c never judge others on their appearance.
2 Uniforms
   a help students to be serious about clothes.
   b make students understand school is important in their lives.
   c make teachers feel students are a part of their school.
3 Uniforms
   a look the same on rich and poor students.
   b are very fashionable.
   c make students have arguments.
4 University students
   a never wear jeans and T-shirts in their final year.
   b often wear white coats over their casual clothes.
   c know it's important to dress well for an important occasion.
5 Clothes can tell people
   a what we think about our work.
   b what someone studied at university.
   c that we are confident.

3 Which is the best summary of the text?

A A person's appearance doesn't tell us anything about them. Most people know a person's clothes can't tell you if they are good at their job.
B We use clothes to help us make decisions about the people we meet. Clothes can show us what other people are like and how serious they are about the things they are doing.
C Clothes give us a lot of information. Teachers use clothes to make quick decisions about their students.

UNDERSTANDING IDEAS

Answer the questions. Look at the text, and use your own words and ideas.

1 Do you think the author is right about school uniforms? Why / Why not?
2 Do you have stereotyped images of the clothes people should wear for particular jobs? Give some examples.
3 What do you think your clothes can tell people about you?
4 Apart from clothes, what other things do you think tell us what a person is like?

VOCABULARY
What to wear

1 Match the highlighted words in the text with the definitions.

1 Prevents something bad from happening.
2 Considered to be acceptable and correct.
3 Clothes that are for informal situations.
4 To go to or be present at an event or activity.
5 Something damaged by pulling it apart.
6 To form an opinion about something, using the information you have.
7 Ideas that are sometimes wrong, about what someone or something is like.
8 Opinions or feelings that you show by your behaviour.
9 The name of a product made by a particular company.
10 To use your money in a way that is good for you.
11 Popular at a particular time.
12 The people who work for a particular company or organization.
13 To think that something will happen.
14 A set of rules about what people should wear.
15 The belief that you can do things well.

2 Do you know these words?

appearance   certain   compulsory   decision
furthermore   occasion   profession   uniform

(●●●○ Workbook: page 4)

What to wear

ACTIVATE

Complete these sentences with the correct form of the words from the box.

> attend attitude avoid brand casual confidence
> dress code expect fashionable invest judge respectable
> stereotypes staff torn

1 I like to wear a suit for work. I think it's important to wear something _____ at work. However, at home I usually wear _____ clothes like jeans or a tracksuit.
2 I try to _____ listening to the _____ that people have of different countries. I know it often rains in Britain but I'm sure people don't spend all their time walking around under an umbrella!
3 There are rules about clothes for the people that work in my company. The _____ says all _____ must wear suits.
4 My boss thinks it's fine if we wear T-shirts and jeans, but they must be clean and they can't be _____ or have holes in them! He says that if someone is dirty and untidy, it shows a bad _____ to their work.
5 When he _____ the interview, he came to the office in very nice clothes. We thought he was perfect for the company and we _____ him to be a good worker. However, he was terrible! I'm not going to _____ people by their appearances any more!
6 People today want to be _____ and dress in the most popular clothes. They are also happy to pay for expensive clothes just because they have the name of a famous _____ on them!
7 I read in a magazine that good clothes can give you _____ and make you feel you can do things well. So I'm going to _____ some money in a few new suits and buy some expensive shoes, too!

EXTEND

dress and *wear*

1 Complete the sentences with the correct forms of the verbs *dress* and *wear*.

1 The students are wearing jeans and T-shirts.
2 My dad usually _____ in dark colours.
3 What were they _____?
4 It's an informal celebration. You don't have to _____ up.
5 My sister needs an hour to get _____ in the morning.
6 She _____ a beautiful white dress at her wedding last Saturday.
7 I love helping my sister to _____ her baby.
8 Don't _____ those football boots in the house!

Uniforms

2 Match the words in the box with the pictures.

> overalls a wig and gown an apron a white coat
> a wetsuit a tracksuit a jumpsuit

1 a white coat   3 _____   5 _____   7 _____
2 _____   4 _____   6 _____

3 Answer the questions with the words in the box.

> a mechanic a diver a judge a coach a chef a physician

Who wears
1 a white coat? a physician   4 an apron? _____
2 overalls? _____   5 a wetsuit? _____
3 a tracksuit? _____   6 a wig and gown? _____

Definitions: advertising

4 Match the words (1–6) with the definitions (a–f).

1 brand   a a short sentence in an advertisement that is easy to remember.
2 design   b the name of a product made by particular company.
3 label   c a symbol or design that a company uses as its sign.
4 logo   d the materials that companies use to cover their products.
5 slogan   e a piece of paper or material that gives information about the product it is on.
6 packaging   f the drawings and plans for a new product before a company makes it.

Prepositions: *in, off, on* and *up*

5 Complete the sentences with the prepositions *in*, *off*, *on* and *up*.

1 It was very hot so I took my coat off.
2 Can you see the girl _____ the red dress? That's my sister.
3 Jack! Put your socks _____ before your shoes!
4 Do your coat _____. It's raining!
5 I don't think you look good _____ that suit.
6 Pull _____ your sleeves before you wash your hands!
7 Yes, I like this dress. Can I try it _____, please?
8 Boys! Take _____ your football boots before you come in the house!

(●●●●● Workbook: page 5)

GRAMMAR

Present simple and continuous

EXPLORE

1 Read the text messages. What does Ed think of the wedding?

> **Pete**
> Hi Ed. Are you having a good time?

> **Ed**
> No, I'm not. I don't know many people here. I'm not talking to anyone. And I'm wearing a silly tie!

> **Pete**
> A tie?! You never wear ties. Send me a photo! I need a laugh. By the way, I'm going to my cousin's wedding next weekend.

> **Ed**
> Do you like weddings? They're so boring. My grandad always falls asleep. He's got the right idea!

2 Look at the table. Find examples of the present simple and present continuous in the text messages.

Present simple	
affirmative	She always wears jeans.
negative	He doesn't like impatient people.
interrogative	Do you want a drink?

Present continuous	
affirmative	She's sending a text message.
negative	They aren't wearing any shoes.
interrogative	Is he playing the keyboard?

3 Complete the rules in the *Learn this!* box with the correct tense.

LEARN THIS!

1 We use the _____ for something that always or regularly happens.
2 We use the _____ for something that is happening now.
3 We use the _____ for a fact that is always true.
4 We use the _____ for arrangements in the future.
5 We don't use the _____ with certain verbs, e.g. *believe, hate, like, love, need, know, prefer, want.*

●○○○○ Grammar Reference: page 94

EXPLOIT

1 What are the people doing? Write sentences, using the verbs in the box.

Useful verbs carry chat drink eat hold laugh listen relax ~~sit~~ smile stand text

A girl is sitting at a table. She's smiling.

2 🎧 (1.03) Complete the dialogue with the present simple or present continuous form of the verbs in brackets. Listen and check.

Dave Hello. [1]*Are you enjoying* (you / enjoy) the music?
Ed Not really. I [2]_____ (prefer) world music. This group is terrible.
Dave It's my dad's group.
Ed Oh, right. Actually, they [3]_____ (not play) badly now. Lots of people [4]_____ (listen). Which one is your dad?
Dave He [5]_____ (play) the guitar.
Ed He's good! Anyway, I [6]_____ (not know) your name.
Dave I'm Dave.
Ed I'm Ed. Pleased to meet you.
Dave Hey, I [7]_____ (like) your suit. It's cool.
Ed I [8]_____ (not wear) it very often. I have a different suit for work.
Dave I [9]_____ (work) on a farm for the summer so I [10]_____ (wear) jeans every day.
Ed Lucky you!

3 Look at the table. Make two true sentences with each verb, using the present simple and present continuous.

Verbs	Nouns	Time phrases
go	my homework	after school
speak	jeans	every day
wear	English	at the moment
do	computer games	today
play	to town	next week
	to school	at weekends
	this exercise	this weekend

I don't go to school at weekends.
I'm going to town after school.

●●●○○ Grammar Builder: page 95

●●○○○ Workbook: page 6

Personalities
VOCABULARY

1 Look at the photos. Is each person:
- kind or unkind?
- funny or serious?
- lazy or hard-working?
- generous or mean?

I think she is serious.

2 Match the personality adjectives in A with their opposites in B.

Personality adjectives

A
considerate
well mannered
optimistic
assertive
talkative
amusing
lazy
generous
patient

B
bad mannered
timid
pessimistic
quiet
thoughtless
mean
hard-working
earnest
impatient

3 🎧 (1.04) Listen, repeat and check.

4 Match an adjective from exercise 2 with each definition.
1 Not wanting to work. lazy
2 Wanting to keep money for yourself rather than share it with others.
3 Expecting bad things to happen.
4 Having good manners and showing respect for others.
5 Making very little noise.
6 Making people smile or laugh.
7 Caring about other people.
8 Being calm when there is a problem or when you have to wait.

5 What type of person is being described? Circle the correct adjectives.
1 'I don't want to speak to any of your friends.'
   unfriendly / lazy
2 'Here, take the money and give it me back when you can.'
   shy / generous
3 'I'm sure we'll win the match and that you'll score two goals!' unkind / optimistic
4 'He just pushes people out of the way and he never says "please" or "thank you!" rude / talkative
5 'He's in the office at 6 a.m. every day and he doesn't leave until 8 p.m.' hard-working / friendly
6 'I've worked hard and I really think I'll pass the exams.'
   polite / confident
7 'She's really nice but she never smiles or laughs.'
   serious / generous
8 'Mum, is dinner ready? I'm hungry! When will it be ready?'
   mean / impatient

(●●●●●● Workbook: page 7)

LISTEN

🎧 (1.05) Listen to the dialogues and match an adjective in the box with each person in the table. You will not need all the words.

generous	impatient	lazy	pessimistic	rude	shy

1 Martin	
2 Julie	
3 Terry	
4 Emma	

SPEAK

1 Make notes about three friends or relatives. What personality adjectives can you use to describe them? Give reasons.

Ahmed (brother) – lazy – doesn't help around the house
Hana (sister) ...

2 Tell the class about your friends or relatives.

My brother, Ahmed, is very lazy. He never does any work around the house. My sister, Hana, is ...

Verb + infinitive or -ing form

EXPLORE

1 Answer the questions.

Are you FEARLESS or PHOBIC?

1 You want to have a shower but there's a big spider. Do you
  a avoid having a shower?
  b have a shower anyway?

2 You're in a situation where there are a lot of people you don't know. Do you
  a decide to leave?
  b spend time making new friends?

3 Travelling by plane is very safe, but what is your opinion of flying?
  a I can't help feeling nervous.
  b I don't mind flying at all.

4 Somebody offers to give you a free ticket to a big concert. Do you
  a say no because you can't stand being in a very large crowd of people?
  b accept the ticket?

5 You're in a lift when it gets stuck. Do you
  a feel scared because you imagine being in the lift for hours?
  b wait patiently and hope to be free soon?

6 A friend suggests doing a bungee jump. Do you
  a refuse to do it because you're afraid of heights?
  b agree to do it?

2 Look at your answers and count the *a*s and *b*s. Are you fearless (mostly *b*s) or phobic (mostly *a*s)?

3 Study the information in the *Learn this!* box. Find all the verbs in the questionnaire that are followed by the infinitive or *-ing* form of another verb.

LEARN THIS!

1 Some verbs are followed by the infinitive of another verb.
I'm pretending to be ill.

2 Some verbs are followed by the *-ing* form of another verb.
I don't fancy going out tonight.

4 Complete the table with the verbs that you found in the questionnaire.

Verb + infinitive	Verb + *-ing* form
pretend	fancy

●●○○○ Grammar Reference: page 94

EXPLOIT

1 Complete the sentences with the infinitive or *-ing* form of the verbs in the box.

be   chat   feel   pass   ~~help~~   pay   study   wait

1 My dad is really kind. He always offers to help people.
2 I'm quite optimistic. I usually expect _____ my exams.
3 My friend Sarah is really impatient. She can't stand _____.
4 Sammy is really generous. He always offers _____.
5 Jane is very hard-working. She doesn't mind _____ for hours.
6 I'm very ambitious. I often imagine _____ rich and famous.
7 Alex is so talkative! He keeps _____ even when nobody is listening!
8 My sister is so shy. She can't help _____ nervous when a stranger talks to her.

2 Complete the sentences with an infinitive or *-ing* form and true information about yourself.

1 I usually avoid …
2 I really can't stand …
3 I don't mind …
4 I spend a lot of time …
5 I really want …
6 I sometimes pretend …

3 Tell the class your sentences. Does anybody have the same answers?

●●●○○ Grammar Builder: page 95

●●●○○ Workbook: page 8

A personal profile

READ

Read the profiles. Answer the questions for each person.

1 How old are they?
2 What year are they in at school?
3 Which sports do they like?
4 What other hobbies and interests do they have?
5 What personality adjectives do they use to describe themselves?

The real me   by Martin

My name is Martin and I'm from London. I'm 16 years old and I'm in Year 11 at Parkfield School.

I've got lots of hobbies and interests. I love playing chess and computer games with my brother. I also do a lot of sport – I particularly enjoy swimming and karate. I'm also interested in photography.

I'm quite an ambitious person. I want to go to university and then get a job in web design. I think I'm quite hard-working, too. I've probably got a few faults. I think I'm slightly impatient and maybe a little intolerant too.

The real me   by Sarah

My name is Sarah. I'm 17 and I go to Greenhill School. I'm in Year 12. I live with my parents and my brother Jake.

My hobbies are reading and listening to the radio. I'm not very keen on sport, but I play volleyball at school.

I'm not a timid person at all and I prefer talking to other confident people. I think I'm considerate and very loyal to my friends.

PREPARE

1 Read the profiles again. How have the writers organized their information? Use the headings in the box to complete the writing plan. Then add information about yourself.

> Personality   Introduction   Hobbies and interests

> **Paragraph 1:**
> •
> •
>
> **Paragraph 2:**
> •
> •
>
> **Paragraph 3:**
> •
> •

2 Read the *Writing tip*. Underline all the modifying adverbs in the personal profiles.

Writing tip: using modifying adverbs

We use modifying adverbs to make the meaning of adjectives stronger or weaker.

not at all   a little   slightly   quite   very   really

LOOK OUT!

> 1 Modifying adverbs usually go before the adjective.
>   She is really tired.
> 2 *quite* goes before *a / an* when there is a noun.
>   My brother is quite a good football player.
> 3 *not at all* is split by *a / an* and the noun.
>   He's not a hard-working student at all.

3 Rewrite the sentences to include the modifying adverb in brackets.

1 I'm pessimistic. (slightly)
2 My best friend is assertive. (really)
3 He's an impatient person. (not at all)
4 I'm a student at a big school. (quite)
5 I find English difficult. (quite)
6 I'm sometimes shy. (a little)

WRITE

Write your personal profile. Use your writing plan and notes in Prepare exercise 1. Write 80–100 words.

Check your work

Have you

☐ organized your information into paragraphs?
☐ used modifying adjectives?
☐ checked your spelling and grammar?

●●●●○ Workbook: page 9

The real you
LANGUAGE SKILLS

1 🎧 (1.06) Complete the dialogue with the words from the box. Then listen and check your answers.

> prefer ambitious confident on little interests lot interested for at

Sally	Hi, Claire. What are you doing?
Claire	I'm waiting ¹_____ my cousin Anna.
Sally	Is she coming to the theatre with us?
Claire	Yes, she is. She's really ²_____ in the theatre. She's in the school theatre group.
Sally	I love going to the theatre but I'm not keen ³_____ acting. I'm very shy.
Claire	Well, my cousin isn't a shy person ⁴_____ all. She's really ⁵_____.
Sally	What other ⁶_____ has she got?
Claire	She enjoys writing. She writes for the school theatre group. She's very ⁷_____ and she wants to be a writer.
Sally	I'm not very good at writing! It's hard work and I'm a ⁸_____ lazy when I have to write. I ⁹_____ photography. I'm always taking photos.
Claire	You can say a ¹⁰_____ with a photo!
Sally	Yes, and it's easier than writing. Well, it is for me!

2 Decide if the sentences are true or false. Correct the false sentences.

1 Sally isn't going to the theatre with Claire and Anna.
2 Anna enjoys being in the school theatre group.
3 Sally likes acting in front of other people.
4 Claire writes for the school theatre group.
5 Anna wants to do very well as a writer.
6 Sally is always lazy.

3 Circle the correct verb form.

1 **Do you go** / **Are you going** to the gym every day?
2 They **fly** / **'re flying** to Sydney next Sunday.
3 She **doesn't like** / **isn't liking** making her bed.
4 **Are you doing** / **Do you doing** your homework right now?
5 We **finish** / **'re finishing** school early on Fridays.
6 I **play** / **'m playing** tennis on Thursday evenings.
7 He **'s wearing** / **wears** a hat and a scarf in the winter.

4 Complete the sentences with the verb + infinitive or *-ing* form.

1 He refused _____ (tell) me the answer.
2 I can't help _____ (cry) every time I read that story.
3 We wanted _____ (go) home but they made more coffee.
4 My dad decided _____ (change) jobs yesterday!
5 My mum doesn't mind _____ (cook) lunch for all of us.
6 He avoided _____ (talk) about the exams.
7 I spend a lot of time _____ (study) English on the internet.
8 She pretended not _____ (see) me when I entered the shop.

DICTIONARY CORNER

Personality adjectives

1 Check the meaning of the personality adjectives in the box and match them with the descriptions.

> ~~cheerful~~ flexible helpful punctual reliable sensitive

1 Monday morning or Friday afternoon, Jack is always happy.
   cheerful
2 Louise always does what she says she is going to do. Always!
3 Mike is at the office at 8 a.m. every morning. He never arrives late.
4 Sarah is happy to work alone or in a team.
5 Alice does all the work in the house for her mother.
6 Frank thinks about what other people think and feel.

Prefixes and suffixes

2 Add the correct prefix to form the opposite adjective.

> flexible ~~kind~~ patient polite reliable sensitive

un-	im-	in-
¹unkind	³_____	⁵_____
²_____	⁴_____	⁶_____

3 Write the noun forms of the adjectives, using a suffix.

adjective	noun	adjective	noun
kind	¹kindness	patient	⁵_____
rude	²_____	lazy	⁶_____
generous	³_____	flexible	⁷_____
reliable	⁴_____	punctual	⁸_____

I CAN ...

Read the statements. Think about your progress and tick (✓) one of the boxes.

✴ I need more practice.
✴✴ I sometimes find this difficult.
✴✴✴ No problem!

	✴	✴✴	✴✴✴
I can understand an article about uniforms and dress code.			
I can say what I usually do and what I'm doing now.			
I can describe someone's personality.			
I can identify and use different verb patterns.			
I can write a personal profile.			

●●●○○ Workbook: Self check pages 10–11

2 Winning and losing

THIS UNIT INCLUDES ● ● ● ◉

Vocabulary • sports • phrasal verbs with *set* • prepositions of movement • expressions with *play* • *do / play / go* + sports • water sports • sporting terms • football

Grammar • past simple • contrast: past simple and continuous

Skills • listening to sports commentaries • talking about favourite sports

Writing • a magazine article

Surf's up

BEFORE READING

Make a list of some water sports. Which water sports do you think are sometimes dangerous? Why?

READ

> **Reading tip**
>
> Use the title and the pictures to make predictions about what is in the text.

1 Read the *Reading tip*. Look at the title of the article and the photos. Then answer the questions.

1 What do you think the title tells you about the girl in the photo?
2 Do you notice anything unusual about the surfer in the photos? What do you think happened to her?
3 Do you think what happened to the girl has changed her life as a surfer?

Surfing superstar!

On the morning of 31 October 2003 Bethany Hamilton set off to go surfing with some friends in Hawaii. There wasn't a cloud in the sky, the sun was shining and it was a perfect day for surfing on the big waves near the shores of Kauai island.

The 13-year-old surfing star was lying face down on her surfboard about 300 metres from the beach. She was waiting for the next big wave, and her arms were hanging in the clear, blue water. Suddenly a five-metre tiger shark sank its sharp teeth into her left arm and shook her backwards and forwards. Bethany gripped her board with her other hand and battled for her life. Finally, the shark swam away but unfortunately it took

her left arm with it. It also took a huge piece of her board. The attack happened so fast that Bethany didn't even have time to scream.

At that time Bethany was an outstanding teenage surfer, and was planning to become professional. As soon as she was attacked, she started worrying about her future career and thought: 'Will I lose my sponsors?' Fortunately, her survival instinct took control and she slowly headed for the beach. Her friends didn't see the attack, and as Bethany started swimming towards them, using only one arm, they thought at first that she was playing a joke on them. Then they saw her terrible wound and rushed to help.

2 Now read the text and check your answers to questions 1 to 3.

3 🎧 (1.10) Read the text again. Choose the best answers.

1 When Bethany went surfing
   a the weather was cloudy.
   b the conditions were good for surfing.
   c there were dangerous waves around Kauai island.
2 When the shark attacked, Bethany was
   a standing on her surfboard.
   b swimming backwards and forwards.
   c going to surf soon.
3 The shark
   a took all of Bethany's surfboard.
   b left when Bethany screamed.
   c pulled Bethany in different directions.
4 After the attack, Bethany
   a started thinking about her family.
   b swam to the beach.
   c became a professional surfer.
5 Bethany
   a was back in the sea very quickly.
   b spent a long time in hospital.
   c became world champion soon after the accident.

4 Put the events in the correct order.

☐ The shark swam away.
☐ Ten weeks later she took part in a surfing competition.
☐ She started to swim back to the beach.
☐ Bethany decided to go surfing with some friends.
☐ Her friends saw the blood and came to help her.
☐ While she was waiting for a wave, a shark attacked her.

UNDERSTANDING IDEAS

Answer the questions. Look at the text, and use your own words and ideas.

1 Why do you think people like surfing? Try to think of two or three reasons.
2 Bethany didn't immediately swim to the beach after the attack. Why?
3 Bethany was surfing again very soon after the attack. What does this tell you about Bethany? Think of some adjectives to describe her personality.

VOCABULARY

Surfing superstar!

1 Match the highlighted words in the text with the definitions.

1 An injury to a part of the body.
2 Certain to happen.
3 To become healthy again after an illness or accident.
4 Tried very hard to deal with a dangerous situation.
5 In the direction of somebody or something.
6 Left on a journey.
7 Extremely good at something.
8 Held something strongly.
9 Having a thin edge that can cut things easily.
10 Moved in the direction of a place.
11 Went under the surface of a soft object.
12 The natural force that helps us in dangerous situations.
13 Did something quickly.
14 Businesses that pay sports stars to advertise their services or products.
15 With the front towards the ground.

2 Do you know these words?

backwards and forwards   career   compete   champion
professional   shake   shore   surfer   unfortunately

ost people take a long time to recuperate from an attack like the
e Bethany had. However, ten weeks after the shark attack Bethany
as competing again and less than a year after the accident she won
st place in a surfing competition in Hawaii. Before the accident a
of professional surfers thought that Bethany was destined to be
e women's world champion. Very few of them have changed
eir opinion.

(●●●○ Workbook: page 12)

VOCABULARY

Surfing superstar!

ACTIVATE

Complete these sentences with the correct form of the words from the box.

> battle   destined   face down   grip   head for   outstanding
> recuperate   rush   set off   sharp   sink   sponsor
> survival instinct   towards   wound

1 Don't play with that knife! It's very _____.
2 The ambulance quickly _____ the injured man to hospital.
3 He's an _____ player. I think he's the best in the team.
4 When the lion ran _____ us we thought he was going to attack. We were really frightened!
5 When I go to sleep I always lie _____ on my bed.
6 She cut herself badly with a knife and the _____ took a long time to heal.
7 We left the theatre and slowly _____ home.
8 It took me a long time to _____ from the illness. I was in bed for six months.
9 We _____ from home at 10 a.m. but we didn't arrive until late in the evening.
10 That dog is really dangerous. It _____ its teeth into my friend's leg.
11 Our football team has got a new _____. Their name is on the front of our shirts.
12 It was _____ that made me jump out of the way of the car. I didn't think about it!
13 I _____ my bag but the thief was stronger than me and he pulled it from me.
14 My grandmother and my mother were doctors, so I was _____ to be one too.
15 The firemen _____ with the fire for four hours before they could control it.

EXTEND

Phrasal verbs with *set*

1 Complete the definitions for the phrasal verbs with the words in the box.

> start   keep or save   arrive and stay   attack   delay   stop

1 **set sth aside:** to keep or save sth for use later.
2 **set sth back:** to _____ the progress of sb / sth.
3 **set sb down:** to _____ to let a passenger get out.
4 **set in:** to _____ for a period of time, especially an illness or bad weather.
5 **set off:** to _____ a journey.
6 **set on sb:** to _____ sb suddenly.

2 Complete the sentences with the correct form of the phrasal verbs from exercise 1.

1 The cold weather sets in early in Scotland.
2 The taxi driver _____ us _____ at the airport but he forgot to give us our suitcases!
3 The thieves _____ the man as he left the bank.
4 Our teacher _____ the start of the game _____ because the other team arrived late.
5 We've got a school trip tomorrow and the coach _____ at 9 o'clock.
6 My dad _____ some money _____ every month for the holidays.

Prepositions of movement

3 Complete the text with the prepositions of movement in the box.

> towards   through   across   into   along   up

Walk [1] across the road to the building on the other side. Go [2]_____ the building and go [3]_____ in the lift to the tenth floor. There's a long corridor. Go [4]_____ the corridor [5]_____ the big window at the end. Before you get to the end of the corridor turn left and go [6]_____ the big wooden doors. They are waiting for you there, in the meeting room.

Expressions with *play*

4 Match the expressions with their definitions.

1 play a joke on someone   a behave in a silly way
2 play along with something   b play something that is recorded on a machine
3 play the fool   c do something slowly so you have more time to do it
4 play for time   d use your opportunities well
5 play something back   e trick somebody
6 play with fire   f be calm in a difficult situation
7 play it cool   g take a risk
8 play your cards right   h pretend to agree with someone

●●●●● Workbook: page 13

GRAMMAR

Past simple

EXPLORE

1 Read the text and find the following past simple forms.

    1 two affirmative regular verbs
    2 two forms of *be* (singular and plural)
    3 two affirmative irregular verbs
    4 a negative form and an interrogative form

On 21 November 1945, Arsenal played Dynamo Moscow in London. It was very foggy that day. In the first half, the referee sent off an Arsenal player, but he came back on a few minutes later. The referee didn't notice because of the fog! Dynamo Moscow cheated too. At one moment in the second half, fifteen Moscow players were on the pitch at the same time! How did the match finish? Dynamo Moscow 4, Arsenal 3.

2 Complete the table with the correct past simple form of *play*, *go* or *do*.

Past simple
affirmative
I ¹_____ basketball at the gym yesterday.
We ²_____ surfing last Saturday.
negative
My sister ³_____ gymnastics until she was seven.
interrogative
⁴_____ they ⁵_____ swimming in the sea?

3 🎧 (1.11) Listen and repeat the past simple forms. How is the *-ed* ending pronounced? Write the correct sound next to each verb: /d/ /t/ or /ɪd/.

    1 played   d   5 scored   ___
    2 cheated ___   6 competed ___
    3 finished ___   7 passed   ___
    4 kicked   ___   8 watched ___

◖●●●◗ Grammar Reference: page 96

EXPLOIT

1 🎧 (1.12) Complete the stories using the past simple form of the verbs in brackets. Listen and check.

At the Sydney Olympics in 2000, the biggest cheer from the spectators at the swimming pool ¹came (come) when Eric Moussambani ²_____ (finish) the 100-metres freestyle. Eric ³_____ (not win) the event. In fact, his time ⁴_____ (be) 1 minute 53 seconds, the slowest time in Olympic history. Eric, from Equatorial Guinea in Africa, only ⁵_____ (learn) to swim eight months before he ⁶_____ (compete) in the Olympics.

In a tennis match in 1998 between Pete Sampras and Patrick Rafter, Rafter ⁷_____ (become) angry with himself when he ⁸_____ (miss) an easy shot. He ⁹_____ (give) his racket to Chad Little, one of the ball boys, and ¹⁰_____ (shout): 'You play!' Chad ¹¹_____ (not know) what to do, so he ¹²_____ (get) ready to play the next point against Sampras. More than 10,000 spectators ¹³_____ (cheer).

2 Complete the questions about the stories.

    1 Did Eric win the 100 metres freestyle?
       No, he didn't. He finished last.
    2 What _____ time?
       1 minute 53 seconds.
    3 When _____ to swim?
       Eight months before the Olympics.
    4 Why _____ angry?
       Because he missed an easy shot.
    5 What _____ to Chad Little?
       His racket.
    6 What _____ to Chad Little?
       'You play!'

3 Write three sentences about what happened last weekend, two true and one false.

My uncle Stan visited us and we went to a football match.

4 Tell the class your sentences. The class votes on which sentence they think is false.

●●●●◗ Grammar Builder: page 97

●●●●◗ Workbook: page 14

A question of sport

VOCABULARY

1 What sport are they talking about? Match twelve of the words in the box with the sentences.

> **Sports** athletics ~~badminton~~ baseball basketball
> cycling football golf gymnastics ice hockey judo
> karate rugby surfing swimming table tennis
> tennis volleyball weightlifting

1 'You win a game when you get 21 points.' badminton
2 'A player can't touch the ball two times in a row.'
3 'It was a dead heat. Both runners finished in 10.85 seconds.'
4 'It's the final of the ladies' singles at Wimbledon today.'
5 'That's his third goal in the World Cup final. It's a hat trick!'
6 'She's thrown her opponent onto the mat.'
7 'Dribbling is when you run along the court bouncing the ball.'
8 'The fielder is the person who tries to catch the ball.'
9 'She lifted 128 kilograms to break the world record.'
10 'It was very close! The ball stopped 10 centimetres from the hole.'
11 'They don't use a ball. They use a puck.'
12 'He ran 60 metres along the pitch and scored a try.'

2 🎧 (1.13) Listen, repeat and check.

3 Read the information in the *Look out!* box. Match the other sports from exercise 1 to the three verbs.

> **LOOK OUT!**
>
> We normally use
> ***play*** with team sports and ball sports: *play badminton*
> ***go*** with sports that end in *-ing*: *go cycling*
> ***do*** with other sports: *do athletics*

(●●●●● Workbook: page 15)

LISTEN

🎧 (1.14) Listen to eight short sports commentaries. Identify the sports.

1 _____	3 _____	5 _____	7 _____
2 _____	4 _____	6 _____	8 _____

SPEAK

1 Work in pairs. Ask and answer the questions. Make notes of your partner's answers.

1 What sports do you enjoy doing?
2 When do you do them?
3 Where do you do them?
4 What sports do you enjoy watching on TV?
5 Who / What are your favourite players / teams?

2 Tell the class about your partner.

> Laila enjoys doing athletics and going swimming. She ...

3 Work in pairs. Ask and answer the questions. Then check your scores.

Are you a sports fan?

(a)

1 Who are the people in the photos?
a _____
b _____
c _____

2 Who won the 2008 Africa Cup?
a ☐ Cameroon
b ☐ Egypt
c ☐ Ghana

3 Would you prefer to
a ☐ do sport with friends?
b ☐ watch sport on TV?
c ☐ chat with friends?

(b)

4 Would you prefer to be
a ☐ a TV sports presenter?
b ☐ a famous sportsperson?
c ☐ a famous film star?

5 How often do you watch sport on TV?
a ☐ More than once a week
b ☐ About once a week
c ☐ About once a month
d ☐ Never

(c)

ints for each correct answer.

points	b 2 points	c 0 points	
points	b 2 points	c 0 points	
point	b 2 points	c 0 points	
points	b 2 points	c 1 point	d 0 points

5 points You are sports mad!
points You like sport but there are other things in life.
oints You aren't really interested in sport.

Past simple and continuous

EXPLORE

1 Look at the **past continuous forms** in the text. Complete the table with the correct form of the verb *be.*

On 1 August 1976, Niki Lauda **was racing** in the German Grand Prix when he had a terrible accident. The weather was bad – it **was raining**. While Lauda **was going** round a corner, he suddenly lost control of his Ferrari. The car crashed and caught fire. Another driver, Guy Edwards, **was coming** towards the corner when he saw Lauda inside the burning car. He stopped and pulled Lauda out.

Past continuous
affirmative
I ¹_____ sleeping. We ²_____ reading.
negative
It ³_____ raining. They ⁴_____ listening.
interrogative
⁵_____ you playing? What ⁶_____ he doing?

2 Study the information in the *Learn this!* box. Find one example of each use in the text in exercise 1.

> 1 We use the **past continuous** to describe a scene in the past.
> *The sun was shining. Birds were singing.*
>
> 2 We use the **past simple** for a sequence of actions or events that happened one after the other.
> *I stood up, walked to the door and left the room.*
>
> 3 We use the **past continuous** and the **past simple** together when we describe a sudden action or event that interrupted a longer action or event.
> *While I was walking to school, my phone rang.*
> [longer action]   [interruption]

●●●●● Grammar Reference: page 96

EXPLOIT

1 Complete the text with the past simple or past continuous form of the verbs in brackets.

> It was 17 March, 1984. Thousands of people ¹were standing (stand) on the banks of the river Thames in London. They ²_____ (wait) for the start of the annual Oxford and Cambridge Boat Race. But while the Cambridge boat ³_____ (go) under a bridge, it ⁴_____ (hit) another boat. Soon, it was clear that the boat ⁵_____ (sink), so they ⁶_____ (row) to the bank. The race ⁷_____ (take place) the next day – and Cambridge ⁸_____ (lose).

2 Work in pairs. Look at the cartoon story and answer the questions. Use the words in brackets to help you.

1 What was the weather like? (the sun / shine, warm)
   What was the girl doing? (sit / on a bench, watch / baseball match)
2 What did the player do? (hit the ball)
   What did the dog do? (run onto the pitch)
3 What did the dog do next? (catch the ball)
   What happened to the player? (fall over)
4 What did the girl do?   (take the dog off the pitch)
   What were the spectators doing?   (laugh and cheer)

3 Look at the cartoon story for one more minute. Close your books and tell the story around the class. Use the past simple and past continuous.

The sun was shining.   It was a lovely warm day.

●●●●● Grammar Builder: page 97

●●●●● Workbook: page 16

A magazine article

READ

1 Read the article quickly and match the headings with the paragraphs (A–D).

☐ Early successes ☐ Family and early years
☐ Greatest achievements ☐ First experience of sport

Jesse Owens

A Jesse Owens was born in 1913 in Alabama. His family was poor, and Jesse worked in his spare time to support his family.

B Jesse was a fast runner and so he joined the school athletics team. He set a new schoolboys' world record for the 100-yard sprint.

C While at university, Jesse had to work to pay for his studies. He also faced racial discrimination and wasn't allowed to live with white students. On 25 May, 1935, he broke four world records within 45 minutes: the 100-yard sprint, the 220-yard sprint, the long jump and the 220-yard hurdles. He was still a student!

D At the 1936 Olympic Games in Germany, Jesse won the 100-metre sprint, the 200-metre sprint, the long jump and the 400-metre relay. He also broke three Olympic records. It was a fantastic achievement.

2 Answer the questions.

1 When and where was Jesse Owens born?
2 Why did Jesse have to work in his spare time?
3 In which event did Jesse break the world record while he was still at school?
4 In what ways was university life difficult for Jesse?
5 How many world records did Jesse set on 25 May, 1935, and how long did it take him?
6 How many gold medals did Jesse win at the 1936 Olympics, and in which events?

3 Find words in the text that mean:

1 a measure of length used in Britain and the USA which equals 91 centimetres
2 a short, fast race
3 treating people badly because they are a different colour
4 a race in which the runners have to jump over small fences
5 a race between teams of runners, swimmers, etc.

PREPARE

Writing tip: using paragraphs

When you are preparing to write an article, divide the information into different topics. Put all the information about each topic into a separate paragraph.

Match the sentences about Jesse Owens with the four topics in Read exercise 1.

1 By the end of his first year at college, Jesse realized he could compete at the highest level.
2 Jesse was the first American to win four gold medals in a single Olympics.
3 Jesse couldn't do sports after school because he had to work.
4 When Jesse was 8, his father lost his job and the family moved to Ohio.
5 Some Germans hoped to prove at the Games that white people were physically superior to black people.
6 Jesse's school sports teacher realized that Jesse was immensely talented.
7 Jesse had nine brothers and sisters.
8 When he travelled with fellow students he had to stay in 'blacks only' hotels.

WRITE

Write an article (130–150 words) for a student magazine about a famous sportsperson from the past. Include paragraphs on three or four of these topics and your own ideas.

- family
- early years and education
- first experience of sport
- early successes
- greatest achievements
- why you admire him / her

Check your work

Have you

☐ divided your article into paragraphs, each with its own topic?
☐ put the paragraphs in a logical order?
☐ checked your spelling and grammar?
☐ written 130–150 words?

●●●●● Workbook: page 17

Winning and losing

LANGUAGE SKILLS

1 🎧 (1.15) Complete the dialogue with the words from the box. Then listen and check your answers.

> become events medals achievement joined born
> information broke runner named

John Hi, Mike. What are you doing?

Mike I'm looking for ¹_____ for my project on the King of the Mile.

John Who?

Mike The King of the Mile! The ²_____ Hicham El Guerrouj.

John Hicham El Guerrouj? He was the best athlete in the world.

Mike Yes, he was. They ³_____ him best athlete in the world in 2001 and in 2002.

John Where was he ⁴_____?

Mike He was born in Berkane, in Morocco, in 1974.

John So when did he ⁵_____ interested in running?

Mike He saw Said Aouita win gold at the 1984 Olympics so he ⁶_____ an athletics team.

John And why do they call him the King of the Mile?

Mike Because he ⁷_____ the world records for the 1500 metres and the mile.

John Not bad! How many Olympic ⁸_____ did he win?

Mike He won two medals; two gold medals.

John In which ⁹_____ did he win the medals?

Mike In the 1500- and 5000-metre races at the 2004 Olympics.

John Wow, that was a fantastic ¹⁰_____.

2 Read the dialogue again. Then complete the information.

Athletics Fact File

Runner: Hicham El Guerrouj
- Athletics fans call him the ¹_____ of the Mile.
- Born in ²_____ in ³_____.
- Started running in ⁴_____.
- Broke the world ⁵_____ for the 1500 ⁶_____ and the mile.
- Won two ⁷_____ medals at the 2004 Olympics.

3 Put the verbs in brackets in the correct past simple or past continuous form.

We ¹_____ (watch) a DVD when someone ²_____ (ring) the door bell. My brother Tom ³_____ (open) the door and there was a young man. The young man ⁴_____ (hold) a big box in his hands and he ⁵_____ (wear) a T-shirt with the words 'Happy Birthday' on it. When he ⁶_____ (see) my brother, he said, 'Happy Birthday.' My brother ⁷_____ (tell) him it wasn't his birthday and ⁸_____ (ask) the young man about the box. While they ⁹_____ (talk) the man's mobile phone rang. The young man ¹⁰_____ (finish) his telephone conversation and said it was a mistake. The box was for our next-door neighbour!

Water sports

1 Check the meaning of the words in the box and match them with the pictures.

1 windsurfing

> diving rowing scuba-diving snorkelling waterskiing
> ~~windsurfing~~

Sporting terms

2 Look up the words in **bold** and answer the questions with the names of different sports.

In which sport or activity do you:
1 say '**love**' to mean someone has zero points?
2 use a **club** to hit a ball?
3 use a racket to hit a **shuttlecock**?
4 take part in a **track event**?
5 do the crawl, back stroke or **butterfly**?
6 sit on a **saddle** and **pedal**?

Football

3 Check the meaning of the words in the box and complete the text.

> home kit pitch replica stadium ~~support~~ team

I ¹support Arsenal Football Club. They've been my favourite ²_____ for years. I always go with my dad and brothers to the Emirates ³_____ to watch their ⁴_____ games. I get really excited when I see the players in the red and white ⁵_____ of Arsenal come on to the ⁶_____. Of course, I always wear my ⁷_____ Arsenal shirt when I go to the games. I think it gives the team good luck!

I CAN ...

Read the statements. Think about your progress and tick (✓) one of the boxes.

✶ I need more practice.   ✶✶ I sometimes find this difficult.   ✶✶✶ No problem!

	✶	✶✶	✶✶✶
I can understand a magazine article.			
I can describe past events.			
I can talk about sports.			
I can tell a short story using past tenses.			
I can write an article for a student magazine.			

●●○○○ Workbook: Self check pages 18–19

The call of the wild
by Jack London

Biography

Jack London was born in California, USA, in 1876. As a young man in 1897, he took part in the famous Klondike Gold Rush, when a huge number of people rushed to the Yukon in Canada to look for gold. When London returned to California in 1898, he started writing stories. His novels *The Call of the Wild* and *White Fang* are based on his experiences in the Yukon. He died in 1916.

Buck did not read the newspapers. He did not know that trouble was coming for every big dog in California. Men had found gold in the Yukon, and these men wanted big, strong dogs to work in the cold and snow of the north.

Buck lived in Mr Miller's big house in the sunny Santa Clara valley. There were large gardens and fields of fruit trees around the house, and a river nearby. In a big place like this, of course, there were many dogs. There were house dogs and farm dogs, but they were not important. Buck was chief dog; he was born here, and this was his place. He was four years old and weighed sixty kilos. He went swimming with Mr Miller's sons, and walking with his daughters. He carried the grandchildren on his back, and he sat at Mr Miller's feet in front of the fire in winter.

But this was 1897, and Buck did not know that men and dogs were hurrying to north-west Canada to look for gold. And he did not know that Manuel, one of Mr Miller's gardeners, needed money for his large family. One day, when Mr Miller was out, Manuel and Buck left the garden together. It was just an evening walk, Buck thought. No one saw them go, and only one man saw them arrive at the railway station. This man talked to Manuel, and gave him some money. Then he tied a piece of rope around Buck's neck.

Buck growled, and was surprised when the rope was pulled hard around his neck. He jumped at the man. The man caught him and suddenly Buck was on his back with his tongue out of his mouth. For a few moments he was unable to move, and it was easy for the two men to put him into the train.

When Buck woke up, the train was still moving. The man was sitting and watching him, but Buck was too quick for him and he bit the man's hand hard. Then the rope was pulled again and Buck had to let go.

1 Read the text and find out when and where the story is set. Who is the main character of the story?

2 🎧 (1.18) Read the text again and answer the questions.

1 Where did Buck live?
2 Why was he different from the other dogs?
3 Why did Manuel steal Buck from Mr Miller?
4 Where did Manuel and the man put Buck?
5 What did Buck do to the man when he woke up?

3 Answer the questions. Look at the text, and use your own words and ideas to explain your answers.

1 How do you think Mr Miller and his family felt when they found out that Buck had disappeared?
2 Where do you think the man was taking Buck? Why?
3 In what ways do you think Buck's new life will be different from his old life?

4 Imagine it is 1898 and you're a gold prospector. You're travelling to Dawson City in the Yukon to look for gold. Look at the photo and write a paragraph for your diary describing your journey. Include details about the weather, the geographical features and your feelings.

On the river

READ

1 Read the text and answer the questions.

1 When does the race take place?
2 Where does the race take place?
3 Who competes in the race?

The Boat Race

The Boat Race takes place in London every year in the spring. It is a race between two teams – one from Oxford University and the other from Cambridge University. Each team has eight rowers and a 'cox', the person who shouts instructions to the rowers and steers the boat. The rowers are usually very big and strong (often about 200 centimetres tall), but the cox is usually small and light so that the boat doesn't have to carry much extra weight.

The teams spend months preparing for the race. They begin training in September. Then, in December, there are practice races – but not between Oxford and Cambridge. Teams from the same university compete in practice races so that they can choose the best rowers for the 'big' race in the spring.

The race takes place along the river Thames, in west London. The course is 6,779 metres from start to finish. It is an extremely popular event. Every year, about 250,000 spectators watch the race from the banks of the river, and about 200 million people around the world watch it on TV.

2 Answer the questions.

1 How many rowers are there in a team?
2 Why is the cox usually small?
3 When do the teams begin training?
4 What happens in December?
5 How long is the race?
6 How many people watch the race from the banks?

LISTEN

1 🎧 (1.19) Listen to the radio programme about the history of the Boat Race. Number the events in the order you hear about them.

a dead heat

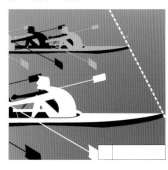

b female cox

c TV broadcast

d crashed

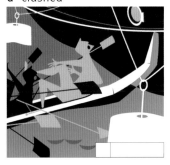

e fastest time

f both sank

2 🎧 (1.19) Listen again and write the correct year next to each picture.

SPEAK AND WRITE

1 Work in pairs. Ask and answer questions about the history of the Boat Race.

What happened in 1912?

Both boats sank.

Who won in ...?

2 Write a short paragraph about a popular sports event.

3 Town and country

THIS UNIT INCLUDES ●●●●

Vocabulary • towns and cities • people on the move • *do* and *make* • homophones • rural and urban landscapes • synonyms • urban or rural
Grammar • quantifiers: *some, any, much, many, a lot of, a little, a few* • definite, indefinite and zero article
Skills • describing landscapes • listening to directions
Writing • a leaflet

Are you lonesome tonight?

BEFORE READING

1 What are the advantages and disadvantages of living in a small town?

2 Do you think you will live in a different town or city when you are older? Why?

READ

Reading tip

The first line of a paragraph usually introduces the subject of the paragraph. By reading the first lines of paragraphs you can quickly find out the subjects the article talks about.

1 Read the *Reading tip*. Read only the first sentence of each paragraph. Match it with the correct title (A–E).

A Everybody has gone
B Where are the jobs?
C It was different in the past
D Happy to be on her own
E A very busy lady

Monowi, population: 1

☐ Elsie Eiler is the mayor of Monowi, a tiny town in northern Nebraska, USA, but that isn't her only job. She is also the town clerk, the town treasurer, the librarian, and she works in the café. Why has she got a
5 lot of different jobs? Because there's nobody else to do them. Monowi has got a population of one – Elsie.

☐ Immigrants from Europe originally founded the town in 1902 but today nobody wants to live there. There are about 12 empty one-storey wooden houses.
10 In one house there is still an abandoned piano. Most of the houses are in ruins and surrounded by a few trees, some old cars and lots of junk. The town is completely silent. An old rusting yellow school bus, with no wheels or seats, stands next to the small school.
15 The school closed 40 years ago. Opposite Elsie's café is an old building, filled with rubbish. It was a shop but it closed in the 1950s. Even the church has been closed since 1960.

☐ Monowi was a thriving town in the 1930s. Then, the
20 population was 150, mostly farmers and their families. There was a railway, too. However, the farmers couldn't compete with the enormous industrialized farms. They left the town to look for other work. In 1971, the railway closed and the town began to die.
25 Three years ago the last inhabitant, apart from Elsie and her husband, moved away. Then Elsie's husband died, and Elsie became the town's only inhabitant.

2 🎧 (1.20) **Read the text. Choose the best answers.**

1 Elsie Eiler
  a does other people's jobs for them.
  b has to do different jobs.
  c works in different towns.
2 The twelve wooden houses in Monowi
  a are all in a bad condition.
  b have car wheels inside them.
  c are not inhabited.
3 In Monowi you can't
  a go shopping.
  b borrow a book.
  c eat or drink.
4 Elsie's son and daughter
  a have jobs in another place.
  b are small farmers.
  c went to live abroad.
5 People still visit Monowi
  a to hunt the wild animals.
  b because they think Elsie is lonely.
  c because of Elsie's cooking.

3 **Read the text again. Are the sentences true or false? Correct the false sentences.**

1 Elsie Eiler has got five jobs.
2 The shop closed first, then the church, then the school.
3 In the past, it was possible to take the train to Monowi.
4 The farmers left Monowi because the railway closed.
5 Three years ago Elsie's husband moved away.
6 In this part of the USA, young people are moving from rural areas to urban areas.
7 Elsie wants to move away from Monowi.

UNDERSTANDING IDEAS

Answer the questions. Look at the text, and use your own words and ideas.

1 What do you think are the advantages and disadvantages of living in a town alone?
2 Which parts of your country have a small population? Why?
3 Where do most people live in your country? Why?

VOCABULARY

Monowi, population: 1

1 **Match the highlighted words in the text with the definitions.**

1 Connected with the countryside.
2 People who come to live in a country from another country.
3 A person who lives in a place.
4 Someone who works with documents in an office, bank, etc.
5 Growing or developing successfully.
6 A floor or level of a building.
7 Something that has been left and not used any more.
8 Having a lot of machines or factories.
9 Being damaged by a red substance that forms on metal.
10 Tiny pieces of a substance.
11 Started building and living in a town.
12 Badly damaged or destroyed.
13 Someone who is in charge of an organization's money.
14 Old things that do not have much value.
15 Went to another place usually to find a job.

2 **Do you know these words?**

> enormous mayor memory originally railway
> region surrounded by tiny

(●●●○○   Workbook: page 20)

☐ Elsie's son and daughter migrated years ago to find work in bigger towns. 'The small farmers and
30 businessmen can't make any money here,' says Elsie. It is the same in other small towns in the region. Between 1996 and 2004, almost 500,000 people left the rural states of Nebraska, Kansas, Oklahoma, North Dakota, South Dakota and Iowa, and went to live in
35 big cities.

☐ Now Elsie lives alone, but she isn't lonely. Her food is good and farmers and truck drivers travel a long way to eat at her café. And the town is often visited by wild animals such as deer. 'One day Monowi will just
40 be memories, and it will probably turn to dust,' she says. 'But I like it here, and as long as I can take care of myself, I'll stay here.'

Monowi, population: 1

ACTIVATE

Complete these sentences with the correct form of the words from the box.

> abandoned clerk dust found immigrants industrialized inhabitant in ruins junk migrate rural rusting storey thriving treasurer

1 The house is _____ as nobody has lived there for years. The rooms are full of old _____ and they are very dirty. In fact, the building is _____ and it's dangerous to go into the house.
2 I went to look at a car yesterday. It was really old and _____. There were holes in the metal! The inside was worse. It was full of dirt and _____. I don't think anyone will buy it.
3 My parents moved here 20 years ago when the town was _____ and doing well. It became _____ very quickly and there were lots of new factories and jobs. My dad _____ the family business in 1975 and today we have five factories in three different countries.
4 When I first came to the town hall I worked as a _____ in the office. I looked after all the documents and paper work. Now I've got a more important job, I'm the _____, and I control all the money that the city spends. I've got a big office on the fifth _____ with a great view of the city centre.
5 A lot of people from the countryside had to _____ to safer places because of the war. Most of them went abroad. Now, they were _____ in a new country. They were farmers so they went to live in small _____ villages. The old _____ were happy to see young people working in their villages again.

EXTEND

People on the move

1 Match the words to complete the sentences.

1 An immigrant…	a leaves their country because of a war or natural disaster.
2 A commuter…	b travels a long way to visit a religious place.
3 A nomad…	c comes into a country from abroad to live and work there.
4 A refugee…	d travels a lot and visits a lot of countries.
5 A pilgrim…	e leaves their country to go and live and work in another.
6 An emigrant…	f moves with their family and animals from place to place.
7 A globetrotter…	g travels to and from work every day.

do and make

2 Put the words in the box in the correct columns.

> money ~~badly~~ a living harm a job maths a mistake well a bad impression an appointment

do	make
1 badly	6 _____
2 _____	7 _____
3 _____	8 _____
4 _____	9 _____
5 _____	10 _____

My home town

3 Complete the text with the words in the box and answer the question.

> blocks harbours local neighbourhood cosmopolitan resort ~~urban~~ suburbs

I live in the second biggest [1]urban area in my country. The city is on the Mediterranean coast and it has an important port, which has two [2]_____. The city has a population of over four million inhabitants and it is a [3]_____ city, with people from all over the world living here. Although there are a lot of factories in the industrialized [4]_____ outside the city centre, my city is also a popular tourist [5]_____, because of its beautiful beaches. I live in a [6]_____ in the city centre where there a lot of [7]_____ of flats, small [8]_____ shops and businesses. Do you know the name of my city?

a Beirut   b Alexandria   c Athens   d Istanbul

Homophones

4 Homophones are words that have the same pronunciation but have different spellings and meanings. Complete the sentences with homophones of the words in italics.
1 a We live in a five-**storey** block of flats.
    b He told me a really good ~~story~~ about his family.
2 a My grandfather **died** 10 years ago.
    b My mum has _____ her hair a different colour.
3 a We saw a beautiful **deer** at the park.
    b _____ John, I'm writing this letter to ask you…
4 a He didn't say anything. He just **sighed**!
    b Look! There's Anne on the other _____ of the road.
5 a What a beautiful **blue** sky!
    b The wind _____ away the children's balloons.
6 a Let's have a short coffee **break**.
    b I've put a new front _____ on my bicycle.
7 a You always **groan** when I ask you to help me!
    b You've _____ a lot! How tall are you now?
8 a Jane's bought a **new** camera.
    b I _____ the answer but I couldn't remember it.

●●●●○ Workbook: page 21

GRAMMAR

Quantifiers: *some, any, much, many, a lot of, a little, a few*

EXPLORE

1 Fiona is playing a computer game called *SimCity*. Read the description of her ideal town. Find two examples of *some* and four examples of *any* in the text. Then complete the rules in the *Learn this!* box.

Sunshine City

1 Sunshine City is a great city. There's so much to do! There are a lot of **cinemas**, **cafés**, and a few **parks** and **playgrounds**. It's got some great clothes and shoe **shops** too.

2 Sunshine City is very modern and beautiful. There aren't any ugly **buildings** and there's some beautiful **scenery** around the city.

3 Is there any **pollution** in Sunshine City? There isn't much pollution because there isn't any **traffic**. Everyone travels by bike or walks, so there aren't many **accidents**.

4 No one works, so everyone has got a lot of free **time**. Are there any unfriendly **people** in Sunshine City? No – so come and spend a little time here!

LEARN THIS!

1 We use _____ in affirmative sentences.
2 We use _____ in negative sentences and questions.

2 Look at the words in blue in the text in exercise 1. Which are plural countable nouns? Which are uncountable nouns?

3 Find *a little*, *a few*, *many*, *much* and *a lot of* in the text in exercise 1. Complete the table. One quantifier can be used with both countable and uncountable nouns.

With uncountable nouns	With plural countable nouns
1 _____	4 _____
2 _____	5 _____
3 _____	6 _____

LOOK OUT!

We often use *much* and *many* in negative sentences and questions. We don't often use them in affirmative sentences. We use *a lot of* (or *lots of*) in both affirmative and negative sentences.

⬤⬤◦◦◦ Grammar Reference: page 98

EXPLOIT

1 🎧 (1.21) Martin is visiting his cousin Ben. Complete the dialogue with *some* or *any*. Then listen and check.

Ben Let's go to the cinema. There are ¹some good films on this week.
Martin I prefer being outside. Let's go mountain-biking. Are there ²_____ hills near here?
Ben No, there aren't.
Martin Oh. Maybe we could go for a walk in the countryside.
Ben There isn't ³_____ countryside near here, but there are ⁴_____ interesting parts of town.
Martin Great. Let's go and look at ⁵_____ traffic lights.
Ben Don't be silly. There are ⁶_____ streets in the centre where there isn't ⁷_____ traffic. You just hate cities!

2 🎧 (1.22) Choose the correct words in the text. Then listen and check.

I live in a small village in the south of Ireland. There are ¹**much / a lot of** old houses in the village, but there aren't ²**many / much** modern buildings. There are ³**a few / a little** farms around the village. Everybody's got a car, so there is ⁴**a little / much** pollution, but much less than in the city. There isn't ⁵**many / much** entertainment, but there's ⁶**much / a lot of** beautiful scenery and it's very peaceful. I love living here.

3 Work in pairs. Imagine you are playing *SimCity*. Describe your ideal town. Write six sentences. Use some of these words: *some, any, much, many, a lot of, a little* and *a few*.

There are a few ...
You can find some ...

⬤⬤◦◦◦ Grammar Builder: page 99

⬤⬤◦◦◦ Workbook: page 22

Landscapes

VOCABULARY

1 🎧 (1.23) Label the pictures with the words in the box. Listen and check.

> **Rural landscapes** cottage field footpath gate hedge ~~hill~~ lane stream valley wood
> **Urban landscapes** advertisement bus stop pavement pedestrian crossing postbox road sign roadworks rubbish bin street lamp traffic lights

1 hill
2
3
4
5
6
7
8
9
10

2 Label the pictures with the prepositions in the box.

> **Prepositions of movement** across over past through along

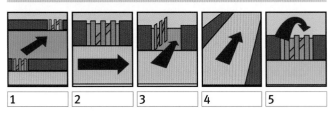

1   2   3   4   5

(●●●●● Workbook: page 23)

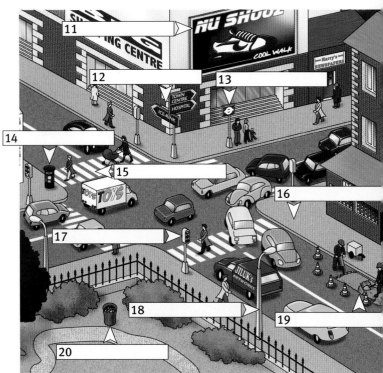

11
12
13
14
15
16
17
18
19
20

LISTEN

🎧 (1.24) Listen and mark the route on the picture below.

SPEAK

Work in pairs. Student A: Give directions using the picture in Listen. Student B: Follow the directions on the picture.

> Walk along the edge of the lake ... /
> Walk across the field to ...

GRAMMAR

Definite, indefinite and zero article

EXPLORE

1 Read the text and match the rules in the *Learn this!* box below with the words in blue.

I live in **a** town on **the** east coast of England. **The** town is called Grimsby. It's **a** nice place, and I like living by **the** sea. My dad's **a** fisherman and he's got **a** boat. I sometimes go fishing with him on **the** boat. But it's **a** small boat so we can't go out in (**x**) stormy weather.

LEARN THIS!

1 We use *a* when we talk about something for the first time. We use *the* when we talk about something again. (*There's a café near my house. I often go to the café at the weekend.*)

2 We use *a* when we say what someone's job is (*She's a doctor*), or when we describe what somebody or something is. (*He's a nice man. / It's a lovely day.*)

3 We use *the* when there is only one of something. (*the sun / the president / the cinema*)

4 We use the zero article when we are making generalizations.
What's the weather like?
I don't like (x) hot weather.
The lanes near our cottage are very narrow.
Don't drive fast in (x) narrow lanes.

2 Are the sentences generalizations or not? Choose the correct answers.

1 **Life / The life** in a small village can be very boring.
2 **Weather / The weather** in Scotland was terrible last weekend.
3 This crossing isn't for **bicycles / the bicycles**, it's for **pedestrians / the pedestrians**.
4 I love **Indian food / the Indian food**.
5 **Fields / The fields** around the village are full of cows.
6 I hate **advertisements / the advertisements**. They're usually so boring.

●●●●●● Grammar Reference: page 98

EXPLOIT

1 Choose the best answer, *a* or *the* or zero article (x).

MyTown.com   Chatroom

Jess22	I live in [1]**a / the** small village. It's near [2]**a / the** sea. It's [3]**a / the** really boring place.
Amy76	Hi Jess. I love [4](**x**) **/ the** villages. They're so quaint. What's the name of your village?
Jess22	Thurlbury. It's in Scotland. Where do you live, Amy?
Amy76	Ashford. It's [5]**a / the** small town in [6]**a / the** south of England.
Jess22	Is that [7]**a / an** exciting place to be at [8](**x**) **/ the** weekends?
Amy76	It's OK here. There's [9]**a / the** sports centre and [10]**a / the** cinema, but [11]**a / the** cinema's only got one screen.
Jess22	Cinema! We haven't even got [12]**a / the** café.

2 Complete the text using *a*, *an*, *the* or the zero article (x).

I have [1]a very responsible job. I am [2]_____ mayor of Newington City. This is [3]_____ great city – [4]_____ people here are friendly, [5]_____ weather is fantastic and we have [6]_____ very modern facilities. There are [7]_____ parks, [8]_____ enormous shopping centre and [9]_____ leisure centre with [10]_____ lake. So [11]_____ people love living here. However, there is [12]_____ problem. [13]_____ population of the city is relatively young. So we need to build more schools and [14]_____ university. And to do that, I need [15]_____ money!

3 Ask and answer questions using the table. Don't use *the* if it's a generalization.

Do you like	the (x)	big cities?
		weather today?
		scenery in your country?
		Italian food?
		talkative people?
		reading topic in Unit 1?
		optimistic people?

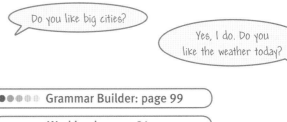

Do you like big cities?

Yes, I do. Do you like the weather today?

●●●●●● Grammar Builder: page 99

●●●●●● Workbook: page 24

A leaflet
READ

Read the two leaflets. Which place would you prefer to visit?

(A) *Devon* – **something for everyone**

Come and visit Devon, in the south-west of England. There are miles of sandy beaches, where you can swim, surf, dive or windsurf. Or just relax on the sand with a good book. If you like walking, cycling or horse riding, spend some time on Dartmoor, with its vast stretches of open moorland. Devon has got lots of interesting historic buildings. Visit Castle Drogo or the atmospheric castle at Totnes.

(B) Visit the historic city of York

- Wander through the winding streets and walk along the ancient city walls, which are over 700 years old.
- Don't miss the famous Clifford's Tower, first built in the eleventh century.
- Visit the fascinating Jorvik Museum and learn about the history of York.
- Take a trip to the wonderful Yorkshire Dales and marvel at the stunning scenery.

PREPARE

1 Which leaflet consists of:
   1 a single paragraph?
   2 short bullet points?

   Which is more effective in your opinion?

2 Which grammatical structure does each bullet point in leaflet B begin with?

3 Rewrite leaflet A as three bullet points.

4 Find adjectives in the leaflets that mean:
   1 very big
   2 important in history
   3 with a special feeling
   4 very old
   5 well-known
   6 very interesting
   7 fantastic
   8 very impressive

WRITE

Writing tip: writing a leaflet

When you are writing a leaflet:
- think of a good title to attract the readers' attention.
- use bullet points and short, informative sentences.
- use adjectives to make the descriptions more interesting.

Write a tourist leaflet (70–80 words) about some beautiful or interesting places in your country. Use the *Writing tip* to help you. Include information on some of these things:

- historic towns
- beautiful landscapes
- interesting buildings
- holiday activities
- tourist attractions (e.g. museums, monuments)

Check your work

Have you
- [ ] used bullet points?
- [ ] used short, informative sentences?
- [ ] used a variety of adjectives?
- [ ] written 70–80 words?

●●●●● Workbook: page 25

Town and country
LANGUAGE SKILLS

1 🎧 (1.25) Complete the dialogue with the words from the box. Then listen and check your answers.

> town fascinating wander mean atmospheric setting
> miss keen historic tickets

Angela You're ¹_____ on the theatre, aren't you, Sara?

Sara Yes, I am. Why?

Angela Because we're going to Stratford-upon-Avon on Saturday. Do you want to come?

Sara You ²_____ you're going to Shakespeare's home ³_____? Of course, I want to come!

Angela Great! My mum and dad have got ⁴_____ for the theatre in the evening.

Sara What time are you ⁵_____ off?

Angela At 10 o'clock in the morning. We want to see some of the ⁶_____ buildings in the town.

Sara Good. We can't ⁷_____ Anne Hathaway's cottage.

Angela Who was Anne Hathaway?

Sara She was Shakespeare's wife. Her cottage is outside Stratford. They say it's really ⁸_____.

Angela I'm sure my parents will want to see that. We're also going to ⁹_____ along Henley Street.

Sara Ah, yes. There are lots of ancient buildings in Henley Street and it's very ¹⁰_____, just like in Shakespeare's time.

Angela Well, it has probably changed a bit but I'm sure we'll have a good time.

2 Decide if the sentences are true or false. Correct the false sentences.

1 Sara enjoys watching plays.
2 Stratford-upon-Avon is Sara's home town.
3 They are going to the theatre at 10 a.m.
4 Shakespeare was Anne Hathaway's husband.
5 Anne Hathaway's cottage isn't in Stratford-upon-Avon.
6 Angela doesn't think Henley Street has changed since Shakespeare's time.

3 Complete the sentences with the words in the box.

> lot much any few some many little

1 There are a _____ of cars in the city centre.
2 Are there _____ cafés in the street?
3 How _____ people were in class today?
4 I only take a _____ milk in my coffee. That's enough!
5 We haven't got _____ food in the fridge.
6 We've got _____ apples. Do you want one?
7 I've only got a _____ computer games; just two or three.

Synonyms

1 Circle the adjective which is different in each group and say why it's different.

1 enormous huge (tiny) vast
  Tiny means very small. The other adjectives mean very big.
2 celebrated famous infamous well known
3 dreadful magnificent marvellous wonderful
4 antiquated contemporary current up-to-date
5 fascinating monotonous tedious tiresome

2 All the words in the box are synonyms of *old*. Check the usage of the words and complete the sentences.

> ~~antique~~ archaic elderly obsolete second-hand

1 This antique furniture is from the 18th century. It's very expensive.
2 No, my computer isn't new. It's _____. I bought it from a friend.
3 These poems were written in the 16th century. The language is _____ and difficult to understand.
4 Black and white TVs are _____. Nobody uses them today.
5 My grandparents are _____ now but they still travel a lot.

Urban or rural?

3 Put the words in the correct columns.

> ~~barn~~ crops irrigation pedestrian crossing
> parking meter plough square traffic jam

urban life	rural life
1 _____	5 barn
2 _____	6 _____
3 _____	7 _____
4 _____	8 _____

I CAN ...

Read the statements. Think about your progress and tick (✓) one of the boxes.

| ✳ | I need more practice. | ✳✳ | I sometimes find this difficult. | ✳✳✳ | No problem! |

	✳	✳✳	✳✳✳
I can understand a newspaper article.			
I can talk about quantities.			
I can describe a place in the town or country.			
I can use definite, indefinite and zero articles correctly.			
I can write a leaflet describing places of interest.			

●●○○○ Workbook: Self check pages 26–27

4 Heroes

THIS UNIT INCLUDES ●●●●

Vocabulary • challenging jobs • extreme adjectives • *-ed* and *-ing*
adjectives • human qualities • describing success
Grammar • comparatives and superlatives • *(not) as...as, too, enough*
Skills • listening and talking about heroes
Writing • a book report

An ordinary hero

BEFORE READING

What does it mean to be a hero? Who is your hero? Why?

AN AWARD FOR BRAVERY

The George Cross is the highest award for bravery that a civilian
in the UK can receive. It's named after King George VI, who
decided to create the award in 1940. Since then, fewer than
160 people have received it, all of them for performing acts of
exceptional heroism. The youngest recipient is John Bamford.
John received the award in 1952, at the age of 15, after he
suffered dreadful injuries while rescuing members of his family
from a horrific fire at their home in Nottinghamshire.

The fire broke out in the early hours of the morning of 19
October, 1952. In the house at the time were John, his parents
and his five younger brothers and sisters. When John and his
father realized that something was wrong, they went downstairs
to investigate. They opened the living room door and were
horrified to see the interior of the room suddenly burst into
flames. The heat was so intense that John and his father couldn't
get back upstairs to help the rest of the family. Instead, they

climbed up the front of the house and managed to help John's
mother and three of the children out of the bedroom window
and on to a flat roof. They knew that two children remained
inside the burning building.

John and his father climbed inside. They could hear the
distressed cries of the two remaining children, who were
only 4 and 6 years old, coming from a back bedroom.
The father covered himself with a blanket and made a heroic
attempt to reach the children. But before he could get to them,
the blanket caught fire and the searing flames drove him back.
Telling his father to wait outside at the back of the house,
15-year-old John then crawled through the flames and into
the bedroom. Despite the agonizing burning sensation as the
flames set fire to his shirt, he carried on until he reached his
two younger brothers. They were on the bed, terrified. John
picked them up and dropped the younger of the two boys out

READ

1 Read the *Reading tip*. What words do you expect to find in this text? Make a list.

2 Read the text quickly. Who did John Bamford save from the fire (a) with his father's help, (b) on his own?

3 🎧 (1.28) Read the text again. Choose the best answers.

1 How many people receive the George Cross?
  a Only a few each year.
  b About 160 each year.
  c Nearly 15 have received it since it first appeared.

2 John Bamford is unique among recipients of the George Cross because:
  a he showed amazing bravery in the face of danger.
  b he rescued his family from a terrible fire.
  c he was under the age of 16.

3 The fire at the Bamfords' house started
  a when everybody was out.
  b when everybody was in bed.
  c when everybody was in the living room.

4 John's mother escaped from the fire by
  a running down the stairs.
  b climbing through a window at the front of the house.
  c jumping out of a window at the back of the house.

5 John managed to reach the two younger children by
  a covering himself with a blanket.
  b going outside and round the back of the house.
  c getting down on his hands and knees.

6 Why did one boy run away when John was trying to rescue him?
  a Because he thought he could escape down the stairs.
  b Because he didn't understand what was happening.
  c Because he didn't recognize his brother through the thick smoke.

of the window and into his father's arms. But the elder boy was so dazed that he ran back through the burning room.

John knew that he could jump to safety, but he refused to leave without his brother. He chased the panic-stricken 6-year-old through the flames and eventually managed to catch him and drop him down to their father.

By this time, John was almost unconscious from the heat, the thick smoke and the pain. But somehow he managed to get one leg through the open window and fall to the ground below, exhausted. An ambulance rushed all three boys to hospital. The two younger boys soon recovered, but John did not return home until February of the following year, after countless operations. While still in hospital, he received the George Cross for his outstanding bravery and the newspapers printed the gripping story of his heroism.

UNDERSTANDING IDEAS

Answer the questions. Look at the text and use your own words and ideas.

1 Why is it surprising that John Bamford sent his father to wait outside?

2 What choice did John Bamford have when he was standing at the back bedroom window?

3 At which point in the events did John Bamford show the most courage, in your opinion?

VOCABULARY

An award for bravery

1 Find the best adjectives in the text to match the definitions.

1 Unhappy and upset	9 Very bad and frightened
2 Shocked and frightened	10 Frightened and unable to think
3 Seeming to be asleep because of an injury	11 Unusually good
4 Painful	12 Brave
5 Strong	13 Confused
6 Very bad and unpleasant	14 Frightened
7 Holding your attention	15 Tired
8 Very many	

2 Do you know these words?

award   burst into flames   civilian   crawl   heroism
investigate   outstanding   recipient   rescue

(●●●○○   Workbook: page 28)

An award for bravery

ACTIVATE

Read the text. Match the highlighted adjectives with the words from the box.

agonizing   countless   dazed   distressed   dreadful
exceptional   exhausted   gripping   heroic   horrific
horrified   intense   panic-stricken   terrified

Last month, news programmes reported on the ¹interesting story of a young woman in the town of Bridgeport who showed ²uncommon bravery during an ³awful flood. After a hot August day, there was a night of ⁴strong rain which caused a nearby river to break its banks. Residents were ⁵shocked to see the streets fill with water, flooding ⁶many homes. The rescue services took the ⁷confused residents to a local sports centre where it was warm and dry. As 19-year-old Jenny Wilson was preparing to leave her house, she saw that her elderly next-door neighbour was in a ⁸bad situation: he was trapped inside his car, ⁹worried, as the water levels rose all around him. Miss Wilson struggled through the water to reach his car. She needed to break the window but could find nothing to do it with, so she used her hand. The cuts were ¹⁰painful. Before she could help her neighbour to get out of his car, a rush of water carried her across the street. She had to use all her strength just to stay on her feet. But although she was ¹¹tired, she made one final, ¹²brave attempt to rescue her ¹³frightened neighbour. She managed to get back to the car and help him to get free. He was cold, wet and ¹⁴unhappy, but at least he was safe.

EXTEND

Adjectives ending in -ed and -ing

1 Study the *Look out!* box and complete the table with adjectives ending in -ed and -ing.

> **LOOK OUT!**
>
> -ed adjectives describe how a person feels about something.
> -ing adjectives describe a person or thing which causes a feeling.
> The film is boring.
> They are bored.

if a person or thing is ...		then you are ...	
boring		bored	
annoying		annoyed	
1 _____		embarrassed	
thrilling		2 _____	
3 _____		mesmerized	
astounding		4 _____	
5 _____		bewildered	
disappointing		6 _____	
7 _____		frightened	
exhausting		8 _____	

2 Describe the people in the photos. Use -ed adjectives.

1 I think he looks exhausted. I don't think he looks ...

① ② ③ ④

3 Choose the correct adjectives: -ed or -ing.
1 I don't like this piece of music. It's **bored** / (**boring**.)
2 This article is very **interested** / **interesting**.
3 I love parties. They're really **excited** / **exciting**.
4 I forgot her name. It was really **embarrassed** / **embarrassing**.
5 I'm really **annoyed** / **annoying** because I can't find my mobile phone.
6 I'll be **surprised** / **surprising** if England win the World Cup.
7 It was an **exhausted** / **exhausting** tennis match, but I won in the end.
8 I worked hard last term, but my exam results were **disappointed** / **disappointing**.

4 Write sentences that include -ing adjectives to describe these things and experiences in your life.
1 a horror film
   It was frightening. It was also exciting.
2 your English book
3 a shopping trip
4 the result of your last exam
5 a football match
6 an argument with a friend

●●●●○ Workbook: page 29

GRAMMAR

Comparatives and superlatives

EXPLORE

1 Read the text. Are these sentences true or false? Correct the false sentences.

1 Amr Zaki joined Wigan on a temporary contract.
2 He waited a long time for success in England.
3 He is almost at the end of his career.

The names of the overseas footballers in the English Premiership can be more difficult to pronounce than British names. However, Amr Zaki is one of the simpler names for commentators and fans to say. Zaki, one of the most talented footballers from Egypt, joined the Premiership's Wigan Athletic in 2008 on a one-year loan. At £1.5 million, he was cheaper than most players, and he turned out to be one of the best deals the manager made that year. Zaki was regularly scoring the most spectacular goals. He became known as one of the hottest strikers in the Premiership, and some of the better known, wealthier clubs in the Premiership became interested in him. With impressive speed, strength and fighting spirit, Zaki has a lot further to travel on the path of his football career. Things certainly could be worse in a footballer's career!

2 Find the comparative and superlative adjectives in the text. Then complete the table.

	Comparative	Superlative
Short adjectives		
cheap	¹_____	cheapest
hot	hotter	²_____
simple	³_____	simplest
wealthy	⁴_____	wealthiest
Long adjectives		
difficult	⁵_____	most difficult
talented	more talented	⁶_____
Irregular adjectives		
good	better	⁷_____
bad	⁸_____	worst
well known	⁹_____	best known
far	¹⁰_____	furthest

3 Look at the short adjectives in exercise 2. What are the spelling rules for the comparative and superlative forms?

(●●○○○ Grammar Reference: page 100)

EXPLOIT

1 Complete the chatroom texts with the comparative or superlative form of the adjectives in brackets.

Socceraddicts.com

Join in the chat .... *last night's soccer*

I saw Wigan play yesterday evening. It was their ¹ best (good) result of the season, and against one of the ²_____ (wealthy) clubs in the league, too! Fantastic!
martin@hkinternet.com   posted 22.39 5 July

Sure, but the performance was ³_____ (bad) than the result. I think they were lucky, frankly. Chelsea's goalkeeper is probably the ⁴_____ (reliable) in the Premiership, but he made big two mistakes last night.
kate32@demonmail.co.uk   posted 22.42 5 July

I reckon Wigan showed more fighting spirit. Their players were ⁵_____ (brave), ⁶_____ (determined) and ⁷_____ (well-organized) than Chelsea's. And, as kate32 said, they were ⁸_____ (lucky) too!
dg77@swiftmail.net   posted 22.44 5 July

It's true, Wigan worked hard. They're one of the ⁹_____ (fit) sides in the league, even if they aren't the ¹⁰_____ (talented). I'm sure this season will be ¹¹_____ (good) than last. They're definitely a ¹²_____ (entertaining) side to watch than they were last year.
kate32@demonmail.co.uk   posted 22.42 5 July

2 Write questions, using comparative forms and the words below. Then ask and answer the questions.

1 exciting – parachuting / bungee jumping?
   Which is more exciting, parachuting or bungee jumping?
2 fit – footballers / ballet dancers?
3 dangerous – crocodiles / sharks?
4 entertaining – football / basketball?
5 well-paid – TV presenters / footballers?
6 gripping – history / geography?
7 bad for your health – chocolate / chips?

3 Complete the sentences using a superlative form of the adjective and your own opinion.

1 The most talented (talented) footballer in the world is …
2 The (important) football competition is …
3 The (aggressive) sport to play is …
4 The (fascinating) sport to watch is …
5 The (well known) sports person in this country is …
6 The (spectacular) sports event I have ever seen is …
7 The (healthy) sport to play is …
8 The (impressive) football stadium is …

(●●●●○ Grammar Builder: page 101)

(●●●○○ Workbook: page 30)

Personal heroes

VOCABULARY

1 Find two negative qualities among the positive qualities in the list below.

> **Human qualities** loyalty cowardice meanness generosity education patience intelligence leadership courage modesty perseverance sense of humour wisdom

2 Using a dictionary, complete these adjectives related to some of the nouns in exercise 1.

1 gener...
2 courage...
3 intellig...
4 mode...
5 mea...
6 coward...
7 loya...
8 educat...

3 Work in pairs. Add more positive qualities to the list in exercise 1 and write down their related adjectives. Use a dictionary to help you.

4 In pairs, decide which two qualities from exercise 1 are most important for:

1 a sports star
2 a head teacher
3 a charity worker
4 a mountaineer

5 Read about these famous historical figures. Can you say what qualities they possessed, in your opinion?

Mahatma Gandhi
Mahatma Gandhi was an Indian lawyer. For most of his life, he fought for racial equality and for the independence of India from British rule, even though he was imprisoned at times.

Naguib Mahfouz
Naguib Mahfouz was an Egyptian novelist who won the 1988 Nobel Prize for Literature. He wrote about the traditions and culture of his native country and introduced Arabic fiction to the West.

Anwar El Sadat
Anwar El Sadat became the third President of Egypt in 1970. When he led the October War of 1973 and regained Sinai, he became a national hero for many people.

LISTEN

1 🎧 (1.29) Listen to four teenagers talking about a personal hero. Match the speakers with the people they describe and one of their main qualities.

1 teacher
2 charity worker
3 neighbour
4 grandfather

a modesty
b perseverance
c patience
d courage

Speaker 1	
Speaker 2	
Speaker 3	
Speaker 4	

2 🎧 (1.29) Listen again. We can say the same thing using different expressions. Which expressions do the speakers use, *a* or *b*?

1 a He grew up on a farm ...
  b He spent his childhood on a farm ...
2 a He managed to get a university degree ...
  b He ended up with a university degree ...
3 a The most important thing is job satisfaction ...
  b It's all about job satisfaction ...
4 a I really admire her because ...
  b I find her really admirable because ...
5 a It's because of him that I decided ...
  b He's the main reason that I decided ...
6 a What stands out in my memory is ...
  b What I remember most clearly is ...
7 a As if that weren't enough, ...
  b In addition to all that, ...
8 a I think he's an inspiration to all of us.
  b I think he provides an inspiring example for us all.

SPEAK

1 Think about somebody you find inspiring. It could be a famous person or someone you know personally. Make notes using the phrases below.

Name:
Famous person? Personal acquaintance?
What does he or she do?
His / Her main qualities are ...
He / She inspires me because ...

2 Tell the class about the person you chose in exercise 1.

●●●●● Workbook: page 31

GRAMMAR

(not as) ... as, too, enough

EXPLORE

1 🎧 (1.30) Read and listen to the dialogue. Answer the questions.

Harry Look. *Last Action Hero* is on at the cinema.

Mike Yeah, but you have to be 15 to see it. We aren't **old enough**.

Harry I'm old enough. You're not. What about *Everyone's Hero*? It's **not as good as** *Last Action Hero* but we can both see it.

Mike OK. I'll book the tickets online ... Oh, no. We're **too late**. It's sold out.

Harry Try the earlier showing.

Mike That starts in fifteen minutes. There isn't **enough time** to get there.

Harry OK. Let's watch a DVD.

1 Who is old enough to watch *Last Action Hero*?
2 In Harry's opinion, which film is better, *Last Action Hero* or *Everyone's Hero*?
3 Why can't they see the earlier showing?

2 Complete the rules in the *Learn this!* box with *after*, *before* or *between*. Match words in blue from the dialogue with the rules.

1 An adjective comes _____ *(not) as* and *as*. example: _____
2 *too* comes _____ an adjective. example: _____
3 *enough* comes _____ an adjective. example: _____
4 *enough* comes _____ a noun. example: _____

⦿●●●● Grammar Reference: page 100

EXPLOIT

1 Write six true sentences about yourself. Use *not as ... as* and adjectives 1–6.

1 rich *I'm not as rich as Bill Gates.*
2 tall
3 short
4 impatient
5 talkative
6 hardworking

2 Invent two reasons why you can't follow each suggestion. Use *too* in one reason and *enough* in the other.

1 Why don't we go to the cinema?
   I'm too busy. / I haven't got enough money for a ticket.
2 Let's buy a new DVD player.
3 Shall we go to the beach?
4 Why don't we have lunch now?
5 Let's go to Paris for our holidays.
6 Why don't you study maths at university?

3 🎧 (1.31) Complete the conversation between two casting directors. Use *too* and *enough* and words from the box. Then listen and check.

experience	muscle	old	~~tall~~	time	well known

Jack Now, we need an actor for the part of the hero, Brad Peters is certainly talented enough. But is he ¹ *tall enough*?

Micky No, he isn't. He's only about 1 metre 50. What about Tom Delaney? He's very good.

Jack But he hasn't had ²_____. He's only acted in one film.

Micky Well, Michael Lamb is ³_____. He's appeared in lots of popular films.

Jack Yeah, but he's ⁴_____. He'll be 60 next year. And think about his physique – he hasn't got ⁵_____. This is an action film, remember.

Micky What about Dave Wilson?

Jack He's always very busy. I'm sure he hasn't got ⁶_____.

4 Complete the text using an appropriate form of the adjectives and nouns in brackets: comparative, superlative, *too*, *enough*, *not as ... as*.

What if you had a chance to be a hero? Would you be ¹*brave enough* (brave) to take it? The animated feature *Everyone's Hero* was one of the ²_____ (funny) and ³_____ (moving) films of 2006. It tells the tale of a young boy who believes he can make a difference if he just shows ⁴_____ (perseverance).
It is 1930s America and one of the ⁵_____ (well-known) celebrities of the day is baseball star Babe Ruth. Babe has no ⁶_____ (big) admirer than 10-year-old Yankee Irving. Yankee dreams of being a baseball star like Babe, but he soon discovers that he is ⁷_____ (talented) his hero. In fact, he isn't even ⁸_____ (good) to hit the ball! Yankee gives up on his beloved game in frustration. But when a dishonest security guard steals Babe Ruth's bat a few days before the ⁹_____ (important) game of the year, Yankee is determined to get it back before it's ¹⁰_____ (late). In the process, he learns about the value of hope, family and friendship.

⦿●●●● Grammar Builder: page 101

⦿●●●● Workbook: page 32

WRITING

A book report

READ

1 Read the book report. In which paragraph does Joanna:

A give her opinion of the book? _____
B describe what happens in the book? _____
C give information about the book and its author? _____

> The Old Man and the Sea
>
> a book report by Joanna Martins
>
> 1 The Old Man and the Sea is a short novel by the famous American writer Ernest Hemingway. He wrote it in 1951 when he was 52 years old and it is one of his best-known works. Three years later, Hemingway received the coveted Nobel Prize in Literature.
>
> 2 It's the story of an old fisherman called Santiago. After 84 days without catching a fish, he is hungry, impoverished and alone. The other villagers avoid him because they think his disastrous luck might make them unlucky too. Finally, his luck changes and he hooks a huge marlin. After a long and exhausting struggle, he eventually manages to bring it on board his boat. But his troubles are not over. During a terrifying attack, sharks try to steal his catch. He succeeds in fighting off the attackers. However, they eat the marlin, leaving him only the fish's skeleton. In the end, he loses the marlin but regains his pride and his friends.
>
> 3 I liked the book because the story is fascinating. I admired the character of Santiago because he showed a lot of courage and perseverance. The moral of the story is thought-provoking and the style of writing is simple and poetic. I would definitely recommend it to a friend.

2 Are these sentences true or false? Correct the false sentences.

1 The main character in the book is 52 years old.
2 In the story, Santiago catches a large shark.
3 Joanna found the character of Santiago admirable.
4 Joanna says the book has funny and serious parts.

3 Find adjectives in the text which have a similar meaning to:

1 desirable
2 poor
3 bad
4 large
5 tiring
6 frightening
7 interesting

PREPARE

1 Read the phrases. In a book report, which paragraph would you find the information in? Complete the table.

Talking about stories	1	2	3
a I identified with (a character)			✓
b I liked the book because …			
c In the end, …			
d The author's name is …			
e It's a (type of story)			
f It takes place in …			
g It's the story of …			
h There's a film of the book …			
i The main character is (name)			
j There's a twist at the end.			
k You should read it.			

2 Choose a book that you have read. Complete the writing plan using these headings. Include any other information that you think is important.

> **Paragraph 1: General information**
> • Title
> • Author
> • Type of book
>
> **Paragraph 2: Story and characters**
> • Where is it set?
> • Main characters
> • What happens?
>
> **Paragraph 3: Your opinion**
> • Why did you like it? For example:
> • It's funny / moving / exciting / fascinating.
> • It contains lots of interesting characters.
> • I really wanted to know what was going to happen.
> • There are lots of surprises.

WRITE

Read the *Writing tip*. Write a book report using the writing plan from exercise 2.

> **Writing tip: using the present simple tense**
>
> Remember to use the present simple when you re-tell the story of a book or film.

(●●●●○ Workbook: page 33)

Heroes

LANGUAGE SKILLS

1 🎧 (1.32) Complete the dialogue with the words from the box. Then listen and check your answers.

> as best distressing enough generously more
> sense of humour talented although too

Sally Do you have a local hero? You know, someone who helps other people, but is ¹_____ modest to appear in the news.

Naomi Well, a friend of mine is a charity worker. He raises money for a charity that helps homeless people. Actually he's a ²_____ accountant but he's just not motivated ³_____ to work for a big company.

Sally Charity work must be much ⁴_____ rewarding than working for a big company because you feel that you are making a difference. But lots of successful business people or celebrities also donate ⁵_____ to charities.

Naomi That's true, ⁶_____ I'm sure they enjoy the publicity too. And it's not just a question of money. Working with homeless people can be quite ⁷_____. So who's your local hero?

Sally The caretaker at school is my hero. He's not as clever ⁸_____ some of the teachers but he has a great ⁹_____. Whenever we're feeling disappointed about something he always does his ¹⁰_____ to cheer us up!

2 What human quality is being described in each sentence?

1 He never gives up.
2 She's very brave.
3 He stands by his friends and never betrays them.
4 She often buys gifts for people.
5 He never loses his temper.
6 She has a deep understanding of the world.

3 Rewrite these sentences to include the words or phrases in brackets. Don't change the meaning!

1 He's the same height as his brother. (as … as)
2 I was too impatient to wait my turn. (enough)
3 My sister is more cowardly than my brother. (courageous)
4 She wasn't fast enough to catch the thief. (too)
5 I think history is easier than chemistry. (difficult)
6 There's nobody in the class more intelligent than you. (most)

DICTIONARY CORNER

Challenging jobs

1 Check the meaning of the words in the box and match them with the pictures.

2 fund-raiser

> ~~fund-raiser~~ lifeguard mountaineer paramedic
> surgeon surveyor

Describing success

2 Check the usage and example sentences of the words in bold. Then choose the best word in these sentences.

1 Perseverance is one of the **tools** / **keys** to success.
2 His early work wasn't up to **scratch** / **the point** but now he has really improved.
3 She has **accomplished** / **succeeded** a lot in a relatively short space of time.
4 He's finally **fulfilled** / **completed** his dream of becoming an engineer.
5 At 21, she **achieved** / **scored** her goal of becoming a university graduate.

I CAN ...

Read the statements. Think about your progress and tick (✓) one of the boxes.

✷	I need more practice.	✷✷	I sometimes find this difficult.	✷✷✷	No problem!

	✷	✷✷	✷✷✷
I can understand a real-life story.			
I can make comparisons.			
I can talk about human qualities and peronal heroes.			
I can use different structures to make comparisons.			
I can write a book report.			

(●●●○○ Workbook: Self check pages 34–35)

The Railway Children
by Edith Nesbit

Biography

Edith Nesbit was a children's author and poet. She was born in London in 1858. She was not typical of a woman in the late 19th century – she had short hair and she smoked, and she started writing short stories for a magazine to earn money for her husband and children. She went on to write many successful novels.

When the children first went to live at the white house, they talked about Father a lot and were always asking questions about him. But as time passed, their questions seemed to make Mother unhappy, so they stopped asking them. But they never forgot him.

Bobbie thought about Father often. She knew her mother was unhappy, and she worried a lot about that. And why was Father away for so long? Was there something that Mother wasn't telling them?

The answer came on the day she went to the station to fetch the magazines. They were old magazines which people left on trains or in the waiting room. Perks said the children could have them to read, and one day Bobbie went to fetch them.

'I'll just put some newspaper round them to keep them together,' said Perks. And he took an old newspaper from the heap.

The magazines were heavy, and Bobbie stopped to rest on the way home. She sat on the grass and dropped them beside her. As she did this, she looked at the newspaper and read some of the words on the page ... *and it was like a terrible dream.*

She never remembered how she got home. But she went to her room and locked the door. Then she took the newspaper off the magazines and looked at it again. The words seemed to jump out at her:

FIVE YEARS IN PRISON FOR SPY!
And the name of the 'spy' was the name of her father.

Bobbie was very quiet at tea-time.

'Is anything wrong?' Mother asked her.

'I'm all right,' said Bobbie.

But after tea, Mother went up to Bobbie's room. 'What's the matter?' she wanted to know.

For an answer, Bobbie took the newspaper from under her bed and showed it to her mother.

'Oh, Bobbie!' cried Mother. 'You don't believe it, do you? You don't believe Daddy is a spy?'

'No!' said Bobbie.

'He's good and honest and he's done nothing wrong,' said Mother. 'We have to remember that.'

1 Look at the title of the book and the illustration. Which of the words in the box do you expect to find in the text? Read the text quickly and check.

> waiting room prison station shops accident
> train driver station master brother spy lawyer
> newspaper email tea-time dream

2 🎧 (1.35) Read the text again and answer the questions.

1 Why did the children stop asking questions about their father?
2 Why did Bobbie go to the station?
3 When did she first notice the story in the newspaper?
4 How did Mother know that something was wrong with Bobbie?
5 What did Bobbie do to explain what was wrong?

3 Answer the questions. Look at the text, and use your own words and ideas to explain your answers.

1 Why do you think Mother and the children moved to the white house?
2 Do you think the family was rich? Why / Why not?
3 How do you think Bobbie felt when she first read the name of the spy?
4 What do you think Mother's main qualities were?

4 *The Railway Children* has a happy ending. Write a short paragraph about what you think happens.

In the country

READ

Are the sentences true or false? Read the text and check your answers.

1 Wales is an independent state.
2 There are 11 million people in Wales.
3 Britain's highest mountain is in Wales.
4 About 600,000 people speak Welsh.
5 More people in north Wales speak Welsh as their first language than English.
6 Sheep farmers make a lot of money.

Canol y dref
Town centre

North Wales

A Wales isn't an independent state – it is part of the UK. It is situated in the west of Britain. It has a population of about three million and the capital is Cardiff. Most of the population live in the industrial south of the country.

B The north of Wales is one of the most beautiful parts of Britain. There are spectacular lakes, valleys and rivers. There are also wonderful mountains – including Snowdon, Britain's second-highest mountain.

C Two languages are spoken in Wales: English and Welsh. Welsh is a Celtic language and is one of the oldest languages in Europe. Only 20% of the total population of Wales speak Welsh, but in the small villages and towns of west and north Wales, about 75% of people speak it as their first language.

D The two main industries in the north are tourism and farming. Many people come to walk and climb in the mountains or go kayaking on the rivers. There are lots of sheep farms in the hills, but it is difficult to make money from sheep farming, and many farms are closing. Young people have difficulty finding jobs in north Wales and many of them are leaving to get jobs in the city.

Interesting fact
The village with the longest name in the world is in north Wales: Llanfairpwllgwyngyllgogerychwyrndrobwllllantysiliogogogoch. The name means: the church of St Mary in a valley of white hazel trees near a fast whirlpool by the church of St Tysilio of the red cave.

Interesting fact
There are 3 million people in Wales and 11 million sheep.

LISTEN

1 🎧 (1.36) Listen to a radio programme about life in north Wales. Who wants to:

1 leave north Wales?
2 stay in north Wales?
3 stay, but thinks it will be difficult?

a Bryn   b Gareth   c Bethan

Listening tip
Don't take detailed notes while listening. Take short notes and use them to write full sentences later.

2 🎧 (1.36) Listen again and answer the questions.

1 What is Bryn's first language?
2 What does Bryn's father do?
3 What two disadvantages of life on the farm does Bryn mention?
4 Why do tourists visit Llangollen?
5 Why doesn't Gareth enjoy living there any more?
6 What does Gareth plan to do in Cardiff or London?
7 Where is Caernarfon?
8 Why are young people leaving Caernarfon?
9 Is Bethan happy to go and live in another place?

SPEAK AND WRITE

1 Work in pairs. Ask and answer the questions.

1 What are the advantages of living in your village, town or city?
2 What are the disadvantages?
3 Have you lived in the same place all your life?
4 Do you want to live where you are now for the rest of your life? Why? / Why not?

2 Write a short text about your country. Include the following information:

- the population
- the capital city
- the languages spoken
- main industries
- an interesting fact

5 | Gifts

Famous gifts

THIS UNIT INCLUDES ●●●●

Vocabulary • parts of buildings • people and buildings • compound nouns • prepositions of place • retail • synonyms: *cheap* or *expensive*? • shopping
Grammar • present perfect • contrast: present perfect and past simple
Skills • listening to a radio programme
Writing • an informal letter

BEFORE READING

Think of three famous buildings in the world.
Answer the questions.

1 What kind of building is it? Choose from the words in the box.
2 Where is it?
3 Is it a tourist attraction today?

Buildings	castle	concert hall	government building
museum	palace	tower	skyscraper	opera house
temple	stadium		

READ

> **Reading tip**
>
> When you scan a text for information, look for key words to help locate the sentences that you need. For example, information about height and age might include dates, numbers, and the words: *metres, years,* etc.

1 Read the *Reading tip*. Read the texts quickly and find out which of the three buildings is:

  1 the oldest 2 the newest 3 the highest

MONUMENTAL GIFTS

From Russia with Love

Poles either love it or hate it. The Palace of Culture and Science has dominated the Warsaw skyline for over 50 years, and is still one of the tallest landmarks in Europe. It was a personal gift from Joseph Stalin to the Polish people and he sent 3,500 workers from the former Soviet Union to build it. Work on the building lasted from May 1952 until July 1955 and 16 workers died in accidents during construction. It stands 231 metres high and it has got 42 storeys and 3,288 rooms including three theatres, a swimming pool, a museum and a congress hall. Today it hosts exhibitions and concerts and it is the home of a Polish university. It is also one of the city's most popular tourist attractions and every year thousands of people visit the terrace on the 35th floor and enjoy the views across the city.

Taking Liberties

Since 1886, the Statue of Liberty has been one of the most famous monuments in America – in fact, the world. The statue was a gift to America from the French people. They built the statue in France and then shipped it across the Atlantic Ocean in 350 pieces and re-built it in New York. They completed the work in 1886, and about a million people watched the opening parade on 28 October of that year. At the time, the Statue of Liberty was the tallest structure in New York at 93 metres and until 1902 the Americans used it as a lighthouse. Ships' captains could see its electric light from 40 kilometres away. Since then, although they have built many taller buildings, the Statue of Liberty is still an impressive sight, and millions of visitors have climbed the 354 steps to the top.

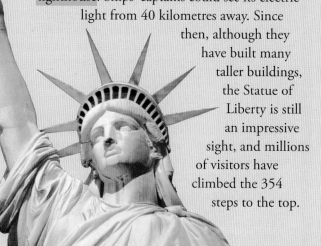

2 🎧 (1.37) **Read the text again and choose the best answers.**

1 The construction of the Palace of Culture and Science took
   a over 50 years.
   b 231 days.
   c over three years.
2 The Palace of Culture and Science
   a has a terrace with good views on the top floor.
   b has a variety of work, educational and leisure facilities.
   c has a university that is visited by thousands of tourists.
3 The Statue of Liberty
   a is the tallest building in New York.
   b was the tallest building in New York.
   c is now taller than it was in 1886.
4 The Statue of Liberty
   a is 40 kilometres away from the coast.
   b is still working as a lighthouse.
   c helped sailors in the past.
5 Today, Balmoral Castle is
   a a tourist attraction and the queen's home in Scotland.
   b a private home for the queen and her family.
   c a place for visitors to have dances and parties.

Queen of the Castle

Balmoral Castle in Scotland was a present for Queen Victoria from her husband, Prince Albert, in 1852. The countryside around the castle is spectacular, and includes Lochnagar, a mountain 1,160 metres high. The royal couple decided that the original castle was too small, so they built a new one. They completed it in 1856, with a beautiful tower about 30 metres high. The castle has belonged to the British royal family since that time, and each new generation has improved the property. Today, the queen and her family always reside at Balmoral when they visit Scotland. The castle grounds have been open to the public for over 35 years, and visitors can also visit the ballroom in the castle.

3 Decide which building each sentence is about: the Palace of Culture and Science, the Statue of Liberty or Balmoral Castle.

1 They built this building next to an older one.
2 This building did a particular job for sixteen years.
3 Some people died when they were working on this building.
4 This building isn't in a city.
5 People visit this building so they can see other buildings.
6 They made this building in one country and re-built it in another.

UNDERSTANDING IDEAS

Answer the questions. Look at the text, and use your own words and ideas.

1 Why do you think tourists like to visit these three places?
2 Which of the three buildings do you think is the most impressive? Why?
3 Are there any buildings in your town that you love or hate? Why?

VOCABULARY

Monumental gifts

1 Match the highlighted words in the text with the definitions.

1 The members of a family that are born and live around the same time.
2 Owned by someone.
3 Organizes an event and provides the things that you need to do it.
4 Something that is constructed or built.
5 A tower next to the sea that uses a light to warn ships of danger.
6 Well known buildings or objects that you can easily see and that help you know where you are.
7 Continued for a period of time.
8 So big or high that it was very easy to see.
9 To live in a particular place.
10 The shapes made by buildings or mountains against the sky.
11 A public celebration where lots of people walk through the streets.
12 The land and gardens around a big house.
13 The buildings and land that someone owns.
14 Sent goods to customers by air, land or sea.
15 The process of building something.

2 Do you know these words?

ballroom   congress hall   exhibition   former
monument   spectacular   storey   tourist attraction

(●●●○ Workbook: page 36)

VOCABULARY

Monumental gifts

ACTIVATE

Complete these sentences with the words from the box.

> belong to construction dominates generation grounds
> host landmark lasts lighthouse parade property
> resides ship skyline structure

1 He's very rich and he's got a lot of _____. He's got houses in London and New York.
2 _____ of the new sports stadium took three years.
3 The palace is a huge building and it _____ the centre of the city.
4 When the team won the cup there was a _____ through the city streets to celebrate.
5 There are a lot of dangerous big rocks under the sea near the _____.
6 We've got a long English class every Monday. It _____ for an hour and a half.
7 The New York _____ with all its skyscrapers is probably the most famous in the world.
8 The gardens in the _____ of the palace are full of beautiful flowers.
9 I don't think our city can _____ the Olympic games. It's an enormous and expensive event to organize.
10 If you get lost, use the Cairo Tower as a _____. You can see it from everywhere.
11 They are going to _____ our furniture to Sydney when our dad has found a flat for us there.
12 The new school will be a three-storey glass and steel _____.
13 The president of France _____ in the Élysée Palace in Paris and works at the French National Assembly.
14 My grandparents are from another _____ and they don't understand computers and the internet.
15 Those trainers _____ me. They're mine, not yours!

EXTEND

Parts of buildings

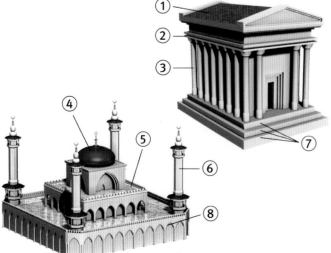

1 Match the names of the parts of buildings with (1–8) in the pictures.

> column terrace dome arch ~~tiles~~ minaret
> beam steps

1 tiles   5 _____
2 _____   6 _____
3 _____   7 _____
4 _____   8 _____

People and buildings

2 Complete the sentences with the words in the box.

> diners ~~spectators~~ audience guests visitors

1 The spectators left the stadium happy after their team's win.
2 A lot of the _____ at the hotel were going to the wedding.
3 We ask _____ to the museum not to take photos in the exhibition.
4 The _____ were disappointed with the musicians' poor performance.
5 _____ had to leave the restaurant because of a fire in the kitchen.

Compound nouns

3 Compound nouns are words that we can make by putting two nouns together. Match the nouns below to make compound nouns.

1 sky   a quake
2 oil   b keeper
3 head   c lord
4 wood   d room
5 earth   e field
6 board   f land
7 house   g line
8 land   h quarters

Prepositions of place

4 Complete the sentences with the prepositions *at*, *in* and *on*.

1 Balmoral Castle is in Scotland.
2 The Statue of Liberty is _____ an island.
3 I'll meet you _____ the door of the congress hall.
4 His office is _____ the top floor of a skyscraper.
5 I like to sit _____ the front when I go to the cinema.
6 The castle is _____ the side of a beautiful mountain.
7 We were sitting _____ his office when he finally arrived.
8 He was standing _____ the terrace looking at the views.

●●●●● Workbook: page 37

GRAMMAR

Present perfect

EXPLORE

1 This sentence is in the present perfect.

The castle has been open to the public for over 35 years.

Read the postcard and find examples of the present perfect.

Dear Dad,

We've been in Cairo since Sunday. We've seen the pyramids and all the sights and I've taken lots of photos. And of course, we've been shopping in Khan Al-Khalili. I haven't bought very much, but Suzie has spent a fortune on presents. She's gone to City Stars, a huge shopping mall. She's been there for hours! She's just sent me a text message. She's tried on four pairs of trainers and six jackets!

Love Amanda

PS. Have you fed my fish?

Colin Smith
17 Barn Street
London
E13 7JX

2 Complete the table with examples from the postcard.

Present perfect
affirmative
We've ¹_____ in Cairo since Sunday.
Suzie ²_____ spent a fortune on presents.
negative
I ³_____ bought very much.
interrogative
⁴_____ you ⁵_____ my fish?

3 Look at the other examples of the present perfect in the postcard. Look at the information in the *Learn this!* box. Which use do they show?

We use the present perfect
1 To talk about recent events and to give news.
2 With *for* to describe a period of time.
I've been here for 45 minutes.
3 With *since* to describe a point of time.
I've been here since 2.30.
4 In questions with *How long...?* to ask about the length of time of a current situation.
How long have you been here?

4 Study the *Look out!* box. Find an example of *been* and *gone* in the postcard.

been and gone
We usually use *have been* instead of *have gone*.
We only use *have gone* when somebody has not yet returned. Compare:
I've been to Paris. Do you want to see my photos?
John isn't here. He's gone to Paris for the weekend.

●●●●●● Grammar Reference: page 102

EXPLOIT

1 Complete the message between Suzie and Amanda. Use the present perfect form of the verbs in brackets.

> Hi, Amanda. City Stars is great! I ¹**'ve tried on** (try on) four pairs of trainers and six jackets. ²_____ (you / buy) anything?
>
> No, I ³_____. I must be careful – I ⁴_____ (spend) enough money this week! Is Mum with you?
>
> No, she isn't. She ⁵_____ (go) to the market to buy some fruit. ⁶_____ (Dad / phone) this afternoon?
>
> I ⁷_____ (not / speak) to Dad, but I ⁸_____ (write) a postcard to him.

2 Complete the sentences with *been* or *gone*.
1 'Where's Maria?' 'She's _____ to the supermarket.'
2 Jake has _____ to the shops. Look at all the books he has bought.
3 'Are you going to the photography exhibition in London?' 'I've already _____ to it. It was fantastic.'
4 Tom has _____ out for lunch. He'll be back about two.

3 Complete the sentences about you. Use *for* or *since*.
1 I've known my best friend _____.
2 I haven't had anything to eat _____.
3 I've been at this school _____.
4 I haven't bought a book _____.
5 I've lived in this town _____.
6 I've had these shoes _____.
7 We haven't had an English test _____.

●●●●●● Grammar Builder: page 103

●●●●●● Workbook: page 38

Retail

VOCABULARY

1 What shops can you see in photos (1–4)? Study the words in the box and write example sentences for eight of them.

1 A corner shop is a convenient place to buy bread and milk.

> **Shops and shopping** browsing cash till
> charity shop clothes rail corner shop delicatessen
> department store food counter hardware store label
> newsagent's price tag queuing up window shopping

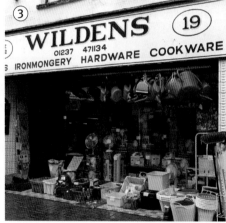

2 Where can you buy these things?

1 a baguette
2 a brooch
3 earphones
4 a folder
5 fresh olives
6 a second-hand book
7 a hairdryer
8 a light bulb
9 a suitcase
10 washing-up liquid

1 delicatessen

(●●●●● Workbook: page 39)

LISTEN

1 🎧 (1.38) Listen to a radio programme about the village of Hale. Number the words in the order you hear them.

a ☐ charity shop
b ☐ corner shop
c ☐ delicatessen
d ☐ price tag
e ☐ queuing up
f ☐ washing-up liquid

2 🎧 (1.38) Listen again and answer the questions.

1 What is Chris Burrows doing in Hale?
2 What does Rachel sometimes go shopping for in the evening?
3 What does the presenter see in a shop window?
4 Why doesn't he buy it?
5 What are people queuing up to buy?
6 What does Rachel have for lunch?

SPEAK

1 Work in pairs. Talk about shops that you like going to and shops that you don't like going to. Give reasons.

> I like going to sports shops because
> I enjoy buying / looking at / trying on trainers.

> I don't like going to computer shops because I'm
> not interested in / I hate buying / I can't afford
> computers and computer games.

2 Imagine you've got £100 to buy gifts. Make notes.

1 Who are you going to buy gifts for? (friends / family members)
2 What gifts are you going to buy? (one or two things for each person)
3 Which shops do you need to visit?

3 Tell the class.

> I'm going to buy gifts for ... , ... and ... .
> First, I'm going to the ... to buy ... for ... .
> Then ...
> After that ...
> Finally, ...

Present perfect and past simple

EXPLORE

1 🎧 (1.39) Read and listen to the dialogue. Which tense are the verbs in blue, present perfect or past simple?

Mark   Have you ever **travelled** abroad?
Alex   Yes, I have. I **went** to South America last year.
Mark   I've **seen** programmes about South America but I've **never been** there. Was it good?
Alex   Yes, fantastic. I **visited** Machu Picchu!

2 Study the information in the *Learn this!* box. Why are the verbs in the dialogue past simple or present perfect?

LEARN THIS!

1 We use the **present perfect** to talk about an experience at any time in the past. The exact time of the experience isn't important.
I've seen the latest adventure film.
Have you ever been to France?

2 We use the **past simple** to talk about a specific occasion in the past.
I saw the latest adventure film last night.
Did you go to France last summer?

LOOK OUT!

present perfect and *past simple*
We often use the present perfect to ask and answer questions about an experience, and then the past simple to give more information about a specific occasion.
'Have you ever been to Japan?'
'Yes, I have. I went there last summer.'

(●●○○○ Grammar Reference: page 102)

EXPLOIT

1 Choose the correct tense.

1 I usually get great presents from my family, but **I've received** / **I received** a few bad ones too!

2 It was my birthday last month, and my parents **have given** / **gave** me a digital camera.

3 We went out for dinner last weekend. **We've had** / **We had** pasta.

4 I love Chinese food, but **I've never eaten** / **I never ate** Japanese food.

5 She's a real fan. **She's seen** / **She saw** all his films.

6 We went to the cinema last night. **We've seen** / **We saw** a very strange film.

2 Complete each dialogue with one verb from the box. Use the present perfect and the past simple.

| eat | find | ~~forget~~ | meet | see |

1 a Have you ever forgotten somebody's birthday?
  b Yes, I have. I forgot my brother's birthday last year.
2 a _____ a Chinese film?
  b Yes, I have. I _____ *Hero* a few weeks ago.
3 a _____ a famous person?
  b Yes, I have. I _____ Bill Gates when he visited our school.
4 a _____ Indian food?
  b Yes, I have. In fact, I _____ chicken curry last night.
5 a _____ money on the pavement?
  b Yes, I have. I once _____ £10.

3 Complete the questions using the present perfect and the verbs in brackets.

1 Have you ever bought (buy) anything in a department store?
2 _____ (have) an argument with your parents?
3 _____ (borrow) money from someone?
4 _____ (hear) a really funny joke?
5 _____ (receive) a present you didn't like?
6 _____ (forget) to do your homework?

4 Ask and answer the questions in exercise 3. If the answer is yes, give more information using the past simple.

(●●●○○ Grammar Builder: page 103)
(●●●○○ Workbook: page 40)

An informal letter

READ

Read the letter. Find three things that Amy got for her birthday.

14 Northbrook Road
Oxford OXI 4RH

24th March 2010

Dear Aunt Susan,

Thank you so much for the scarf that you sent me for my birthday. It's gorgeous! It's very warm and the colour really goes with my eyes. I've worn it every day for the last week. Sophie wanted to borrow it yesterday, but I didn't lend it to her – she never gives things back!

I really enjoyed my birthday. Mum and Dad gave me some money because I'm saving for a holiday in India. (I reckon I've nearly saved enough for the plane ticket!) Sophie gave me a DVD of the programme 'Planet Earth'. Have you seen it? I haven't watched it yet, but my mates say it's brilliant.

I hope you're well. Thanks again for the lovely scarf!

Lots of love,

Amy

PREPARE

1 Find colloquial words and phrases in the letter that mean:

1 beautiful
2 to look good with something
3 to return something
4 I think ...
5 aeroplane
6 friends
7 very good

2 Put what Amy says in the correct paragraph and in the correct order.

a She says that she enjoyed her birthday.
b She says what Sophie gave her.
c She thanks her aunt for the scarf.
d She says what her parents gave her.
e She thanks her aunt again for the scarf.
f She says why she likes the scarf.
g She says how often she's worn the scarf.

Paragraph 1	Paragraph 2	Paragraph 3
1 _____	4 _____	7 _____
2 _____	5 _____	
3 _____	6 _____	

3 Read the *Writing tip* below. What expression does Amy use to end her letter?

> ### Writing tip: informal letter layout
>
> **When you write an informal letter**
> • Put your address in the top right-hand corner
> • Put the date under your address
> • Start with *Dear*...
> • You can use colloquial words and phrases
> • Finish with *Love* or *Best wishes* and your name

WRITE

Imagine that you have received a present from a friend or family member. Write an informal thank-you letter of 120–150 words. Use the writing plan to help you.

Paragraph 1
• Say thank you. Say what the present is and say something about it: What's it like? Why do you like it? Have you used it?

Paragraph 2
• Say what you did on the special occasion. Say what other presents you received.

Paragraph 3
• Say thank you again.

Check your work

Have you
☐ laid out the letter correctly?
☐ used informal language?
☐ included all the information in the task from the writing plan?
☐ written 120–150 words?

●●●●○ Workbook: page 41

Gifts

LANGUAGE SKILLS

1 🎧 (1.40) Complete the dialogue with the words from the box. Then listen and check your answers.

> mates round give seen lend on with glad borrow brilliant

James Hi, Alex. Did you get my birthday present?

Alex Yes, I did, thanks. The tracksuit's ¹_____. Just what I wanted! The colour goes ²_____ the school football kit.

James I'm ³_____ you like it. Did you have a good time ⁴_____ your birthday?

Alex Yes. All my family came for lunch.

James Did they ⁵_____ you lots of presents?

Alex Yes, but the tracksuit was the best! My brother wanted to ⁶_____ it but I didn't ⁷_____ it to him!

James I'll have to buy him one for his birthday! So what other presents did you get?

Alex I got a digital camera and a few books. I also got this great DVD about famous footballers. Have you ⁸_____ it?

James No, I haven't, but my ⁹_____ say it's really good.

Alex Well, why don't we watch it this evening? Come ¹⁰_____ to my house after school!

2 Read the dialogue again, and then answer the questions.

1 What goes with the colour of Alex's new tracksuit?
2 Who did Alex celebrate his birthday with?
3 How did they celebrate Alex's birthday?
4 Who wanted to use Alex's new tracksuit?
5 What other presents did Alex get?
6 What do James's mates say is really good?

3 Choose the correct words.

John How ¹ **long** / **far** have you been a photographer, Kevin?

Kevin Oh, I've been a photographer ² **for** / **since** I left university.

John And you photograph ancient buildings for a travel magazine, don't you?

Kevin Yes, I do. I've worked for *Historic Buildings* magazine ³ **for** / **since** five years now.

John Have you ⁴ **never** / **ever** taken photos of the Alhambra, in Spain?

Kevin Yes, I have. I ⁵ **'ve been** / **went** to the Alhambra last year. It was really impressive. Have you been?

John No, I ⁶ **haven't been** / **didn't go** but I want to go next year. And have you ever visited Petra, in Jordan?

Kevin Yes, I ⁷ **was** / **'ve been** there a few times. I ⁸ **was** / **'ve been** there last month.

DICTIONARY CORNER

Synonyms: cheap or expensive?

1 Check the meaning of the words in the box and write them in the correct columns.

> a bargain costly dear economical extortionate half-price inexpensive pricey

cheap	expensive
a bargain	_____
_____	_____
_____	_____

Exploring vocabulary: shopping

2 Make new words and expressions by adding one word to each group.

1 shopping list	window-shopping	shopping centre
2 flea _____	hyper_____	super_____
3 high _____	low _____	off _____
4 birthday _____	credit _____	identity _____
5 chain _____	_____keeper	department _____
6 estate _____	news _____	travel _____

I CAN ...

Read the statements. Think about your progress and tick (✓) one of the boxes.

| ✴ | I need more practice. | ✴✴ | I sometimes find this difficult. | ✴✴✴ | No problem! |

	✴	✴✴	✴✴✴
I can understand information in a tourist guide.			
I can talk about recent events.			
I can identify different shops and talk about gifts.			
I can talk about past experiences and when they happened.			
I can write an informal thank-you letter.			

●●●●● Workbook: Self check pages 42–43

6 Technology

Nanotechnology

THIS UNIT INCLUDES ●●●●

Vocabulary • technology • health problems • collocations • word building: nouns to adjectives • early and modern devices • affixes
Grammar • *will* and *going to* • zero conditional • *may, might* and *could*
Skills • listening to descriptions of devices
Writing • a formal letter

BEFORE READING

1 **Do you agree or disagree with this statement? Give reasons.**

   Technology is making the world a better place.

2 **Look at the photos and decide which of the inventions have:**

   1 made the world better
   2 made the world worse
   3 made no difference

READ

1 **Read the *Reading tip*. Read the first paragraph. What do you think this text is about?**

> ### Reading tip
> The first paragraph of a text usually introduces the topic. You can find out what the text is about by reading it quickly.

What's the big idea?

When people try to make predictions about the future, they usually get them completely wrong, like the prediction made by T.J. Watson, the head of IBM, in 1943: 'I think there may be a market for five computers in total in the world.' Today, about 45 million PCs are sold every year in the USA alone and computers are part of our everyday lives. But what surprises does technology have in store for us in the future? The answer is nanotechnology.

Nanotechnology is the science of building tiny machines, so small that they are invisible. To give you an idea of the size of these machines, the difference between a nanometre and a metre, two units of length, is the same as the difference between a marble and the planet Earth! Most scientists agree that nanotechnology will change our lives in the future – but how? At the moment it's difficult to predict whether this new technology will be like a wonderful dream, or a terrifying nightmare.

The dream

In the 1966 science fiction film *Fantastic Voyage*, an inventor develops an amazing new way to cure diseases. He shrinks a group of scientists and their submarine and injects them all into a patient. They then travel around the patient's body, visiting the different organs and repairing them. Of course, this is just a film – but the reality of nanotechnology is not very different. Scientists are already making nanobots, tiny robots that are smaller than a virus. In the future, doctors might be able to inject these into a patient, and the nanobots will travel around the body and repair the diseased parts.

2 🎧 (2.02) **Read the text. Choose the best answers.**

1 T.J. Watson said
   a the market for computers was tiny.
   b IBM made five computers a year.
   c IBM computers were the best in the world.
2 Nanotechnology makes
   a tiny marbles.
   b the buildings of the future.
   c machines that people can't see.
3 *Fantastic Voyage*
   a shows a doctor helping tiny patients.
   b was a true story.
   c shows what might happen in the future.
4 Eric Drexler
   a invented nanobots.
   b writes about science.
   c makes copies of science books.
5 In the novel *Prey*
   a people eat nanobots.
   b nanobots destroy the planet.
   c nanobots make a new planet in three hours.

3 **Read the text again. Which paragraphs contain the information to complete the sentences? Complete them in your own words.**

1 Nanobots could make the world a much better place because scientists might be able to …
2 Nanobots could make the world a much worse place because they might …

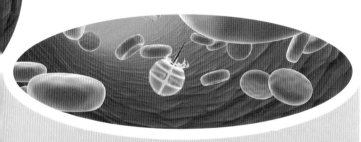

The nightmare

Some people are worried that nanotechnology could be difficult to control. Nanobots might escape into the environment and damage people, plants and animals. Others have even more serious worries. Eric Drexler is a futurist, a scientist who makes predictions about the future. In his book *Engines of Creation* he predicted the invention of nanobots. He also described a special kind of nanobot that can make a copy of itself using the materials around it – and this is where the nightmare begins. In Michael Crichton's book *Prey*, nanobots reproduce themselves so quickly that they consume all the materials around them and then look for more … and more, and more, eventually 'eating' the world. Some people are worried that this might really happen. The most extreme predictions (which very few scientists believe) say that nanobots could destroy the entire planet in about three hours!

4 **Are the sentences true or false? Correct the false sentences.**

1 T.J. Watson was correct about the future of the PC.
2 Most scientists think that nanotechnology will be important in the future.
3 It's easy to predict how nanotechnology will affect our lives.
4 In 1966, an inventor developed an amazing new way to cure diseases.
5 In the future, scientists might be able to cure diseases by injecting nanobots into patients.
6 Eric Drexler is a scientist.
7 Most scientists are worried that nanobots could destroy the world in about three hours.

UNDERSTANDING IDEAS

Answer the questions. Look at the text, and use your own words and ideas.

1 Do you think science fiction books and films really show us what the future will be like?
2 Do you think the positive and negative predictions about nanobots will really happen? Why / Why not?
3 How do you think technology will make our lives different in the future?

VOCABULARY

What's the big idea?

1 **Match the highlighted words in the text with the definitions.**

1 To make a copy of something.
2 A small coloured glass ball that children play games with.
3 The place and conditions that people live and work in.
4 To make an illness end.
5 A bad dream.
6 Something that you can't see.
7 Puts a drug or medicine into someone's body.
8 How big or small something is.
9 A very small living thing that can enter your body and cause disease.
10 Makes something become smaller.
11 A vehicle that can travel under water.
12 Whole or complete.
13 Parts of the body, such as the heart or brain, that do a particular job.
14 To use something such as energy, materials or food.
15 Statements about what you think will happen in the future.

2 **Do you know these words?**

eventually   everyday   futurist   head   material
nanotechnology   patient   science fiction

(●●●○○   Workbook: page 44)

What's the big idea?

ACTIVATE

Complete these sentences with the correct form of words from the box.

> consume cure entire environment inject invisible
> marble nightmare organ prediction reproduce shrink
> size submarine virus

1 Sailors in a _____ live and work in a very small space under the sea for long periods of time. It's a very difficult _____ to be in.

2 I've had this _____ for a week now. I feel really tired and ill. The doctor is going to _____ me in my arm with a different medicine today. I hope it _____ me and that I can go back to work.

3 Did you read that _____ in the newspaper about what scientists will do in the future? It said they will _____ new hearts and brains in laboratories and then give these new _____ to people that are ill. It's incredible!

4 I had this terrible _____ last night! I thought that I was in an enormous washing machine and that I was going to _____! When the washing machine stopped I was the _____ of a small mouse! I was really glad to wake up!

5 They were really hungry after the match. They _____ the _____ meal in five minutes! They didn't leave anything on their plates.

6 Most of my _____ have lines of colour through the middle of them. However, I've got some that you can hardly see because they are just made of glass. They're almost _____ and I often win games with them.

EXTEND

Health problems

1 Put the words in the box in the correct columns.

> virus skeleton outpatient diagnose infection
> prescribe organs epidemic ~~patient~~ cure casualty
> muscle

people	problems	the body	actions
patient	_____	_____	_____
_____	_____	_____	_____
_____	_____	_____	_____

2 Complete the sentences with words from Extend exercise 1.

1 There was a bad car crash but there was only one casualty. An ambulance took him to hospital.

2 When they were building the house they found some bones and the _____ of a strange animal.

3 Can you _____ some tablets for the pain in my back, doctor?

4 She's an _____. She has to go to the hospital every week for three hours.

5 There was a flu _____ at the school last month. Half the children were ill and didn't come to school.

6 He can't run because he's hurt a _____ at the back of his leg. He has to rest for a few weeks.

7 Don't drink dirty water because you will get an _____ and be very ill.

8 The doctors don't know what's wrong with him. They can't _____ his illness.

Collocations

3 Match the verbs with the nouns that we often use them with.

1	cure	a	the environment
2	make	b	tablets
3	protect	c	a disease
4	have	d	technology
5	develop	e	the size
6	prescribe	f	the future
7	predict	g	a prediction
8	increase	h	a nightmare

Word building

4 Complete the table.

noun	adjective
science	[1] scientific
technology	[2] _____
success	[3] _____
medicine	[4] _____
future	[5] _____
environment	[6] _____
infection	[7] _____
muscle	[8] _____

●●●●○ Workbook: page 45

will and *going to*

EXPLORE

1 🎧 (2.03) Read the dialogue and choose *will* or *going to*. Then listen and check.

John	Where's the compass?
Rick	I didn't bring it. ¹**I'm going to** / **I'll** use my new mobile phone instead. It's got a satellite navigation system.
John	OK, fine. So where are we?
Rick	Just a minute. I'm trying to switch it on.
John	Well, hurry up. I'm getting cold.
Rick	²**I'm going to** / **I'll** lend you my coat.
John	Thanks. We're lost, aren't we? And look at that black cloud. ³**It's going to** / **It'll** rain. What are you doing?
Rick	I'm hitting my phone. It isn't working.
John	Do you think ⁴**that's going to** / **that'll** help?
Rick	Probably not.
John	Look, I've got a better idea. ⁵**I'm going to** / **I'll** call a taxi.
Rick	But we don't know where we are!

2 Study the information in the *Learn this!* box. Match examples 1–5 of *will* and *going to* in the dialogue with the uses in the box.

LEARN THIS!

We use *will* for
1 Predictions, especially after *I (don't) think …*
   I think he'll like his present.
2 Offers and promises
   I'll lend you some money.
   I won't tell anyone.
3 Decisions that you make while you are speaking
   He isn't answering his phone. I'll send a text.

We use *going to* for
4 Predictions, especially when they're based on what we can see
   Look out! You're going to drop that computer!
5 Intentions
   I'm going to work hard next term.

●●●●● Grammar Reference: page 104

EXPLOIT

1 🎧 (2.04) Complete the speech bubbles with the correct form of *will* or *going to*. Then listen and check.

Oh no! We ¹_____ hit that tree!

What tree?

Oh no! I've dropped my money!

Don't worry! I ²_____ pick it up for you!

Oh no! My camera!

Don't worry. I ³_____ buy you a new one, I promise.

Why are you wearing those clothes?

I ⁴_____ tidy my room.

It ⁵_____ be another bad day for business.

2 Make notes about your own future. Write down:
- three things you're going to do next week
- three things you think you'll do after you leave school

3 Tell the class your intentions and predictions from exercise 2. How many are the same?

●●●●● Grammar Builder: page 105

●●●●● Workbook: page 46

Early devices

VOCABULARY

1 Look at the photos. What do you think you can do with these devices? What do you think each one is?

- record moving pictures
- play games
- add numbers
- play music
- send messages
- speak to people
- listen to the news

I I think you can send messages. I think it's a ...

2 🎧 (2.05) Listen and check your answers.

3 Match the early devices with the modern devices we use today.

gramophone – CD player

> **Early devices** adding machine cine camera
> crystal radio gramophone Instamatic camera
> telegraph typewriter video game

> **Modern devices** calculator camcorder CD player
> DAB radio digital camera games console
> telephone word processor

4 Choose the correct verbs

1 I'm not surprised it doesn't work. You haven't **unplugged it** / **plugged it in**!
2 Oh no! The computer's crashed and I haven't **deleted** / **saved** my file.
3 You often have to **record** / **reboot** your computer after updating the software.
4 Can you **rewind** / **pause** the camcorder? I'd like to see that bit again.
5 You should **fast forward** / **charge** the battery for eight hours before using the mobile phone for the first time.
6 That old adding machine wasn't electronic so you didn't have to **switch it on** / **turn it up**.

(●●●●● Workbook: page 47)

LISTEN

🎧 (2.06) Listen to four conversations. Which devices from Vocabulary exercise 3 are they describing? Where are the people?

	Device	Location
1		
2		
3		
4		

SPEAK

1 Work in pairs. Which two modern devices in exercise 3 can't you live without? Why? Which two can you easily live without? Why?

2 Tell the class what you think. Vote for the two most and two least essential devices.

Zero conditional

EXPLORE

1 Read the text about the Truth Machine. How many clauses are there in the sentences in blue?

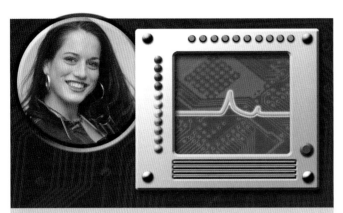

If you tell a lie, your voice contains signs of stress. You can't help it! This gadget is called the Truth Machine. It measures the amount of stress in a person's voice. **If the person is very relaxed, the green lights come on.** The red lights come on if there is some stress in the voice.

2 Look at the sentences in blue in the text. Which tense do we use in the *if* clause? Which tense do we use in the main clause? Complete the rules in the *Learn this!* box.

> **LEARN THIS!**
>
> **1** We use the **zero conditional** to talk about a result which always follows from a particular action. We use the _____ to describe the action and the _____ to describe the result.
>
> **2** The *if* clause can come before or after the main clause. If it comes after, we don't use a comma.
> *Your voice contains signs of stress if you tell a lie.*

(●●●●● Grammar Reference: page 104)

EXPLOIT

1 Work in pairs. Can you complete the facts? Use the zero conditional.

1 If you heat water to 100° Celsius, it boils.
2 If you mix blue paint and yellow paint, ...
3 If you mix green light and red light, ...
4 If you leave a fish out of water, ...
5 If you multiply 1111111 by 1111111, ...

2 Complete the sentences.

1 My teacher gets annoyed if ...
2 I don't sleep very well if ...
3 I speak more in English classes if ...
4 I feel happy if ...
5 I get angry if ...

may, might and *could*

EXPLORE

1 Look at the examples of *may*, *might* and *could* in the text from pages 48–49.

I think there **may** be a market for five computers in total in the world.

In the future, doctors **might** be able to inject these into a patient, ...

... nanobots **could** destroy the entire planet in about three hours.

2 Study the information in the *Learn this!* box. Complete the rules.

> **LEARN THIS!**
>
> **1** To talk about possibility in the present or future, we can use **may, might** or **could** followed by the infinitive without *to*.
> *They may / might / could be at home now.* (present)
> *She may / might / could buy a new DVD recorder.* (future)
>
> **2** We use *may not* or _____ *not* for the negative. We don't use _____ *not*.

EXPLOIT

1 Complete the text with *may*, *might*, and *could* and the verbs in brackets. More than one answer is possible.

Many greengrocer's and butcher's are closing down in the UK because of big supermarkets and people are worried that the same thing [1]_____ (happen) to other small shops.

As more and more big supermarket chains open, more and more people [2]_____ (buy) all their food in them and other shops, such as bakeries, [3]_____ (lose) business and [4] _____ (close). We [5]_____ (not see) small shops like these in ten years time.

One big supermarket [6]_____ (sell) everything we need, including medicine and clothes. We [7]_____ (not have) chemist's or even clothes shops any more!

2 Write down something that you:
- might do this evening.
- may not remember to do next week.
- could have in your pocket or bag.
- may eat this evening.
- might not enjoy doing tomorrow.
- could wear tomorrow.

(●●●●● Grammar Builder: page 105)

(●●●●● Workbook: page 48)

A formal letter

READ

1 Work in pairs. Student A: Read the first letter. Student B: Read the second letter. Ask and answer the questions.

1 What is the name of the gadget?
2 Where did she buy it?
3 When did she buy it?
4 What is the problem with it?
5 What does she want the company to do?

11 Wood Close
Newcastle NE13 7TY

14 May 2010

Customer Services Department
Zenon Electronics
London SW12 7OP

Dear Sir or Madam,

I am writing to report a fault with the new Zenon ZK400 digital camera that I bought from The Gadget Shop in Newcastle on 28th April.

It sometimes stops in the middle of a shot. To make it start, I have to turn the camera off and then turn it on again.

I am returning the camera to you with this letter. I would be grateful if you could repair the fault. If this is not possible, could you please send me a new camera?

I look forward to hearing from you.

Yours faithfully,

Madeline Connor

Madeline Connor

23 Marston Rd
Bolton BO12 4FG

3 January 2010

Customer Services Department
Computer Shop
Manchester M5 5HJ

Dear Sir or Madam,

I am writing to complain about an UltraFast modem that I recently bought from your website.

When it arrived, I connected it to my PC, but it does not work. I cannot access the internet or send emails.

I am enclosing the modem together with the receipt. Could you please replace the modem as soon as possible?

I look forward to hearing from you.

Yours faithfully,

Victoria Swift

Victoria Swift

2 Read the letters. In which paragraph does each writer:
1 explain the problem in detail?
2 say why she is writing the letter?
3 say what she wants the company to do?

PREPARE

1 Read and complete the rules for formal letters with the words in the box.

> Dear Sir or Madam   date   full name   Yours faithfully

1 Write the ¹_____ in full, e.g. *14 May 2010*.
2 Start the letter Dear *Mr / Mrs / Miss, etc.* if you know the name of the person you are writing to, or ²_____ if you don't.
3 Do not use colloquial language or slang, e.g. *My mum bought me a calculator, and it's rubbish.*
4 Finish the letter with *Yours sincerely* if you used the person's name at the start, or ³_____ if you didn't.
5 If you type the letter, include your ⁴_____ at the end of the letter after your signature.

2 Read the *Writing tip* below. Find the set phrases in the letters.

> ### Writing tip: formal letter expressions
>
> We often use these set phrases in formal letters:
> *I am writing to …*
> *I would be grateful if you could …*
> *Could you please …*
> *I look forward to hearing from you.*
> *I am enclosing …*

WRITE

1 Imagine that you have bought a new electronic device. Then choose a fault from the ideas in the box below or invent your own.

> you can't turn it off   the pictures are black and white   there's no sound   it's very slow   you can't switch it on   you can't play your old DVDs / games on it

2 Write a formal letter of 120–150 words to the manufacturer. Include this information:
- say what the gadget is called, and where and when you bought it
- say what the problem is
- tell the company you are returning the gadget.
- ask them to repair it or send you a new one

(●●●●● Workbook: page 49)

Technology
LANGUAGE SKILLS

1 🎧 (2.07) Complete the dialogue with the words from the box. Then listen and check your answers.

> instructions replace device receipt middle possible
> soon connect repair properly

Assistant Good morning. Can I help you?

Peter Yes. I bought this Zircon MP4 player from here last week but it doesn't work ¹_____.

Assistant What's the problem?

Peter Well, it sometimes stops in the ²_____ of a song.

Assistant Are the songs just from your computer?

Peter Yes. And when I ³_____ it to my PC I always follow the ⁴_____.

Assistant I see. Have you got the ⁵_____?

Peter Yes, here you are. Can you ⁶_____ it?

Assistant I'll send the ⁷_____ to the company today.

Peter And if they can't repair it?

Assistant If it's not ⁸_____ to repair it, we'll ⁹_____ it. Now, can I have your name and telephone number, please?

Peter Yes. It's Peter Walton and the number is 322 437 881.

Assistant Thank you, Mr Walton. We'll phone you as ¹⁰_____ as they return it.

2 Read the dialogue again, and complete the repair form.

> Sutton Electronics
>
> Repair request.
>
> Product: Zircon MP4 ¹_____ Receipt: Yes No
>
> Problem: It sometimes ²_____ in the middle of a ³_____.
>
> Client only ⁴_____ his device to his computer.
>
> Action: Sent to company to ⁵_____ it. If they can't, we will replace the device.
>
> Client's name: ⁶_____   Telephone: ⁷_____

3 Complete the sentences with *might*, *going to* or *will* and the verbs in brackets.

1 I can't carry this heavy box.
Don't worry. I _____ (carry) it for you!

2 It's been a hard week.
I agree. I'm really tired! I've only got one plan for this weekend; I _____ (sleep)!

3 Do you think that scientists _____ (build) a car that can fly?
I don't know. Flying cars _____ (be) very dangerous.

4 Where's John? We're meeting in five minutes.
I don't know. He _____ (be) in the library.

Affixes

1 Check the affixes in the box and match them with the definitions.

> ~~bio-~~ micro- -phile -phobe phono- photo-
> tele- thermo-

1 connected with living things bio
2 a person who likes a particular person or thing
3 connected with light
4 a person who dislikes or is afraid of a particular person or thing
5 over a long distance
6 connected with heat
7 very small
8 connected with sound

2 Complete the word in each sentence. Use the affixes in exercise 1.

1 A biometric scanner is a device that identifies people by their fingerprints or their eyes.
2 I can't stand gadgets. I'm a complete techno_____.
3 There's a _____chip inside every computer.
4 Mr Dubois, my French teacher, is also an expert in the _____logy of Arabic.
5 The process by which plants use sunlight to make food is called _____synthesis.
6 I'm such a biblio_____. I can't stop buying books.
7 Do you need to use a _____scope to see that star?
8 The water's too hot. You should turn the _____stat down.

3 Find more words using three of the affixes in exercise 1. Explain what the affix and the words mean.

I CAN ...

Read the statements. Think about your progress and tick (✓) one of the boxes.

✳ I need more practice.   ✳✳ I sometimes find this difficult.   ✳✳✳ No problem!

	✳	✳✳	✳✳✳
I can understand a scientific article.			
I can make predictions, offers, promises and decisions.			
I can describe electronic devices.			
I can talk about outcomes and possibilities.			
I can write a letter of complaint.			

●●○○○ Workbook: Self check pages 50–51

Gulliver's Travels
by Jonathan Swift

Biography

Jonathan Swift was born in Dublin, Ireland, in 1667. During his life he published a great number of books, and *Gulliver's Travels* is the most famous. When it was published in 1726, it was a success with readers of all ages, both children and adults. Today, the amusing and fantastic adventures of its hero are still enjoyed by readers of all ages.

And so in about three weeks I began to speak the language of Lilliput. The King often visited me, and every time he came, I asked him to take off my chains. He explained that first I must promise not to fight against Lilliput or hurt Lilliputians, and that I must be searched for weapons. I agreed to both these things and carefully picked up two of his officers in my hands. I put them first in one pocket, then moved them to all my other pockets, except two which I kept secret. As they searched, they wrote down in a notebook details of all the things they found.

Afterwards I read some of their report:

'In the second coat pocket we found two very large pieces of wood, and inside them were great pieces of metal, very sharp. In another pocket there was a most wonderful engine, at the end of a long chain. The engine was inside a huge round container, which was made half of silver and half of another metal. This second metal was very strange as we could see through it to some mysterious writing and pictures. The engine made a continuous loud noise.'

The officers could not guess what these things were, but they were, of course, my two pocket knives and my watch. They also found my comb, a purse with several gold and silver coins, my gun and bullets.

The King wanted to know what the gun was used for.

'Bring it out,' he ordered me, 'and show me how it works.'

I took the gun out and put a bullet into it. 'Don't be afraid,' I warned the King. Then I fired the gun into the air.

It was the loudest noise the Lilliputians had ever heard. Hundreds of them thought they were dead, and fell down. The King himself was very frightened. As I gave my gun to the officials to keep, I warned them to be careful with it. They allowed me to keep all my other things, and I hoped that one day soon I would be free.

1 Gulliver has travelled to a fictitious country called Lilliput. Read the text and say how the Lilliputians are different to humans. Do you think Gulliver is having a good time there?

2 🎧 (2.10) Read the text again and answer the questions.
1 What did Gulliver want the King to do?
2 What were the officers looking for in Gulliver's pockets?
3 How did they get into his pockets?
4 What was the device with an engine?
5 What did the Lilliputians do when Gulliver fired the gun?

3 Answer the questions. Look at the text, and use your own words and ideas to explain your answers.
1 How do you think Gulliver felt when he first saw the Lilliputians? Why?
2 What type of person do you think the King was?
3 What do you think Swift's message was about guns?
4 Do you think Gulliver became free? Explain your answer.

4 Imagine you are a Lilliputian. Choose a modern device and write a short description of it.

The joy of txt

1 The British love sending text messages. They send more than 2.5 billion every month. And most people now understand the language of text, with its numbers and missing letters. In fact, when a student at a Scottish school wrote an essay entirely 'in txt', his teacher gave him 'C+ 4 f4t' ('C+ for effort').

2 Although texting is a convenient and cheap method of staying in touch with your friends, it can also bring problems. In 2005, a British teenager became the first person in the world to receive treatment for an addiction to text messaging. In one year, the 19-year-old spent about £4,500 on texts. (He was sending about 700 texts a week.) He was also addicted to email, and sent 8,000 messages in one month from his computer at work. The treatment is working well, however, and he now spends no more than £10 a week on texts.

3 For some people, text messaging has changed their lives. For example, James Trusler from Sussex, in England, travels around the world taking part in texting competitions and TV shows. He's the world's fastest texter and recently set a new world record while he was appearing on Australian TV. He texted: 'The razor-toothed piranhas of the genera Serrasalmus and Pygocentrus are the most ferocious freshwater fish in the world. In reality they seldom attack a human.' It took him 67 seconds. (That's fast. Try it!) James sends a lot of text messages – about 2,500 a month. Fortunately, he doesn't get big bills because he works for a large mobile phone company!

The razor-toothed piranhas of the genera Serrasalmus and Pygocentrus are the most ferocious freshwater fish in the world. In reality they seldom attack a human.
Options   Send   Clear

A text education

READ

1 Look at the photos in the text and the title. What does 'txt' mean? Why is it written like this?

2 Read the text. Which paragraph (1–3) mentions:
   1 a TV show?
   2 a school essay?
   3 an addiction?
   4 the fastest texter in the world?
   5 emails?
   6 a mobile phone company?
   7 the language of text?
   8 competitions?

3 Work in pairs. Try to say these words and phrases from text messages. How would you write them in normal English?
   1 cu soon
   2 call me b4 2moro
   3 ur gr8
   4 im @ home

LISTEN

🎧 (2.11) Listen to four teenagers talking about how they use a mobile phone. Answer the questions.

Paula   Ethan   Darren   Cindy

1 Who loves texting?
2 Who loves ringtones?
3 Who has got a 3G phone?
4 Who talks for a long time on the phone?

SPEAK AND WRITE

1 Work in pairs. Ask and answer the questions.
   1 How often do you use a mobile phone?
   2 What do you use it for?
   3 What do you think you will use it for in the future?

2 What are the advantages and disadvantages of having a mobile phone? Write a short paragraph.

Unusual festivals

BEFORE READING

Look at the photos. What are the people doing? Why do you think they are doing it? Use the title and headings of the text to help you.

READ

1 Read the *Reading tip*. Read the sentences (1–9) and find the key words that you should look for in the text. Match the sentences with the three festivals. Write WT for Water Throwing, CR for Cheese Rolling or BR for Bull Running.

1 Nobody knows when the tradition began.
2 Old people don't take part.
3 They banned it because too many people got injured.
4 It's part of a longer festival.
5 It takes place at eight o'clock in the morning.
6 It takes place on the same day every year.
7 Participants have to chase something.
8 Participants have to throw something.
9 Participants have to escape from something.

Reading tip

In matching exercises, start by reading the whole text. Then try to match the statements to appropriate parts of the text. Read the parts of the text carefully to see if they match the statements. If they don't, look for the answers in other parts of the text.

Cheese rolling

Nobody knows exactly when this tradition at Cooper's Hill in the centre of England started, but it was centuries ago. The rules are simple: you have to chase a large, round cheese down a very steep hill. This dangerous event takes place every year at the end of May. Participants often break limbs or suffer from concussion, and even the spectators are at risk: one year, a cheese soared into the air and hit a 59-year-old grandmother on the head. 1997 was a particularly bad year for casualties; up to 37 people were injured. So in 1998, the local authorities banned the cheese rolling. However, because of all the protests, the ban only lasted a year and the tradition started again in 1999. To reduce the number of injuries, participants and spectators had to obey a few simple safety rules. Even so, about twelve people a year get injured.

The traditions they tried to ban

Water throwing festival

If you are visiting Thailand in April, it might be a good idea to take an umbrella with you. Why? Well, although April is the hottest month in Thailand, it is also when Thais, on 13 April, celebrate New Year. How do they celebrate it? By dousing people with water! Originally the Thais gently poured water over each other's hands as a sign of respect. This then developed into young people throwing water at each other to relieve the heat. Today, however, young people run or drive through the streets with buckets of water or enormous water-guns and throw water at anybody they see. So, if you don't want to get soaked, don't stand in the street. Fortunately, there are some rules. Firstly, participants mustn't throw water at elderly people. Secondly, they mustn't touch people. Thirdly, they mustn't throw water at car drivers. Every year people get killed or injured in road accidents during the festival and some people want to ban it.

2 🎧 (2.12) Read the text again. Choose the best answers.

1 In Thailand
  a it rains a lot in the month of April.
  b water is an important part of New Year celebrations.
  c old people can't throw water at young people.

2 At Cooper's Hill
  a people throw cheese at their grandmothers.
  b people have to run and eat cheese at the same time.
  c fewer people injure themselves now.

3 Cheese rolling
  a starts at the bottom of a hill.
  b started in 1999.
  c is an ancient event.

4 The bulls
  a die after they have run.
  b have red handkerchiefs around their necks.
  c weigh a hundred kilos each.

5 Participants
  a run in groups of six.
  b can't escape from the bulls.
  c can receive serious injuries.

Bull running

It is the most famous part of the Fiesta de San Fermín, a week-long festival that is held every July in Pamplona, Spain. Every morning at 8 o'clock, participants run through the streets in front of a small herd of six bulls, each about 600 kilos. Anybody can take part. You needn't sign up – you just have to stand in the street and wait for the bulls. However, most participants wear white clothes with a red handkerchief tied around their necks. The event is extremely dangerous. In 2004, eight participants were injured when the bulls caught them with their horns. All spectators must stay behind the double line of fences along the road. This is because the participants need to leap over the first line of fences into an empty space to escape from the bulls. Each year, there are people who want to ban the bull running. They aren't concerned about the number of injuries to the participants – they're protesting because, after the bull running, the bulls are killed in bull fights.

UNDERSTANDING IDEAS

Answer the questions. Look at the text, and use your own words and ideas.

1 Which event do you think is the most dangerous? Why?
2 Why do you think some people like to take part in dangerous events like these?
3 The three events in the text are traditions. Do people in your country take part in any dangerous events or traditions?

VOCABULARY

The traditions they tried to ban

1 Match the highlighted words in the text with the definitions below.

1 To jump.
2 With a gradient that rises or falls very quickly.
3 Made a liquid flow from a container.
4 To join a course, an organization or an event.
5 To run after someone or something so you can catch them.
6 Rose high in the sky.
7 Fastened by pulling two ends together.
8 Covering someone or something with a liquid.
9 Two hard pointed parts that grow on the heads of some animals.
10 To make an unpleasant situation better.
11 The feeling that someone is important and that you should be polite to them.
12 A head injury that makes people lose consciousness.
13 Old.
14 Actions that show that people are against something.
15 A group of animals that live and eat together.

2 Do you know these words?

> authorities ban bucket casualties
> concerned about limb safety rules spectator

(●●●○○   Workbook: page 52)

The traditions they tried to ban

ACTIVATE

Complete these sentences with the correct form of the words from the box.

chase   concussion   douse   elderly   herd   horns   leap
pour   protest   relieve   respect   sign up   soar   steep   tie

1 Could you _____ some water into my glass, please?
2 Only one goat on our farm has got big _____, and he's not dangerous.
3 The little boy fell of his bicycle and hit his head. He had _____ and his parents took him to hospital.
4 There isn't a bridge but the river is very narrow. We can _____ from one side to the other.
5 Children should always show _____ to older people and speak politely to them.
6 On safari we saw a _____ of elephants drinking water at a lake.
7 I threw the paper plane into the sky and it _____ high into the air.
8 A lot of _____ people find it difficult to move around.
9 It took me thirty minutes to cycle up the _____ hill and five to cycle down the other side!
10 He wants to study Arabic so he has _____ for a course at the Arab Studies school.
11 These tablets _____ the pain of headaches and soon stop them.
12 The firemen had to _____ the fire with water for three hours before they could control it.
13 Our dog always _____ cats but he never catches them!
14 The laces on his trainers were unfastened so he _____ them together.
15 The people don't want a new road and they've organized a _____ against it in the city centre.

EXTEND

Prohibition and permission

1 Match the verbs with the definitions.

1 prohibit   a to refuse to buy goods from a particular company or to take part in a particular event
2 allow   b to make someone live in another country, usually for political reasons
3 boycott   c to give official permission to do something
4 authorize   d to give a person permission to do or have something
5 censor   e to remove the parts of a book or film for moral, political or religious reasons
6 exile   f to stop people doing something

2 Complete the sentences with the correct forms of the verbs from exercise 1.

1 We're boycotting that shop and not buying anything from there. The owner was really rude to my mum.
2 The education department said there is some violence in the film and they have _____ parts of it.
3 My parents only _____ me to watch TV at the weekends.
4 The British _____ the French leader Napoleon to a small island in the Atlantic Ocean.
5 The government has _____ the building of a new hospital. Work will start next month.
6 You can't smoke in the library. The town hall has _____ smoking in public buildings.

Groups of animals

3 Complete the phrases with the words in the box.

herd   ~~pride~~   pack   troop   school   flock

1 a pride of lions
2 a _____ of cows
3 a _____ of birds
4 a _____ of monkeys
5 a _____ of wolves
6 a _____ of sardines

Dependent prepositions

4 We use some words with just one or two particular prepositions. Complete the text with the prepositions in the box.

with   from   for   to   around   in   of   ~~about~~

Camel fighting

They talk [1] about bullfighting in Spain but in fact it is a man waiting [2] _____ a bull to run at him. However, camel fighting in the ancient city of Ephesus consists [3] _____ one camel fighting [4] _____ another. The day before the fights, the camel owners participate [5] _____ a festival. The next day thousands of people crowd [6] _____ to watch the fights. However, the fights are not very violent and there are very few injuries [7] _____ the camels: they just push each other. Although, when a camel escapes [8] _____ the fight and runs at the crowd, it can be very dangerous! Fortunately, there are never many accidents.

●●●●● Workbook: page 53

must, mustn't and needn't

EXPLORE

1 🎧 (2.13) Complete the text with *must*, *mustn't* or *needn't*.
Then listen and check.

How to be polite at a Chinese meal

You ¹_____ start your food until the host picks up his or her chopsticks. In general, if your host offers you food, you ²_____ accept it. (It's better to leave it in your bowl than refuse it.) Periods of silence during a meal are not considered embarrassing in China, so you ³_____ talk just to fill the gaps. As the Chinese proverb says: 'Your speech should be better than silence. If not, be silent.'

2 Study your answers to exercise 1. Complete the rules in the *Learn this!* box with *must*, *mustn't* or *needn't*.

1 We use _____ to express **necessity** (something that is very important to do).
2 We use _____ to express **lack of necessity** (something that isn't necessary but isn't against the rules).
3 We use _____ to express **prohibition** (something that is very important not to do).

●●●●● Grammar Reference: page 106

EXPLOIT

1 Write sentences about your school with *must*, *mustn't* and *needn't*. Use phrases from the box.

run in the corridor   study English
copy your friend's homework
switch off your mobile phone in class   wear a uniform
stand up when the teacher comes in

At our school we mustn't ...

2 Work in pairs. How many more sentences can you make about rules in your school?

3 Complete the facts about customs around the world with *must*, *mustn't* or *needn't*.

1 In Japan you must remove your shoes before entering somebody's house – it is offensive to wear them indoors.
2 In many parts of Asia, you _____ touch or pat somebody on the head – it is considered offensive.
3 In many Asian countries, you _____ eat with your right hand because it's wrong to use your left hand.
4 In many countries, you _____ use your index finger to beckon somebody – it is very rude.
5 If you are invited to somebody's home in Brazil, you _____ take a gift, but it's normal to send a thank-you note the next day.
6 In many Middle Eastern countries, you _____ show the soles of your feet – it is offensive.
7 In Indonesia, you _____ use a knife and fork at mealtimes – you can use your fingers if you prefer.
8 In most European countries, you _____ put your elbows on the table when your eating, because it's rude.

4 Work in pairs. Think about the customs in your country when you visit somebody's house for a meal. Are the ideas in the box things you *must* do, *mustn't* do or *needn't* do?

arrive exactly on time   bring flowers
take your shoes off when you enter the house
eat everything that you are given   eat with your fingers
eat with a knife and fork

5 Write a short note to somebody who is visiting your country. Explain how to be polite when you go to somebody's house for a meal. Use your ideas from exercise 4.

Hi _____,
Here's some advice about how to be polite when you go to somebody's house for a meal.
You must ...
You mustn't ...
You needn't ...
Best wishes,
_____

●●●●● Grammar Builder: page 107

●●●●● Workbook: page 54

Body language

VOCABULARY

1 Describe the body language of the people in the pictures. Use expressions from the box.

> **Gestures** beckon bow cross your legs embrace
> fold your arms frown gesticulate hold hands nod
> pat somebody on the back / head
> point (at somebody / something) raise your hat
> shake hands shake your head wave goodbye

2 🎧 (2.14) Complete the text with some of the verbs in the box in exercise 1. Then listen and check your answers.

Traveller's tales: Bulgaria

An American tourist is in a local street market in Bulgaria when a flower-seller ¹beckons her, so she goes over to his stall. He ²_____ at some flowers and ³_____ with his hands. She doesn't want to buy them, so she ⁴_____ her head to say no. Immediately, the flower-seller starts wrapping the flowers. When the woman walks away, he looks angry. He ⁵_____ at her and ⁶_____ his arms with indignation. Someone should have explained to her that in Bulgaria you shake your head to say yes, and do the opposite, ⁷_____, to say no. That's why the flower-seller thought the woman wanted to buy the flowers!

3 Which of the gestures and greetings in exercise 1 do people use in your country?

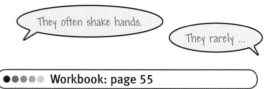

They often shake hands.

They rarely ...

●●●●● Workbook: page 55

LISTEN

1 🎧 (2.15) Listen to three people talking about customs in their country. Match the two halves of the sentences.

1 Lucy thinks that Australian people are ...
2 Haruko thinks that Japanese people are ...
3 Ludmila thinks that Russian people are ...

a quite formal and very polite.
b very warm and friendly.
c informal and treat everyone the same.

2 🎧 (2.15) Choose the correct words. Then listen and check.

1 In Australia, you **should** / **shouldn't** sit in the front of a taxi.
2 In Australia, it's rude to **point at** / **hold hands with** people.
3 In Japan, you shouldn't **cross your legs** / **fold your arms** when you're in a formal situation.
4 In Japan, you **must** / **mustn't** shake hands with a woman when you meet her for the first time.
5 When you visit a Japanese house, you shouldn't look in the **kitchen** / **bathroom**.
6 In Russia, men **and** / **but not** women greet each other in public with an embrace.
7 In Russia, close friends kiss **twice** / **three times** when they meet.

SPEAK

Work in pairs. Answer the questions.

- How do you greet people you see every day?
- How do you greet friends and family that you haven't seen for a few weeks?
- Do you shake hands with people when you meet them for the first time?
- Do you use any other forms of greeting (for example, a 'high five')?

First conditional

EXPLORE

1 **Work in pairs. Answer the questions.**

1 Do you know any superstitions?
2 Do you believe in any superstitions?
3 Do you know anyone who is very superstitious? How does it affect their behaviour?

2 **Read the text. Are any of the superstitions familiar to you?**

Superstitions

Some superstitions are part of British culture. **If a black cat walks in front of you, you will have good luck.** On the other hand, **you will have seven years of bad luck if you break a mirror**. A lot of people don't really believe in superstitions, but at the same time, nobody likes to take chances: if you look at the seats on some aeroplanes, you won't find the number 13. According to a survey, people who believe in superstitions have worse luck than people who don't believe in them. In other words, if you believe in bad luck, you'll probably have it!

3 **Study the information in the *Learn this!* box. Look at the *if* clauses and main clauses in blue in the text above and find two more examples.**

LEARN THIS!

1 We use the **first conditional** to predict the result of an action. We use the present simple to describe the action and *will* + verb to describe the result.

If a black cat walks in front of you, you will have good luck.
↑ action ↑ result

2 The *if* clause can come before or after the main clause. If it comes after, we don't use a comma.

You will have bad luck if you break a mirror.

Grammar Reference: page 106

EXPLOIT

1 **Complete the sentences about superstitions around the world. Use the present simple or *will* form of the verbs in brackets.**

1 (UK) If a cat washes behind its ears, it ________ (rain).
2 (Venezuela) If you ________ (give) somebody handkerchiefs as a gift, you won't have a good relationship with that person.
3 (Brazil) If you eat lentils on 1 January, you ________ (make) a lot of money during the year.
4 (Korea) If a man ________ (smile) a lot during his wedding, his first child won't be a boy, it will be a girl.
5 (UK) If you see a spider in your house, it is a sign that you ________ (get) some money.
6 (Thailand) If a woman ________ (sing) in the kitchen, she will marry a very old man.

2 **Complete the text with the correct form of the verbs in brackets.**

Superstitions around the world

Different countries have different superstitions. For example, in England, it's unlucky to see one magpie on its own, but in Korea, it's the opposite. If you [1]________ (see) a magpie in the morning, you [2]________ (get) good news that day. Another Korean superstition says that you mustn't wash your hair on the morning of an exam. If you [3]________ (wash) it, you [4]________ (not remember) what you've learned!

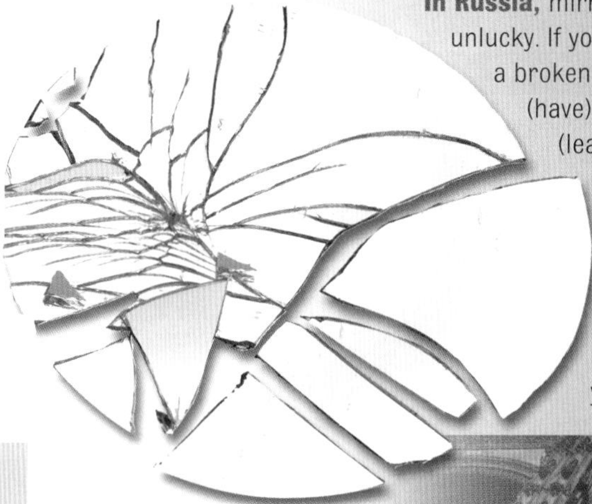

In Russia, mirrors can be lucky or unlucky. If you [5]________ (look) in a broken mirror, you [6]________ (have) bad luck. If you [7]________ (leave) something at home by mistake and have to go back for it, you [8]________ (have) bad luck. But you [9]________ (not be) unlucky if you [10]________ (look) in a mirror when you go home to get it.

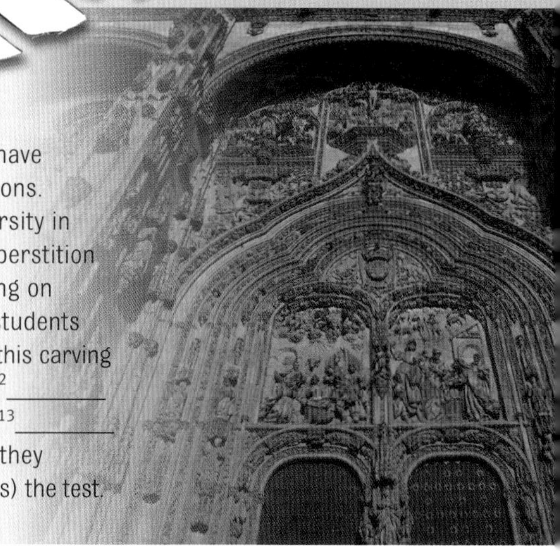

Sometimes, cities have their own superstitions. At Salamanca University in Spain, there is a superstition about a stone carving on one of the walls. If students [11]________ (touch) this carving before a test, they [12]________ (do) well. But if they [13]________ (forget) to touch it, they [14]________ (not pass) the test.

3 **Work in pairs. Ask and answer the questions. What will you do if:**

- you can't sleep tonight?
- it rains all weekend?
- you can't do your homework?
- you feel ill tomorrow?
- there's nothing good on TV this evening?

What will you do if you can't sleep tonight?

I'll read a book.

Grammar Builder: page 107

Workbook: page 56

WRITING

A note

READ

1 Read the notes. Which note is (a) making, (b) accepting, and (c) declining an invitation?

(1)

Hi Janet,

Thanks very much for your note. It's very kind of you to invite me to your sister's graduation do, but I'm afraid I won't be able to make it. My grandparents are coming to visit us that weekend. It's my grandma's birthday on Saturday, and we're going for dinner at Giovanni's in Marsh Rd. It's too bad, because I'd love to come!
Anyway, I hope you have a great time!
See you soon.
Louise

(2)

Dear Jack,

It's my birthday next Sunday and I'm going to have some mates round. Would you like to come? If the weather's good, we'll have a barbecue in the back garden. There'll be lots of burgers, chicken, crisps, etc. so you needn't bring any food. Just bring a few CDs. I haven't got many, and my sister's CDs are rubbish!

Hope you can make it.

Mike

PS RSVP asap! Tel. 643492

(3)

Hi Tania,
Great to hear from you. And thanks very much for the invitation to come to lunch on Saturday. I'll definitely be there!
Greek food is a great idea. I'm really looking forward to it!
Love,
Gloria

PS Shall I bring some food, e.g. a cake?

2 Answer the questions.
1 What kind of celebration is Janet having?
2 What is Louise going to do on the evening of Janet's do?
3 How is Mike going to celebrate his birthday?
4 What does Mike want Jack to bring?
5 What day is Tania's lunch?
6 What food is Tania going to cook?

PREPARE

> **Writing tip: informal language**
>
> We often use abbreviations and colloquial expressions when writing short messages.

1 Match the words in the box with the abbreviations below.

| and so on   as soon as possible   compact disc   for example |
| I also want to say   Please reply   Road   telephone number |

1 CD   3 Tel.   5 RSVP   7 PS
2 Rd   4 e.g.   6 etc.   8 asap

2 Match the highlighted colloquial expressions in the notes with the definitions below.
1 friends   4 very bad
2 come   5 a pity
3 receive a note, email, etc. from you

WRITE

1 Imagine you are a friend of Mike's and have received his invitation. Plan two different notes: (a) declining the invitation, (b) accepting the invitation. Think about:
- what phrase you can use to accept / decline the invitation
- what reason you have for declining it (e.g. other plans)
- what questions you could ask when you accept the invitation

2 Write your two notes. Use the writing plans to help you.

- Begin *Dear Mike* or *Hi Mike*
- Thank him for the invitation
- Decline the invitation
- Give your reason for declining it
- End with *Love* or *See you soon* and your name

- Begin *Dear Mike* or *Hi Mike*
- Thank him for the invitation
- Accept the invitation
- Ask a question about the occasion
- End with *Love* or *See you soon* and your name

> **Check your work**
>
> **Have you**
> ☐ used some colloquial expressions?
> ☐ used some abbreviations?
> ☐ written 50–70 words?
> ☐ checked your spelling, punctuation and grammar?

●●●●● Workbook: page 57

Cultures and customs
LANGUAGE SKILLS

1 🎧 (2.16) Complete the dialogue with the words from the box. Then listen and check your answers.

> anyway   forward   make   classmates   pity   invitation
> bad   afraid   speaking   celebrate

Angela   Hello. Angela Manley ¹_____.

Jane   Hi, Angela. It's Jane.

Angela   Hi, Jane. Did you get my ²_____?

Jane   Yes, I did. In fact I'm phoning about it. I'm ³_____ I won't be able to ⁴_____ it.

Angela   Oh, that's a ⁵_____. Why can't you come?

Jane   Well, it's my parents' wedding anniversary on Saturday and we're going to ⁶_____ it with all the family.

Angela   You can't miss that!

Jane   No, I can't! It's too ⁷_____, because I'd love to come to your meal.

Angela   Well, we can have another one next month.

Jane   Yes, we can have one at my house. ⁸_____, who's going on Saturday?

Angela   Our ⁹_____ from school: Ann, Sara, Mary and Lisa.

Jane   Well, I hope you have a good time.

Angela   Thanks. I'm really looking ¹⁰_____ to it.

Jane   Bye.

Angela   Bye. See you next week.

2 Decide if the sentences are true or false. Correct the false sentences.

1   Angela sent Jane an invitation.
2   Jane is going with her parents to a wedding on Saturday.
3   Jane will see people from her family on Saturday.
4   Jane is going to miss the wedding anniversary.
5   Angela says they can have a meal at Jane's house next month.
6   Angela and Jane have the same friends.

3 Complete the sentences with *must, mustn't* or *needn't*.

1   They _____ study because they haven't got any exams.
2   They _____ buy some food because the fridge is empty.
3   Students _____ talk in the library.
4   Dad, you _____ wear a seatbelt when you're driving!
5   He _____ go on the bus because he can walk to school in five minutes.
6   You _____ go to bed late because you've got an exam at 8 o'clock tomorrow morning.

4 Answer the questions, using the first conditional and the words in brackets.

1   Will she come to the meal? (you / ask her)
2   Will they walk to school? (they / miss the bus)
3   Will they watch TV? (they / not have got homework)
4   Will he pass the exam? (he / study hard)
5   Will they win the match? (they / play well)
6   Will he play tennis? (it / not rain)

Expressions: the body

1 Check the definition of the words in **bold** and complete the sentences.

If someone
1   **yawns**, they are tired.
2   **sneezes**, they've got _____.
3   **snores**, they make a noise when they _____.
4   **blinks**, they close and open their eyes _____.
5   **giggles**, they think something is _____.
6   **sobs**, they are _____.

2 Look at the information about the verbs and match them with the parts of the body. Then write an example sentence.

In this exercise you need to bend your knees.

1 bend ————	a	your knees
2 blow	b	your fingers
3 clap	c	your head
4 click	d	your legs
5 nod	e	your nose
6 shut	f	your hands
7 stretch	g	your eyes

3 Check the meaning of the words in the box and put them in the correct columns.

> fist   forearm   gums   heel   knuckles   lobe   nostril
> shin   sole   temple   thigh   wrist

head	arm and hand	leg and foot
_____	fist	_____
_____	_____	_____
_____	_____	_____
_____	_____	_____

I CAN ...

Read the statements. Think about your progress and tick (✓) one of the boxes.

| ✳ | I need more practice. | ✳✳ | I sometimes find this difficult. | ✳✳✳ | No problem! |

	✳	✳✳	✳✳✳
I can understand a description of different cultural traditions.			
I can talk about prohibition and necessity.			
I can describe body language and customs in different countries.			
I can talk about a future situation and its consequences.			
I can write a note replying to an invitation.			

●●●○○ Workbook: Self check pages 58–59

What if ...?

Disaster

BEFORE READING

Work in pairs. Match the countries with the volcanoes. Can you name any other volcanoes?

Turkey   Indonesia   Italy   Japan   Mexico

1   Mount Fuji (last eruption: 1707)
2   Vesuvius (last eruption: 1944)
3   Krakatoa (last eruption: 2001)
4   Popocatepetl (last eruption: 2006)
5   Mount Ararat (last eruption: 1840)

Reading tip

If the text includes a diagram, look at it closely before you read. If you understand the diagram, it will be easier to understand the text.

READ

1   Read the *Reading tip*. Look at the diagrams and the map. Are the sentences true or false?

1   The volcano is on an island near Africa.
2   Waves made by an eruption would reach London in three hours.
3   An eruption would make rock fall into the sea.

2   Scan the text. What do the numbers refer to?

1   6   2   500 billion   3   800   4   90   5   8

Wave power

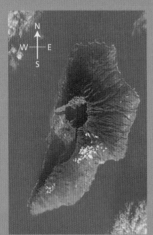

This is a picture of Cumbre Vieja, a huge, active volcano on La Palma, the steepest island in the world, in the Canary Islands. Every few decades it erupts and scientists are worried because the walls of the volcano are getting weaker. Scientists fear that when it erupts, an enormous chunk of the volcano could collapse and fall into the sea. If this happened, it would be a catastrophe. Why? Because it would unleash a giant wave – a tsunami – the biggest ever recorded in history.

How would it happen?

The volcano is by the sea, and the water next to the volcano is about six kilometres deep. If the volcano collapsed, a landslide of 500 billion tonnes of rock would fall into the sea. This would create a huge tsunami about 100 metres high. (See Diagrams 1 and 2.)

What would happen next?

The wave would travel away from the Canary Islands in all directions at about 800 km/h. The other Canary Islands would immediately be covered by water. In less than an hour a 90-metre wave would flood north-west Africa.

The side of the volcano faces west, across the Atlantic Ocean, which would protect Africa and Europe a little. However, a 12-metre tsunami would still crash against Lisbon within three hours and after five hours the tidal wave would reach Britain. The wave could travel a kilometre inland and devastate towns and villages. London would be flooded. (See map.)

How far would it travel?

The wave would have enough energy to cross the entire Atlantic Ocean. Eight hours after the eruption it would smash into the east coast of America. It would still be about 30 metres high. Boston would be hit first, followed by New York, then the coast down to Miami. The wave would create havoc in the Caribbean and Brazil too. It would travel for several kilometres inland because of the low coastline. It would flatten everything and kill thousands of people.

What can we do about it?

Nothing much, it seems. The scientists believe that it is not a question of if, but when. The volcano will collapse at some time in the future, but it could be hundreds or thousands of years from now. Furthermore, if only part of the volcano plunged into the sea, the tsunami would be much smaller. Scientists want to put better equipment on Cumbre Vieja, so that they can predict the volcano's eruptions in the future and give us an early warning of possible problems. Although nobody could stop the tsunami, at least the authorities could then evacuate the towns and cities that would be in danger and save thousands of lives.

Diagram 1

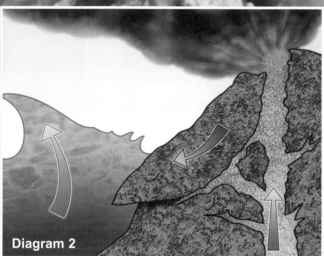

Diagram 2

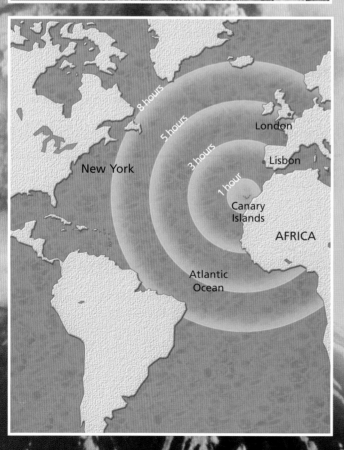

8 hours
5 hours
3 hours
1 hour
London
Lisbon
New York
Canary Islands
AFRICA
Atlantic Ocean

3 🎧 (2.20) **Read the text. Choose the best answers.**

1 A tsunami would be caused by
   a a volcanic eruption.
   b a large rock.
   c a flood.
2 The side of the volcano that could fall
   a faces Africa and Europe.
   b would protect the other Canary Islands.
   c faces America.
3 The tsunami would
   a hit Boston before London.
   b affect towns that are not on the coast.
   c be 12 metres high when it hit New York.
4 Scientists
   a are sure an eruption will happen in the next 100 years.
   b want to tell people what is going to happen.
   c are not sure if there will be an eruption.
5 Scientists want to use better equipment so that
   a the tsunami will be smaller.
   b they can prevent an eruption.
   c they can help people avoid the disaster.

UNDERSTANDING IDEAS

Answer the questions. Look at the text, and use your own words and ideas.

1 If Cumbre Vieja erupted, where would the tsunami travel to?
2 What damage do you think a tsunami would cause to a city?
3 What do you think people would do if scientists told them that a tsunami was coming?

VOCABULARY

Wave power

1 **Match the highlighted words in the text with the definitions.**

1 To move people from a place because it isn't safe.
2 To make something flat.
3 Explodes and throws out fire and rocks.
4 To destroy or damage something badly.
5 To cause something that has a very dangerous effect.
6 A large piece of something.
7 To hit something with a lot of force.
8 When rocks suddenly fall down the side of a mountain.
9 To cover and fill a place with water.
10 A disaster that causes a lot of damage and suffering.
11 Fell quickly from a high place.
12 Something telling people about possible danger.
13 To suddenly fall down.
14 A very large moving part of sea water that destroys the coast.
15 A situation when there is a lot of confusion and damage.

2 **Do you know these words?**

coastline   decade   entire   face   inland   steep
record   volcano

(●●●○○   Workbook: page 60)

Wave power

ACTIVATE

Complete these sentences with the correct form of the words from the box.

> catastrophe chunk collapse devastate erupt evacuate
> flatten flood havoc landslide plunge smash
> tidal wave unleash warning

1 The _____ came up the beach and hit the coastal resort hard. It _____ into trees and buildings and it didn't leave anything standing. It _____ everything and _____ the town, covering the land in water.

2 It was a very hot summer and the town hall sent a _____ to local people about possible forest fires. Unfortunately, there was a big fire and they decided to _____ everybody that lived near the forest and move them to a safer place. However, there was a lot of confusion and all the cars on the roads caused _____ for the fire brigade.

3 When the volcano Krakatoa in Indonesia _____ in 1883 it caused terrible damage. It _____ five tsunamis that _____ local towns. It was a _____ that killed thousands of people and destroyed thousands of homes.

4 There was a storm and a big _____ of wood fell off a tree and hit a man on the head. He _____ but he soon got up again, although he was badly cut.

5 First, a big rock at the top of the hill _____ 500 metres and fell onto a car. Fortunately, nobody was hurt. More rocks started falling and then suddenly everything moved. It was a _____!

EXTEND

Word building

1 Complete the table.

verb	noun	adjective
1_____	action	2_____
create	creation	3_____
4_____	destruction	destructive
5_____	devastation	6_____
7_____	information	8_____
9_____	prediction	10_____
11_____	protection	12_____

Natural phenomena

2 Match the words with the natural phenomena.

> avalanche drought tornado earthquake
> thunderstorm ~~hurricane~~

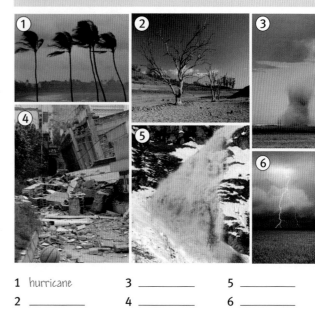

1 hurricane   3 _____   5 _____
2 _____   4 _____   6 _____

Periods of time

3 Match the periods of time with the words in the box.

> millenium decade fortnight quarter
> ~~leap year~~ century

1 366 days = a leap year   4 10 years = a _____
2 2 weeks = a _____   5 100 years = a _____
3 3 months = a _____   6 1000 years = a _____

Water

4 Complete the sentences, using the verbs in the box in the correct form.

> irrigate dribble splash ~~soak~~ water
> spill drip squirt

1 Please soak your dirty football kit in hot water before putting it in the washing machine.
2 That glass of water is very full. Don't _____ it!
3 We need water to _____ the dry fields so we can grow food.
4 I've turned off the tap but water continues to _____ from it. Can you repair it?
5 Children, don't _____ when you're in the bath. I don't want water all over the bathroom floor!
6 You only need to _____ this plant once a week.
7 She accidently squeezed the carton and the juice _____ out all over the table.
8 'You should be careful when you're drinking milk. Look, you've _____ milk down your top!'.

●●●●○ Workbook: page 61

Second conditional

EXPLORE

1 🎧 (2.21) Complete the text with the words in the box. Then listen and check.

> had   used   wouldn't produce   would earn

Darryl Hannah cares about the environment. Her car is very unusual because it doesn't use petrol – it uses vegetable oil, which produces very little carbon dioxide.
'If all our cars [1]_____ it, we [2]_____ so much CO₂. It's also renewable – we can grow it. If more people [3]_____ cars like mine, the world's farmers [4]_____ more money.'

2 Study the information in the *Learn this!* box. Complete the text with *would* and verbs from the box below. You will have to use some of the verbs more than once.

1 We use the **second conditional** to describe an imaginary situation or event, and its result.

2 We use the past tense in the *if* clause, and *would / wouldn't* + verb in the main clause.

If all our cars used vegetable oil, we wouldn't produce so much CO₂.

↑ imaginary situation / event   ↑ result

3 In the *if* clause, we can use *were* instead of *was* as the past tense of *be*, singular.
If the weather were nicer, I'd go out.

> be   consume   earn   own   speak   not be   not have

There are 6.3 billion people in the world. Numbers as big as this are difficult to understand. However, if the world were a village of 100 people, ...

- 61 [1] *would be* Asian and 12 [2]_____ European.
- 22 [3]_____ Chinese and 9 [4]_____ English.
- 20 [5]_____ less than $1 a day.
- 24 [6]_____ any electricity in their home.
- 7 [7]_____ a car.
- 20 [8]_____ 80% of the energy.
- 67 [9]_____ able to read.

●●●●●● Grammar Reference : page 108

EXPLOIT

1 Match the halves of the sentences. Complete them with the correct form of the verbs in brackets.

1 If we _____ (not produce) so much CO₂,
2 I _____ (give) a lot of money to charity,
3 We _____ (save) millions of lives,
4 The world _____ (be) a safer place,
5 If we _____ (not pollute) our rivers,

a if scientists _____ (be able to) stop diseases like cancer.
b they _____ (be) full of fish.
c we _____ (reduce) global warming.
d if I _____ (be) very rich.
e if we _____ (stop) piracy.

1 *If we didn't produce so much CO₂, we would reduce global warming.*

2 Complete the sentences with the correct form of the verbs in brackets.

If we [1]_____ (recycle) more plastic bottles, we [2]_____ (not have to) produce so much plastic.

If we [3]_____ (produce) less plastic, we [4]_____ (burn) less oil.

If we [5]_____ (burn) less oil, there [6]_____ (not be) so many 'greenhouse gases' in the atmosphere.

If there [7]_____ (not be) so many greenhouse gases in the atmosphere, we [8]_____ (be able to) reduce global warming.

If we [9]_____ (reduce) global warming, the Earth's climate [10]_____ (not change) so fast.

3 What would you do in these situations? Make notes. Then tell the class.

1 If you found £100 in the street ...
2 If you could live anywhere in the world ...
3 If you saw someone attacking an old man in the street ...
4 If you didn't have to go to school ...
5 If you could choose any job you wanted ...
6 If you borrowed a friend's computer and accidentally broke it ...

> If I found £100 in the street, I'd ...

●●●●●● Grammar Builder: page 109

●●●●●● Workbook: page 62

Global issues

VOCABULARY

1 Match the photos (1–6) with words from the box.

> **Global issues** child labour disease
> endangered species famine floods and landslides
> global warming homelessness
> piracy pollution poverty racism

2 🎧 (2.22) Listen and repeat all the words.

(●●●●● Workbook: page 63)

LISTEN

🎧 (2.23) Listen to the radio programmes. Which issues are the six people talking about?

Speaker 1	Speaker 2	Speaker 3

Speaker 4	Speaker 5	Speaker 6

SPEAK

1 Read the *Speaking tip* below and look at photo 1. Which words from the box do you need to describe it?

> cold dangerous home mud poor sleep
> sleeping bag smoke street

Speaking tip

Look at the photo closely before you answer. Think what English words you will need to describe it.

2 Answer the questions about photo 1. Use the words in exercise 1 to help you.

1 Where is he?
2 Why is he there?
3 What's he doing?
4 How do you think he's feeling?

3 Work in pairs. Which three issues in Vocabulary exercise 1 do you think are the most serious for (a) your country? (b) the world?

We think the three most serious issues for our country are ...

We think the three most serious issues for the world are ...

GRAMMAR

I wish ...

EXPLORE

1 Look at the cartoons. Answer the questions.

I wish I didn't have so much homework.

1 Does the boy have a lot of homework?

I wish I could fly.

2 Can the cat fly?

3 Is the girl's friend there?

2 Which tense do we use after *wish*? Study the information in the *Learn this!* box. Choose the correct tense to complete the rule.

> **LEARN THIS!**
>
> 1 We use *wish* + **the present / past / future** to say that we want something to be different from how it is now.
>   *I wish I could play the piano.*
>   *Do you ever wish you had a lot of money?*
>   *I wish it wasn't so hot.*
>
> 2 We can use *were* instead of *was* after *I*, *he*, *she* and *it*.
>   *I wish I were 21.*

(●●●○○ Grammar Reference: page 108)

EXPLOIT

1 Write sentences starting with *I wish*.

1 I can't drive.
  I wish I could drive.
2 I don't have a laptop.
3 I don't like vegetables.
4 I'm not very good at maths.
5 I don't speak French.
6 I can't play the guitar.
7 I've got a lot of homework.
8 I'm not very tall.

2 Complete the sentences by using the verbs in the box in the correct form.

be ~~run~~ play read drive have be know

1 I wish I was on holiday.
2 I wish I could _____ faster.
3 I wish I _____ more people.
4 I wish my mum and dad _____ here.
5 I wish I _____ a better computer.
6 I wish I could _____ for the school team.
7 I wish I _____ a bigger car.
8 I wish I could _____ Chinese.

3 🎧 (2.24) Listen and complete the song with the phrases in the box.

be like a bird   break all the chains   break all the chains
know how it feels   say all the things   say all the things
share all the love   soar to the sun

(I Wish I Knew How It Would Feel To Be) Free
I wish I knew how it would feel to be free
I wish I could ¹_____ holding me
I wish I could ²_____ that I should say
Say them loud say them clear
For the whole wide world to hear
I wish I could ³_____ that's in my heart
Remove all the bars that keep us apart
And I wish you could ⁴_____ to be me
Then you'd see and agree that every man should be free
I wish I could ⁵_____ in the sky
How sweet it would be if I found I could fly
Well I'd ⁶_____ and look down at the sea
And I'd sing cos I'd know how it feels to be free
I wish I knew how it would feel to be free
I wish I could ⁷_____ holding me
And I wish I could ⁸_____ that I wanna say
Say them loud say them clear
For the whole wide world to hear
Say them loud say them clear
For the whole wide world to hear
Say them loud say them clear
For the whole wide world to hear

4 Complete the sentences with your own ideas.

1 I wish I were ...
2 I wish I weren't ...
3 I wish I had ...
4 I wish I lived ...
5 I wish I knew ...
6 I wish I could ...
7 I wish I spoke ...

(●●●●○ Grammar Builder: page 109)

(●●●○○ Workbook: page 64)

An essay

READ

1 Read Cathy's essay. Which global issues does she mention?

- ☐ the arms trade
- ☐ disease
- ☐ homelessness
- ☐ endangered species
- ☐ famine
- ☐ racism
- ☐ global warming
- ☐ terrorism

If I ruled the world   by Cathy

If I ruled the world, the first thing I'd do is prevent famine and disease in the developing world. In my opinion, that's one of the most serious problems we face. I'd make sure that poor farmers could sell their food to the rest of the world. I'd also make more medicines available to people in poor countries. I believe we could save millions of lives by vaccinating children, so I'd make drugs companies do that.

The next thing I'd do is invest in wind, water and solar power. We would then have clean energy that wouldn't pollute the planet. In my view, if we could also make petrol-driven cars illegal, we would reduce pollution even more and this way we could stop global warming.

There are some less serious things I'd do too. I'd ban rap music because I think it's terrible and I'd reduce the number of sports programmes on television. Finally, I'd make my brother change his socks every day because they smell awful.

2 Answer the questions.

1 How would Cathy help farmers in the developing world?
2 What would she make drugs companies do?
3 Why would she make petrol-driven cars illegal?
4 What would she ban?
5 What kind of TV programme doesn't she like?
6 What would she make her brother do?

PREPARE

1 Read the *Writing tip*. How many of the phrases can you find in the essay?

> ### Writing tip: expressing your opinion
>
> We can use these phrases for expressing opinions:
> | | |
> |---|---|
> | I think (that) … | I don't think (that) … |
> | I believe (that) … | I don't believe (that) … |
> | In my view, … | In my opinion, … |
> | I'm convinced that … | As I see it, … |

2 Find examples of these structures in the essay.

1 make somebody do something
2 make somebody / something + adjective
3 make sure that …

3 Complete the sentences with the verbs and adjectives in the box.

> found   illegal   optional   pick up   reduce   smaller   was

1 I'd make smoking in all public places _____.
2 I'd make sure that the government _____ a home for every homeless person.
3 I'd make factories _____ the amount of pollution they produce.
4 I'd make cars _____ and cleaner.
5 I'd make people _____ their own litter.
6 I'd make sure that clean water _____ available to everyone in the world.
7 I'd make school _____ instead of compulsory.

WRITE

Do this writing task. Include some serious and some less serious ideas, and use some of the phrases and structures in exercises 1 and 2. Follow the writing plan below.

> Write an essay about what you'd do if you ruled the world. Write 130–150 words.
>
> - The first thing I'd do is …
> - I'd also …
> - The next thing I'd do is …
> - There are some less serious things I'd do too.
> - Finally, I'd …

> ### Check your work
>
> **Have you**
> - ☐ divided your essay into paragraphs?
> - ☐ used phrases for expressing opinions?
> - ☐ used expressions with *make* correctly?
> - ☐ written 130–150 words?
> - ☐ checked your spelling, punctuation and grammar?

●●●●○ Workbook: page 65

What if ...?

LANGUAGE SKILLS

1 🎧 (2.25) Complete the dialogue with the words from the box. Then listen and check your answers.

> my wouldn't idea opinion convinced true could make see thing

Peter Do you know that the government wants to ban cars in the city centre at the weekends?

Mark Well, in my ¹_____ it's a good idea. I'm ²_____ everyone should use a bicycle.

Peter You're not serious, are you? What about elderly people? Are you going to ³_____ them cycle?

Mark That's ⁴_____. But we have to do something. Cars are polluting our cities.

Peter As I ⁵_____ it, the first ⁶_____ I'd do is make buses cheaper.

Mark Well, in ⁷_____ opinion, public transport should be free.

Peter Free? Who would pay for the buses and the bus drivers?

Mark Well, with less traffic the government ⁸_____ have to spend so much money on repairing the roads.

Peter That's true. The money they would save from the repairs ⁹_____ be spent on the buses.

Mark Exactly! Don't you think it's a good ¹⁰_____?

Peter It's not bad. Who told you about it?

Mark Nobody did! It's mine!

2 Read the dialogue again, and then answer the questions.

1 What does Mark think about the government's plan?
2 Who does Peter think will have problems with bicycles?
3 What does Mark say cars are doing to our cities?
4 What would Peter do with the buses?
5 What does Mark say should be free?
6 What wouldn't the government have to spend money on?

3 Write second conditional sentences.

1 If / I be you / I do my homework now
2 If / we live in London / we learn English faster
3 They go to the theatre / if / they have tickets
4 What / you buy / if / you have a lot of money?
5 She send us an email / if / she have a computer
6 If / he tell them / they not believe him

4 Complete the sentences.

1 I'm really tired. I wish I _____.
2 I can't play in the match today. I wish I _____.
3 We live in a small village. I wish we _____ in a city.
4 Mum never makes pizzas. I wish she sometimes _____ them.
5 I haven't got a computer. I wish I _____ a computer.
6 I don't know the answer to the exercise. I wish I _____ it.

Exploring vocabulary: global problems

1 Check the meaning of the words in the box and complete the sentences.

> ~~conservation~~ discrimination recycling slavery starvation vaccinations

1 Conservation aims to protect nature.
2 As I see it, child labour is a type of _____.
3 _____ is one way we can fight against pollution.
4 _____ can stop diseases if doctors have enough to give people.
5 Racism is one of the most common forms of _____.
6 The famine has caused lots of people to die of _____.

Word building: en- and -en

2 We can make some words into verbs by adding the prefix *en-* before, or the suffix *-en* or *-n* after them. Make verbs to match the definitions, using the words in the box.

> ~~bright~~ courage danger flat force large quiet rich sweet worse

1 brighten to make something brighter
2 _____ to cause danger to someone or something
3 _____ to make something flat
4 _____ to make somebody or something quiet
5 _____ to improve the quality of something
6 _____ to become worse
7 _____ to give hope, support or confidence
8 _____ to make people obey a law or rule
9 _____ to make something sweet by adding sugar etc.
10 _____ to make something bigger

I CAN ...

Read the statements. Think about your progress and tick (✓) one of the boxes.

| ✹ | I need more practice. | ✹✹ | I sometimes find this difficult. | ✹✹✹ | No problem! |

	✹	✹✹	✹✹✹
I can understand an article about a natural disaster.			
I can talk about an imaginary situation and its consequences.			
I can identify global problems.			
I can talk about situations I would like to change.			
I can write an essay on a global issue.			

⬤⬤⬤⭕⭕ Workbook: Self check pages 66–67

THE THIRTY-NINE STEPS
by John Buchan

Biography

John Buchan was born in Perth, Scotland, in 1875. He started writing stories when he was at university, and wrote over a hundred books during his life. Some of them were about real events and people in history, but around forty of them were fiction. These were often gripping adventure stories such as *The Thirty-Nine Steps* (1915), which has been made into a film several times.

I came into a village and I saw a policeman standing outside the Post Office and reading something carefully. He looked up at the car, and stepped into the road, and held up a hand to stop me.

I almost did stop. But then I realized that the policeman had been reading about me. I supposed the police at the hotel had worked quickly, and contacted all the local villages. I drove faster, the policeman jumped out of my way, and I was soon out of the village.

I left the main road as soon as possible and tried a smaller one. It was not easy without a map, and I realized that I had been stupid to steal the car. It would help the police and the Black Stone to find me in any corner of Scotland. If I left it, and went off on foot, they would find me in an hour or two.

I took a road that went along a narrow valley, and then up onto the moor again. I was very hungry; I had eaten nothing since morning. And now, as I drove, I heard a noise in the sky, and there was a plane.

On the moor it would see me in a minute. I drove as fast as I could down into another valley, and towards a wood. Suddenly, a car appeared in front of me from a side road. There was no time to stop. I did the only thing possible and drove off the road into a hedge, hoping to hit something soft beyond. But I was out of luck. The car went through the hedge like a knife through butter,

and immediately began to fall. I jumped out and was caught by the branch of a tree, while the car disappeared into a river fifteen metres below.

A hand helped me out of the tree, and a frightened voice asked me if I was badly hurt. The speaker was a young man who was very alarmed and very sorry. I was more pleased than angry; it was a good way for the car to disappear.

1 The main character in *The Thirty-Nine Steps* is called Hannay. Read the first paragraph of the story. What do you think happened next?

a ☐ Hannay stopped the car and spoke to the policeman.
b ☐ Hannay drove faster and got out of the village quickly.
c ☐ Suddenly, a car appeared in front of him.

2 🎧 (2.29) Read the text again and answer the questions.

1 What was the policeman doing?
2 Why didn't Hannay stop for him?
3 Why was it difficult for Hannay to find his way?
4 Why did Hannay regret taking the car?
5 What happened to the car in the end?

3 Answer the questions. Look at the text, and use your own words and ideas to explain your answers.

1 Why do you think the police were chasing Hannay?
2 Who or what do you think the Black Stone was?
3 How do you think Hannay felt when he heard the plane?
4 Why was Hannay pleased about losing the car?

4 Buchan uses the simile *like a knife through butter* to mean 'very easily'. We use similes to compare things, using the words *like* or *as*. Match (1–4) with (a–d) to make similes.

1 as white   a the wind
2 as quick   b as snow
3 drive like   c as a flash
4 run like   d a maniac

Going green

LISTEN

1 🎧 (2.30) Do the environment quiz. Listen and check your answers.

Environment Quiz

1 How long does it take a plastic bag to decompose?
a up to 10 years b up to 100 years c up to 1,000 years

2 The ozone layer
a stops ultraviolet light from the sun.
b causes global warming.
c is pollution in the atmosphere.

3 How much of our energy comes from oil, coal and gas?
a 30% b 60% c 90%

4 On average, how much rubbish do EU countries recycle?
a 35% b 45% c 65%

5 In which of these foods has the British government found a lot of pesticides?
a baby food b bread c chips d all of these

2 🎧 (2.30) Listen again. Answer the questions.
1 What should we do when we go shopping?
2 How high above the surface of the Earth is the ozone layer?
3 When we burn oil, coal and gas, what problem does it cause?
4 How much rubbish does the EU want to recycle?
5 How many pesticides are regularly used in non-organic farming?

READ

Complete the text with the words in the box.

countries energy environment letters rubbish
turn off use

Teen action!

In 2004, 120 young people between the ages of 14 and 17 from ten European [1]_____ met in Berlin at the first Youth Eco-Parliament. Before going to Berlin, they made plans for improving the [2]_____ in their own towns and villages. They focused on areas like recycling, saving [3]_____, and reducing pollution. After that they went to Berlin and discussed their plans. Then they wrote [4]_____ giving ideas for improving the environment, locally, nationally and globally. Here are some of the things they think we should do:

1 recycle more [5]_____ (for example, glass, paper, plastic, metal)
2 use our cars less – use public transport and bikes, or walk
3 stop polluting rivers and streams
4 pick up rubbish in parks and in the street
5 save energy – [6]_____ lights and TVs when we're not using them
6 don't use too many pesticides on farms
7 use recycled paper
8 [7]_____ shopping bags instead of plastic bags

The Youth Eco-Parliament is going to meet every two years. To find out more about it, visit their website: www.eyep.info

WRITE

Write an email to people, telling them how to improve the environment in your town or village.

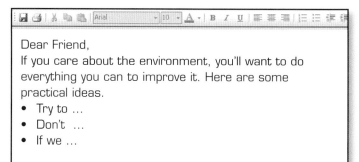

Dear Friend,
If you care about the environment, you'll want to do everything you can to improve it. Here are some practical ideas.
• Try to …
• Don't …
• If we …

9 Crime scene

Computer crime

BEFORE READING

1 Look at the photos on page 77. What can you see? How are these things related to computers?

2 What's a computer virus? What are the consequences of a computer virus?

READ

1 Read the *Reading tip*. Then skim the text and decide what type of text it is.

1 an article
2 an essay
3 a letter

2 Match the titles (A–F) with the paragraphs.

A A second chance
B Creating havoc
C Hard work
D Not a genius
E Happy, but not for long!
F Serious consequences

3 🎧 (3.02) Read the text. Choose the best answers.

1 How far did the Sasser virus spread?
  a All around Germany.
  b All around Europe.
  c All around the world.
2 Why wasn't Sven sent to prison?
  a Because he was too young.
  b Because he wasn't found guilty.
  c Because he admitted his guilt to detectives.
3 How did he feel after he'd released the virus?
  a At first he was frightened, then he was delighted.
  b He was delighted that he'd caused a lot of damage, but terrified that he might be caught.
  c At first he was delighted, then he became frightened.
4 How did the police catch him?
  a One of his classmates told Microsoft about him.
  b Detectives came to his home to ask questions.
  c The police offered a $250,000 reward.
5 How did Sven's teachers react?
  a They contacted Microsoft to receive the reward.
  b They were surprised because Sven wasn't the best student in information technology lessons.
  c They weren't surprised because Sven was very clever.

Reading tip

We skim a text quickly to decide what type of text it is.

An online threat

☐ On the evening of his 18th birthday, a teenager from a tiny village in northern Germany clicked 'send' on his computer. Within three hours, the postal service in Taiwan was in chaos, computers in hospitals and banks in Hong Kong had crashed, and trains in Australia and planes in the USA had come to a halt. How could a young man cause so many problems for people in places that were thousands of kilometres from his home? Of course, there was only one answer. He was the inventor of the terrible computer virus 'Sasser'.

☐ After a three-month long investigation the police traced the virus to teenager Sven Jaschan's computer and they charged him with criminal damage. In court a few months later the judge found him guilty of putting the 'Sasser' computer virus on the internet and he received a 21-month suspended sentence. He avoided a 5-year prison sentence because he was only 18 when he committed the crime. The virus infected millions of computer systems across the world, and caused millions of dollars of damage.

☐ Sven admitted his guilt to the detectives who finally found his home after a long search for the author of the virus. They had started looking for him in Russia because of false clues that Sven had written in the program. He had spent an enormous amount of time creating the 'Sasser' virus on the computer in his bedroom. He often spent ten hours a day in front of his computer but his parents hadn't known what he was doing at the time.

☐ When he released the virus on the internet, he didn't realize it would cause so much damage. He was just delighted that it had worked. 'I felt as if I had written a first-class essay,' said Sven, a student at a computer science school. 'I told my classmates – they thought it was terrific.' But his feelings changed very quickly. He was terrified when he saw a TV news report about the virus and the damage it had caused.

☐ Detectives arrested Sven after one of his classmates contacted Microsoft with a tip-off about his activities. Microsoft had offered a $250,000 reward for information about the virus. However, Sven's teachers at school were astonished that Sven had created the virus. They said that he wasn't a brilliant computer student. 'There are others in the class who are better than him,' one teacher said!

UNDERSTANDING IDEAS

Answer the questions. Look at the text and use your own words and ideas.

1 Why do you think Sven created the Sasser virus?
2 Why do you think people create computer viruses?
3 Sven didn't go to prison and he got a job because of his crime. Do you think this is correct? Why? / Why not?

☐ While he was waiting for his trial to start, Sven left school and started work. A German computer company asked him to help them fight against the makers of computer viruses. Sven's new job is to make 'firewalls' – vital pieces of software that protect computers against the type of viruses that Sven created. After causing so many problems for so many people's computers, Sven now has the opportunity to find ways of protecting them and repairing some of the damage he caused.

VOCABULARY

An online theat

1 Match the highlighted words in the text with the definitions below.

1 A delayed punishment a person will only receive if they do something bad or illegal again during a certain period of time.
2 Money someone receives for helping to find someone or something.
3 Suddenly stopped working.
4 A situation when something stops moving or happening.
5 An examination in court to decide if somebody is guilty of a crime.
6 Took someone to a police station.
7 A situation when everything is disorganized and confused.
8 Very important.
9 Secret information that you give to someone.
10 A process to find out who or what caused something.
11 Found something or someone you were looking for.
12 Pieces of information that help someone in an investigation.
13 Accused someone of doing something bad or illegal.
14 Being responsible for doing something bad or illegal.
15 Let something spread in a particular place.

2 Do you know these words?

admit   click   court   criminal damage   delighted
detective   infect   within

(●●●○ Workbook: page 68)

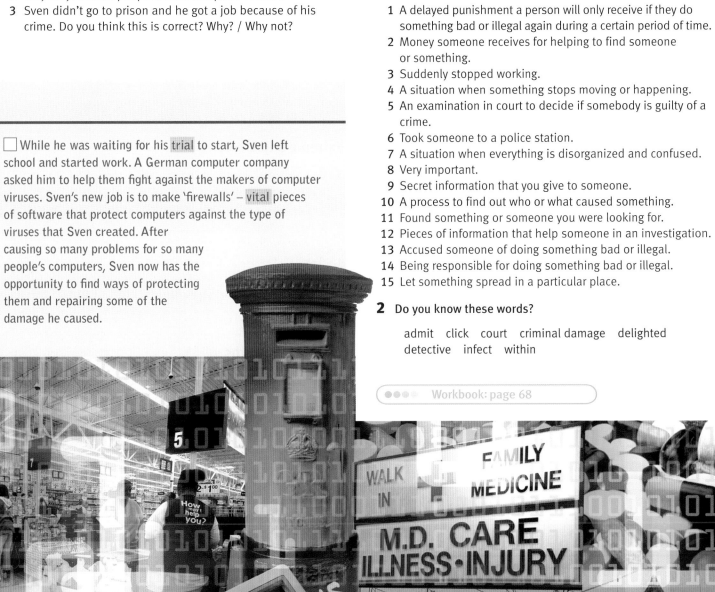

An online threat

ACTIVATE

Complete these sentences with the correct form of the words from the box.

> arrest   chaos   charge   clues   crash   guilty   halt
> investigation   release   reward   suspended sentence
> tip-off   trace   trial   vital

1 The electricity went off and all the machines came to a _____ and stopped working in the factory. In the office all the computers _____. There was a lot of confusion and the factory was in complete _____.

2 There will be an _____ to find out who took the painting from the gallery. We have received a _____ and will be using the information to help the police find the painting. The gallery is also offering a _____ of £50,000 to anybody who can give us more information.

3 The police _____ the young man that took my car to a house in Birmingham. They found him in bed. They _____ him and took him to the police station. After asking him some questions, they _____ him with taking my car. At the _____ he admitted he was _____ but because he was 17 he didn't go to prison. He got a _____.

4 In the film a scientist _____ a dangerous virus that will destroy the planet. A group of students find some _____ about where the virus is but they only have 10 hours to use this _____ information to save the planet!

EXTEND

Computers

1 Complete the text with the words in the box.

> attach   backups   install   protect   update   software
> files   ~~delete~~

Just like medical viruses, there are lots of computer viruses. If a virus gets into your computer it can ¹delete your ²_____ and programs. How can you ³_____ your computer against viruses? Well, people who make viruses usually ⁴_____ them to an email and send it to lots of computers, so don't open emails from unknown people. You should also buy and ⁵_____ anti-virus ⁶_____ on your computer. And ⁷_____ your computer programs regularly so you can stop the newest viruses. You should also make ⁸_____ and copy all your documents so you don't lose them if you do get a virus. Look after your computer and you should be safe!

Compound adjectives: numbers

2 We can put a number and a singular noun together to form a compound adjective. We use a hyphen between the two parts. Write compound adjectives using the words in italics.

1 There was an investigation for *three months*.
  a three-month investigation.
2 We had a wait of *two hours*. _____
3 They stayed in a hotel with *five stars*. _____
4 It's a walk of *ten minutes*. _____
5 There is a motorway with *five lanes*. _____
6 You have to write an essay of *300 words*. _____
7 He works in a building with *ten storeys*. _____
8 They want a car with *four doors*. _____

Extreme adjectives

3 Find extreme adjectives in the text on pages 76–77 that match the definitions.

1 very big   *enormous*
2 very small   _____
3 very surprised   _____
4 very clever   _____
5 very happy   _____
6 very bad   _____
7 very good   _____
8 very scared   _____

Collocation: verbs

4 We use some verbs to express more than one idea. Which word or expression do we not use with each of the verbs below?

1 to spend
  a time ✔
  b food ✘
  c money ✔
2 to release
  a a prisoner
  b a lesson
  c a film
3 to charge
  a a battery
  b someone with a crime
  c an opinion
4 to commit
  a yourself to something
  b a job
  c a crime
5 to receive
  a a gift
  b a warning
  c an illness
6 to leave
  a the weather
  b a meal
  c a place

(●●●●○ Workbook: page 69)

GRAMMAR

Past perfect

EXPLORE

1 Read the text. Look at the verbs in blue. Did these events happen *before* or *after* the man called the radio station?

> Listeners to a radio programme in Chicago were very surprised when a man phoned the programme and said that he was a bank robber. At the beginning of the programme, the presenter **had asked** listeners to call in and confess to any 'small crimes' they **had committed**.
>
> The man described the crime exactly. Five months earlier, he and four other men **had gone** to a bank in Chicago and **had stolen** $81,000. A woman who worked in the bank **had** also **helped** in the robbery. The man was obviously very proud of himself. He didn't give his name on the radio, but police later discovered the man's telephone number and arrested him.

2 Complete the rule in the *Learn this!* box with *before*, *after* or *at the same time as*.

> 1 We form the **past perfect** with *had* or *hadn't* + past participle.
>
> 2 We use the **past perfect** to talk about an event that happened _____ another event in the past.
> *When the police arrived at the house, the burglar had escaped.*
> *I was sure I hadn't met him before.*
> *Had she already left the house when you phoned?*

(●●●●○ Grammar Reference: page 110)

EXPLOIT

1 By the time you arrived at school this morning, which of these things had you done? Write sentences.

I had had a shower.
I hadn't had a shower.

1 have a shower	4 finish all your homework
2 have breakfast	5 send an email
3 watch TV	6 make a phone call

2 Complete the text with the past perfect form of the verbs in brackets.

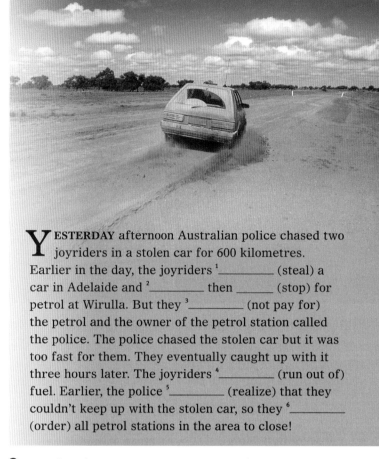

YESTERDAY afternoon Australian police chased two joyriders in a stolen car for 600 kilometres. Earlier in the day, the joyriders ¹_____ (steal) a car in Adelaide and ²_____ then _____ (stop) for petrol at Wirulla. But they ³_____ (not pay for) the petrol and the owner of the petrol station called the police. The police chased the stolen car but it was too fast for them. They eventually caught up with it three hours later. The joyriders ⁴_____ (run out of) fuel. Earlier, the police ⁵_____ (realize) that they couldn't keep up with the stolen car, so they ⁶_____ (order) all petrol stations in the area to close!

3 Complete the sentences. Use the past perfect and your own ideas.

1 I was upset because I had failed the exam.
2 I felt really happy because …
3 I suddenly realized that …
4 I was angry because …
5 I forgot that …

4 Imagine one bad thing that happened yesterday, and write it down. Look at the examples to help you.

– Somebody stole my bike.
– My sister broke my computer.

5 Memory Game! Take it in turns around the class to repeat the whole sentence and add your idea from exercise 4. Remember to use the past perfect.

> When I got home yesterday, somebody had stolen my bike.

> When I got home yesterday, somebody had stolen my bike, and my sister had broken my computer…

(●●●●○ Grammar Builder: page 111)

(●●●●○ Workbook: page 70)

Crimes and criminals

VOCABULARY

1 Look at the photos. Can you name any of the crimes?

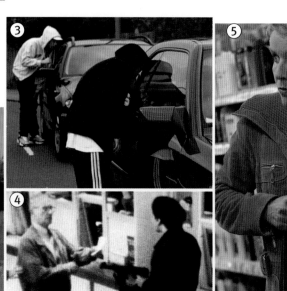

2 Match the extracts from the newspaper reports with the photos.

(a)
Joyriders stole four cars in Oxford last night …

(b)
A shoplifter stole a DVD from a department store …

(c)
The police are questioning a group of vandals who smashed bus shelters in the town centre …

(d)
Police arrested a burglar who broke into three houses on Friday evening …

(e)
Robbers robbed a bank in Liverpool yesterday morning. They took £1,000,000 …

LOOK OUT!

rob and *steal*
You *rob* a place or a person.
Two men robbed a bank yesterday.
You *steal* something from a person or a place.
Thieves stole jewellery from the shop.

●●●●● Workbook: page 71

LISTEN

🎧 (3.04) Listen to the dialogues. Which crimes are the people talking about? Choose the correct answers.

1 a burglary   b vandalism
2 a robbery   b shoplifting
3 a fraud   b theft
4 a robbery   b shoplifting
5 a joyriding   b vandalism

SPEAK

1 Work in pairs. Decide which three of the crimes in Vocabulary exercise 3 are the most serious, and why. Make notes.

2 Tell the class which crimes you have chosen, and why.

We think _____ is the most serious crime because …

3 🎧 (3.03) Complete the table with the words in the box. Which two crimes aren't in the photos above? Listen and check.

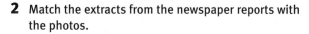
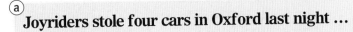

~~burglary~~ cheat joyriding murder robbery steal theft vandalize

Crime	Criminal	Verb
¹burglary	burglar	burgle a house
fraud	fraudster	² _____ someone
³ _____	joyrider	go joyriding
murder	murderer	⁴ _____ someone
⁵ _____	robber	rob someone / a bank, shop, etc.
shoplifting	shoplifter	⁶ _____ something from a shop
⁷ _____	thief	steal something
vandalism	vandal	⁸ _____ something

Reported speech

EXPLORE

1 Read the text. Who said the following things? Find the parts of the text that give you the answers.

1 'I'm robbing the bank.'
2 'You are in the Wells Fargo Bank.'
3 'You need to take the form to the Bank of America.'
4 'A man tried to rob the bank.'

Crime doesn't pay

A man walked into the Bank of America and wrote on a bank form, 'This is a robery. Put all yur munney in this bag.' Then he waited in the queue. But he was worried that someone had seen him write the note, so he left the Bank of America and crossed the street to the Wells Fargo Bank. He gave the note to a bank assistant there, and said that he was robbing the bank. The assistant read the note. She noticed his spelling mistakes, and decided that he wasn't very clever. She said that he was in the Wells Fargo Bank and said that he needed to take the form to the Bank of America. The man looked upset, but he left the Wells Fargo Bank. The assistant then quickly called the police. She told the police that a man had tried to rob the bank. The police arrested the man a few minutes later. He was waiting in the queue at the Bank of America.

2 Compare the quotations with the parts of the text that you found. How do the verbs and pronouns change? Look at the information in the *Learn this!* box and complete the rules.

> When you change **direct speech** to **reported speech**
> 1 verbs in the present simple usually change to
>   a the future.   b the past simple.
> 2 verbs in the present continuous usually change to
>   a the present simple.   b the past continuous.
> 3 verbs in the past simple usually change to
>   a the past perfect.   b the present perfect.
> 4 pronouns
>   a always change.
>   b sometimes change, depending on the context.

⬤⬤○○○ Grammar Reference : page 110

EXPLOIT

1 Rewrite the quotations in reported speech. Change the pronouns if necessary.

1 'I want to catch the thief,' the policeman said.
  The policeman said that he wanted to catch the thief.
2 'She stole a book from the book shop,' he said.
3 'The police arrested a thief,' she said.
4 'I go joyriding at weekends,' he said.
5 'We are questioning two teenagers about the burglary,' the policeman said.
6 'A boy in my class vandalized a phone box,' my brother said.
7 'Jake is a fraudster,' said Mark.
8 'The police are looking for the bank robbers,' she said.

2 Write down three short sentences using the present simple, present continuous and past simple.

I like English.
It isn't raining.
I went to school yesterday.

3 Work in pairs. Read the sentences to your partner. Your partner reports them to the class.

> I like English.

> Laila said that she liked English.

4 Find the reported speech in the text. Change it to direct speech.

> An old lady had spent the morning with a friend at a shopping centre in Los Angeles. When they returned to the car, they found four men sitting in it. The old lady was very angry and said to the men that they were sitting in her car. She said that she wanted them to get out. When the men refused, she took a gun out of her bag, and the terrified men ran away.
>
> Then she and her friend got into the car but she couldn't start the car. She said that it was the wrong key and that it didn't fit. Then she noticed an identical car nearby. She said to her friend that this wasn't her car. They went to the police station and said to the police officer that they had accidentally stolen a car. The police officer laughed and pointed to four frightened men. He said that they had arrived at the police station a few minutes ago and had reported the theft of the car by two dangerous old ladies.
>
> The old lady said to the men, 'You're ...

⬤⬤⬤○○ Grammar Builder: page 111

⬤⬤⬤○○ Workbook: page 72

A story

READ

Read the story quickly. Why did Jeremy want to buy a sat nav system (satellite navigation system)?

The careless thief

One evening last week, Jeremy Watkins was trying to buy a second-hand sat nav system for his car from an online auction site.

Two weeks earlier, a thief had stolen the sat nav system from Jeremy's car. Unfortunately, since the car wasn't locked, the insurance company had refused to replace the system.

After a while Jeremy found some sat nav systems for sale. As he was looking at them, he was astonished to see his own system for sale. Jeremy immediately bought it and emailed the seller to say that he would come round to his house the following day to collect it. Then he phoned the police.

The next day, a police officer called at the man's house. He pretended to be Jeremy. As soon as the man gave him the sat nav system, the police officer arrested him. So in the end Jeremy got his system back!

PREPARE

Writing tip: using time expressions

Use time expressions to order the events in a story.
For example: *in the end   after a while   at first   immediately   soon   then   one (evening)   last (week)   (two weeks) earlier   the following (day)   the next (day)   as soon as   as   while*

1 Read the *Writing tip* and find eleven time expressions in the story.

2 Choose the correct time expressions.
  1 There's a fire – please leave the building **in the end / immediately.**
  2 The police arrested her because **a week earlier / the following week** she'd stolen a mobile phone.
  3 Somebody attacked him **as / as soon as** he was walking through the park.
  4 **At first / After a while** I thought he was innocent, but **immediately / in the end** I realized he was lying.
  5 The witness identified the criminal **as soon as / while** she saw him.

3 Use the pictures to retell the story.

WRITE

Do the writing task. Make notes, using the writing plan below to help you.

> Write a crime story. Write 130–150 words.
> • What was the crime?
> • Who were the criminals?
> • What did they do?
> • Who was the victim?
> • Were there any witnesses?
> • Did the police catch the criminals? If so, how?

Check your work

Have you
☐ used some time expressions to order the events?
☐ thought of a good title for your story?
☐ written 130–150 words?
☐ checked your spelling, punctuation and grammar?

●●●●● Workbook: page 73

Crime scene

LANGUAGE SKILLS

1 🎧 (3.05) Complete the dialogue with the words from the box. Then listen and check your answers.

how told immediately last had earlier when while stolen asked

Jessica Hi, Sara. Why didn't you come to the cinema yesterday?

Sara Because I was at the police station.

Jessica Why? What ¹_____ you done?

Sara Nothing! Somebody had ²_____ my purse.

Jessica I'm sorry. How did it happen?

Sara ³_____ I was crossing the street, a man stopped me.

Jessica What did he do?

Sara Well, a few seconds ⁴_____ I had heard some keys falling and this man had some keys in his hand.

Jessica And he ⁵_____ you if they were yours.

Sara Yes, he did. I said 'no' and I forgot about it and went to buy a dress.

Jessica And ⁶_____ you wanted to pay, you couldn't find your purse.

Sara Exactly! Of course, I ⁷_____ remembered the man and the keys.

Jessica And the police ⁸_____ you that while the man was asking you about the keys, another person was taking your purse from your bag.

Sara Yes! ⁹_____ do you know all this?

Jessica It happened to my mum ¹⁰_____ month. The police told her it happened all the time.

2 Decide if the sentences are true or false. Correct the false sentences.

1 Jessica thought Sara was going to the cinema yesterday.
2 Sara went to the police because she had lost her purse.
3 Sara was walking along the street when a man stopped her.
4 Sara dropped her keys.
5 Sara thought about the man and the keys when she couldn't find her purse.
6 The man with the keys stole Sara's purse.

3 Rewrite the direct speech as reported speech.

1 You told me, 'Dale isn't working.'
2 My parents told me, 'We saw your teacher yesterday.'
3 Yousef said, 'I'm learning to ski.'
4 Sam told Steve, 'I don't like your new trainers.'
5 Alice said, 'I'm not tired.'
6 My friend said, 'I had a good time on holiday.'

DICTIONARY CORNER

Police equipment

1 Check the meaning of the words in the box and match them with the photos.

~~baton~~ bulletproof vest handcuffs helmet shield torch

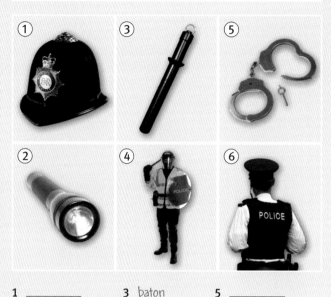

1 _____   3 baton   5 _____
2 _____   4 _____   6 _____

Law and order

2 Look at the information about words (1–6) and match them with (a–f). Then write an example sentence.

They sold the stolen jewels on the black market.

1 black —————— a market
2 death b officer
3 law-abiding c detective
4 petty d crime
5 plain-clothes e citizen
6 police f penalty

I CAN ...

Read the statements. Think about your progress and tick (✓) one of the boxes.

| ✳ | I need more practice. | ✳✳ | I sometimes find this difficult. | ✳✳✳ | No problem! |

	✳	✳✳	✳✳✳
I can understand and react to an article about a crime.			
I can describe an event using different past tenses.			
I can describe different crimes.			
I can report what other people have said.			
I can write a story describing a crime.			

(●●●●● Workbook: Self check pages 74–75)

THIS UNIT INCLUDES ● ● ● ○

Vocabulary • journeys • at the station • phrasal verbs • inventions and discoveries • parts of a car
Grammar • the passive (present simple) • the passive (other tenses)
Skills • listening to teenagers talking about important inventions
Writing • an article

Great explorers

BEFORE READING

Read the *Reading tip*. Do you know these famous explorers? Where did they travel to? Do you know any other explorers?

1 Ferdinand Magellan
2 Christopher Columbus
3 James Cook
4 Neil Armstrong
5 Roald Amundsen
6 ...

Reading tip

Explore the topic before you begin reading the text. Use your general knowledge and discuss your ideas.

READ

1 Read the texts quickly and match the three explorers with the routes (A–C) on the map.

Great journeys

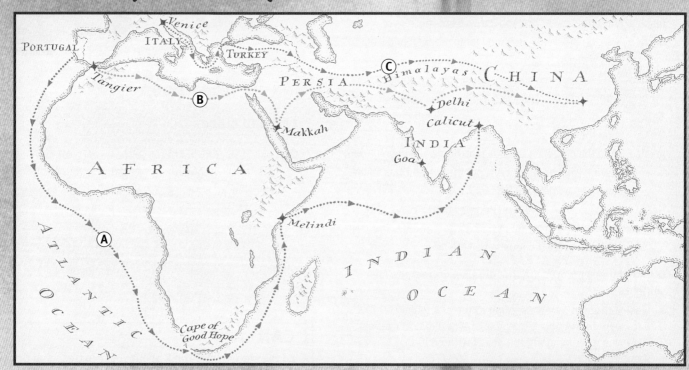

Marco Polo

In 1271, 18-year-old Marco Polo set off from his hometown of Venice with his father and uncle, who were wealthy merchants, to visit China. They went by ship to Anatolia, and travelled the rest of the way overland. They followed the Silk Road, along which merchants from China brought silks to Europe. The road runs north of the Himalayas and the journey took four years. The Emperor Kublai Khan welcomed them warmly and Marco became a civil servant and diplomat. After 17 years working for the emperor, the Polos decided to travel home. At first, the Khan refused to let them go, but in 1292 they received permission and returned home by sea, arriving in 1295. Marco spent the rest of his life as a merchant in Venice. At one time he was imprisoned and while in jail wrote an account of his travels which inspired other explorers such as Christopher Columbus.

Ibn Battuta

As a boy, Ibn Battuta studied the Holy Qur'an and became an expert in Muslim theology. When he was 21, he set off from Tangier on the pilgrimage to Makkah, and during the next 28 years he travelled more than 120,000 kilometres, even further than Marco Polo. After visiting Makkah he joined a caravan of pilgrims which was returning to Persia (now Iran). He continued to travel around the Middle East, studying the people and culture, and writing down anything that interested him, and he eventually arrived in Delhi. He stayed there for eight years working for the Sultan. In 1342 he was sent by the Sultan as his ambassador to China. Having survived a number of shipwrecks, he reached his destination in 1344. He was impressed by Chinese culture and their use of paper money, but after a year he decided to return home. Back in Tangier, Ibn Battuta wrote an account of his adventures called *Rihla*. Many of his contemporaries refused to believe the story of his travels and it was only long after his death that he came to be appreciated.

Vasco da Gama

In 1497 Vasco da Gama was sent by the King of Portugal to find a sea route to India. With four ships and 170 men, he sailed down the Atlantic Ocean, and after surviving a terrible storm, finally reached the Cape of Good Hope, the southern tip of Africa. There he abandoned his largest ship, and sailed up the coast of East Africa, stopping at various ports. The Portuguese were surprised to find rich Arab towns with stone houses on the coast. The Sultan of Melindi welcomed him and supplied two Arab pilots to guide him to India. Thanks to them he was able to cross the Indian Ocean to Calicut in southern India. Shortly after that, da Gama departed for home with a rich cargo of spices, but he lost 110 men and two ships. He sailed to India again in 1502 and after this voyage he retired. However, at the age of 64, he decided to return to India but died in Goa shortly after arriving there in 1524.

2 🎧 (3.08) Read the text. Match the sentences with the three explorers. Write *MP* for Marco Polo, *IB* for Ibn Battuta, and *VG* for Vasco da Gama.

1 Some people didn't believe the account of his travels. IB
2 He returned home not long after reaching his destination.
3 He came from a rich family.
4 He first left home in order to visit a religious site.
5 He worked for the Emperor of China.
6 He did not die in his home country.
7 He didn't write a famous account of his travels.
8 He spent a number of years in India.
9 He wrote abut his travels while he was in prison.

UNDERSTANDING IDEAS

Answer the questions. Look at the text, and use your own words and ideas.

1 Why did it take Marco Polo so long to reach China?
2 Why didn't people believe Ibn Battuta's account of his travels?
3 What do you think motivated the three explorers?

VOCABULARY

Great journeys

1 Match the highlighted words in the text with the definitions below.

1 The place where you are going.
2 People who help to guide ships.
3 The goods that a ship carries.
4 The way from one place to another.
5 Finished working for life.
6 The study of religion.
7 A journey to a holy place.
8 A group of people and animals travelling together, especially across a desert.
9 People who were alive at the same time.
10 People who buy and sell goods.
11 Left forever.
12 The land next to the sea.
13 Accidents at sea that destroy ships.
14 Someone who represents their country.
15 Gave somebody the confidence to do something.

2 Match the verbs (1–8) with phrases (a–h). They are all in the text.

1	set off	a	his destination
2	return	b	from his hometown
3	join	c	the ocean
4	reach	d	a caravan
5	sail	e	home
6	cross	f	up the coast

3 Do you know these words?

account   appreciate   civil servant   depart   diplomat
imprison   impressed   wealthy

(●●○   Workbook: page 76)

Great journeys

ACTIVATE

Complete the texts with the correct form of the words from the box.

> abandon ambassador caravan cargo coast contemporary
> destination inspire merchant pilgrimage pilot retire
> route shipwreck theology

1 The ship sailed from Port Said with a _____ of fresh fruit. It's _____ was London docks. When it arrived, a _____ guided the ship safely into port.
2 The study of _____ has become very popular, and has _____ many students to think deeply about religious issues.
3 More than 250 migrant workers died in a _____ off the _____ of Libya in 2009. The ship was on a _____ bound for Italy.
4 Mansa Musa, the emperor of Mali, made a famous _____ to Makkah in 1324. His impressive _____ consisted of 600 men, thousands of slaves and 80 camels, each carrying 300 pounds of gold!
5 Christopher Columbus and his _____ knew that the Earth was round, even though some people at that time still believed that the world was flat.
6 'The _____ of Venice' is a popular play by Shakespeare.
7 The role of a modern _____ is to represent his or her own country and at the same time maintain good diplomatic relations with another country.
8 When the mayor _____, the plans to build a local airport were _____. Many people had protested against it and the new mayor preferred to use the money for a new sports complex.

EXTEND

At the station

1 Label the picture below with the words in the box. Which items aren't illustrated?

> passengers departures board guard cafeteria
> ~~locomotive~~ platform carriage sleeping car
> ticket office waiting area information desk

1 locomotive

Phrasal verbs: travel

2 Write the phrasal verbs from the box next to their definitions.

> set off check out get off touch down
> ~~get back~~ get on pick sb up drop sb off
> check in blast off

1 arrive again at a place that you left earlier get back
2 leave _____
3 arrive at a hotel reception _____
4 (of a rocket) leave the ground _____
5 step onto (e.g. a bus or train) _____
6 come back to the ground _____
7 stop and let somebody out of a car _____
8 pay a hotel reception and leave _____
9 step off (e.g. a bus or train) _____
10 to collect somebody in a car / bus _____

3 Match the two halves of the sentences and complete them with the correct form of verbs from the box. (The phrasal verbs in each half are opposite in meaning.)

> get ~~set~~ get touch pick check blast check
> drop get

1 We _____ off at six in the morning and
2 We _____ in at the hotel.
3 You're allowed to _____ passengers off in this area
4 You should _____ off the train at Euston station
5 The space shuttle _____ off from Cape Canaveral and

a _____ down three days later.
b _____ back at seven the following day.
c just as our friends were _____ out.
d but you can't _____ them up from here.
e then _____ on a bus that will take you to the city centre.

1 We set off at six in the morning and get back at seven the following day.

⬤⬤⬤⬤⬤ Workbook: page 77

The passive (present simple)

EXPLORE

1 Look at the example of the passive in blue in the text. Then read and complete the rule in the *Learn this!* box.

> Oil is found deep under the ground. It is formed from tiny plants and animals that lived in the sea millions of years ago. Oil has many uses. **It is used** to power vehicles such as cars, planes and trains, and many plastics are made from oil. Scientists believe that global warming is caused by the burning of oil and other fossil fuels, so they are trying to develop alternative sources of energy.

LEARN THIS!

Present passive

1 The present passive is formed with the correct form of the verb _____ and the past participle.

These lorries are made in Sweden.

Mobile phones aren't sold in that shop.

Is this book printed in China?

2 When we want to say who performed the action, we use *by*.

These cars are built by robots.

2 Find three more examples of the passive in the text in exercise 1. Are they singular or plural? Find an example of the passive with *by*.

(●●●●● Grammar Reference: page 112)

EXPLOIT

1 Choose the correct words to complete the sentences.

1 Computers **is** / **are** used in most schools.
2 Coffee **is** / **are** grown in Kenya.
3 The Olympic Games **is** / **are** watched by millions of people around the world.
4 Plastic bags **isn't** / **aren't** provided to customers in our local supermarket.
5 Arabic **is** / **are** spoken in Algeria.
6 Wood **is** / **are** used to make paper.
7 Millions of items **is** / **are** bought and sold on the internet every day.
8 Paris **is** / **are** known as the City of Light.

2 Complete the sentences with the present simple passive. Match the description of the process (1–5) with pictures (A–E).

How oil is refined

1 ☐ The ground [1] is surveyed (survey) by geophysicists. The oil [2] _____ (locate) deep underground.

Ⓐ

2 ☐ Once oil [3] _____ (locate), derricks [4] _____ (erect), and holes [5] _____ (drill) into the ground.

Ⓑ

3 ☐ The oil [6] _____ (pump) from underground to the surface. The oil [7] _____ (carry) by pipeline to an oil refinery.

Ⓒ

4 ☐ At the refinery, the oil [8] _____ (separate) into different products, such as gasoline, kerosene and diesel oil. Most of these [9] _____ (use) to power vehicles.

Ⓓ

5 ☐ Some of the products [10] _____ (combine) with other things to make plastics and chemicals.

Ⓔ

3 Write questions for these answers. Use the words in brackets and the present simple passive.

1 Deep underground. (Where / the oil / locate?)
Where is the oil located?
2 It is pumped. (How / the oil / bring to the surface?)
3 By pipeline. (How / the oil / carry / to the refinery?)
4 Gasoline, kerosene and diesel oil. (What products / the oil / separate into?)
5 To power vehicles. (What / gasoline, kerosene and diesel oil / mostly use / for?)
6 To make plastics and chemicals. (Why / some of the products / combine / with other things?)

(●●●●● Grammar Builder: page 113)

(●●●●● Workbook: page 78)

Inventions and discoveries

VOCABULARY

1 Match the inventions and discoveries in the pictures with the words in the box.

1 combustion engine

Inventions and discoveries   ~~combustion engine~~
contact lenses   frozen food   gravity   nuclear power pasteurized milk   penicillin   printing press telescope   X-rays

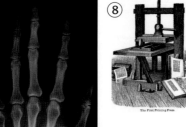

2 Categorize these inventions and complete the table. Add words from exercise 1 and add three more of your own ideas to each category.

airplane   antibiotics   bicycle   camera   dishwasher waterwheel   freezer   hovercraft   microwave oven mobile phone   MP4 player   paper   telegram   telephone

Transport	car, ...
Domestic appliances	fridge, ...
Media and entertainment	television, ...
Communication	computers,
Science and medicine	vaccination, ...
Energy	electricity, ...

●●●●● Workbook: page 79

LISTEN

1 🎧 (3.09) Listen to two teenagers discussing inventions. Which do they think are the three most important?

2 🎧 (3.09) Listen again and complete the sentences.

1 So _____ three inventions and discoveries shall we choose?
2 I think we _____ include the telephone.
3 _____ the invention of the telephone, ...
4 Let's _____ the mobile phone, then, because ...
5 What about our second _____?
6 I think antibiotics, like penicillin, is a more _____ invention.
7 Yes, I _____ with you.
8 I think antibiotics should be on our _____.
9 That's _____ a very important invention.
10 Let's _____ include those two.

SPEAK

1 Work in pairs. Discuss your top three inventions and discoveries and make a list. Use the phrases in Listen exercise 2 to help you.

2 Present one of the discoveries you listed in exercise 1 to the rest of the class. Explain why it is important. Make notes, using the phrases below to help you.

It helps us to ...
It's useful for ...-*ing* ...
It's important because ...
Without it, we couldn't ...
It saves lives / time / money ...

The passive (other tenses)

EXPLORE

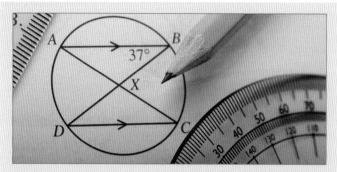

Arab mathematicians have made a significant contribution to the development of geometry and algebra. Nowadays we take the number 'zero' for granted, but it wasn't invented until 967 AD by Mohammed Bin Ahmed. In fact, all the numbers (1, 2, 3, etc.) that are used throughout the world today are based on Arabic numbers. The mathematician Al-Khwarizmi is considered to be the 'father of algebra'. The word 'algebra' comes from the Arabic word 'al-jabr', and was taken from the title of a book that Al-Khwarizmi wrote in 820 AD. Another very influential scholar was Nasīr al-Dīn al-Tūsī. He will always be remembered as the founder of modern geometry, but he was also an expert in many other subjects, including chemistry, biology and astronomy. A crater on the moon has been named after him (Nasireddin) in recognition of his achievements.

Find the passive forms in the text and match them with the tenses. Complete the table.

The passive	
1 present simple affirmative	are used
2 past simple affirmative	
3 past simple negative	
4 present perfect affirmative	
5 future affirmative	

(●●●●● Grammar Reference: page 112)

EXPLOIT

1 Match and complete the active and passive sentences with the same meaning.

Active

1 Alfred Nobel invented dynamite in 1867.
  e Dynamite was invented by Alfred Nobel in 1867.
2 They have discovered a number of planets outside our solar system.
3 In the past sailors _____ stars to navigate.
4 People will remember Johann Gutenberg for the invention of the printing press.
5 Many people _____ James Cook to be the greatest ever explorer.
6 Scientists have developed many forms of renewable energy.

Passive

a In the past, stars were used by sailors to navigate.
b Many forms of renewable energy _____ by scientists.
c James Cook is considered by many people to be the greatest ever explorer.
d A number of planets _____ outside our solar system.
e Dynamite _____ by Alfred Nobel in 1867.
f Johann Gutenberg _____ for the invention of the printing press.

2 Complete the text with the correct passive form of the verbs in brackets.

Wiki Websites

'Wiki' means 'quick' in Hawaiian. The word [1]is used (use) to describe websites that [2]_____ (write) by the people who use the site. Anyone who visits a wiki website can add or change the information on the page. The first wiki website [3]_____ (create) by Ward Cunningham in 1995. Since then, wiki guidebooks, wiki dictionaries and wiki encyclopaedias [4]_____ (publish) on the Internet. The most popular online encyclopaedia is 'Wikipedia'. Over 22 million entries [5]_____ (add) since it started, and it is now the most detailed encyclopaedia in the world. According to the creator of Wikipedia, the work [6]_____ (do) by 20,000 people who regularly edit the pages. The amazing thing is that the information is completely free.

3 Complete the questions with the correct passive form of the verbs in brackets.

1 What item of clothing _____ (wear) by doctors?
2 Who _____ (attack) by a shark in Hawaii in 2003?
3 Who _____ (call) King of the Mile?
4 Which town in Nebraska _____ (found) in 1902?
5 Which prize _____ (receive) by fewer than 160 civilians in the UK?
6 Which club _____ Amr Zaki _____ (choose) to play for?
7 What _____ (win) by Ernest Hemingway in 1954?
8 Name the building in New York which _____ (use) as a lighthouse until 1902.

4 Write the answers to the questions. The answers are all in units 1–5 of this book.

(●●●●● Grammar Builder: page 113)
(●●●●● Workbook: page 80)

An article

READ

Things I'd like to 'uninvent'

Many inventions have certainly made the world a better place. Where would we be without antibiotics, for example? However, there are two things that I would 'uninvent' if I could.

The first thing I'd 'uninvent' is plastic bags. Admittedly, they are convenient, but the problem with plastic bags is that there are too many of them. People don't reuse them, they just throw them away. Furthermore, most bags are not biodegradable, so it will take many years for them to decompose.

The second thing I'd 'uninvent' is mobile phones. Again, they can be useful, especially in an emergency. However, the reason I'd like to ban them is that the ringtones are so irritating. What is more, people always shout when they're using them.

To sum up, there are other irritating inventions, but if just these two things were 'uninvented', in my view the world would be a better place.

Read the article and answer the questions in your own words.

1 What example does the writer give of a useful invention?
   Antibiotics
2 What is the main reason the writer objects to plastic bags?
3 What additional reason does he give?
4 What is the main reason the writer objects to mobile phones?
5 What additional reason does he give?

PREPARE

1 Match phrases in the article with these functions.

   1 starting the main two paragraphs
     The first thing I'd 'uninvent' is ...
     The second thing I'd 'uninvent' is ...
   2 introducing the reasons for 'uninventing' plastic bags and mobile phones
   3 introducing additional information
   4 starting the conclusion
   5 giving an opinion
   6 giving an example
   7 making a contrast

2 You are going to write an article about two things that you would like to 'uninvent'. Make notes under these headings.

- First thing I'd like to 'uninvent':

- Reasons:

- Second thing I'd like to 'uninvent':

- Reasons:

WRITE

Read the *Writing tip* then write your article (130–150 words), using your notes from exercise 2 and phrases from exercise 1.

Writing tip: planning an article

- Start with a short introduction and attract your readers' attention. One way of doing this is to include a question.
- Divide the main part of the article into two paragraphs.
- Finish by summarizing your views and feelings.

Check your work

Have you
☐ divided your article into four paragraphs?
☐ used phrases from Prepare exercise 1?
☐ written 130–150 words?
☐ checked your spelling, punctuation and grammar?

●●●●○ Workbook: page 81

Discovery

LANGUAGE SKILLS

1 🎧 (3.10) Complete the dialogue with the words from the box. Then listen and check your answers.

> abandoned back destination inspired killed named
> route set shipwrecked was

Harry Have you done any research for your school project?

Joe Yes, I've been ¹_____ by an article about an explorer called Ferdinand Magellan.

Harry Ferdinand Magellan. The Magellan Strait was ²_____ after him – is that right?

Joe Yes, that's right. Magellan discovered the ³_____ from the Atlantic Ocean to the Pacific Ocean through the southern part of South America.

Harry So where did the expedition ⁴_____ off from?

Joe Magellan left Spain in 1519 with five ships and 234 sailors. They crossed the Atlantic Ocean and reached the coast of South America. While Magellan was looking for the route to the Pacific, one of his ships was ⁵_____ in a sudden storm. Another ship ⁶_____ the expedition and returned to Spain.

Harry And did they reach their final ⁷_____?

Joe Yes, three years later they returned to Spain with just one ship and 18 men after crossing the Pacific and Indian oceans. It was the first voyage to sail around the world.

Harry So I suppose Magellan ⁸_____ greeted as a hero when he got ⁹_____?

Joe Well, no. Unfortunately he was ¹⁰_____ in a battle with local people on an island in the Pacific.

2 Read the dialogue again and answer the questions.

1 What is Joe doing?
2 Who was Ferdinand Magellan?
3 What did Magellan discover?
4 Was the expedition successful? Why? Why not?
5 Why didn't Magellan compete the journey around the world?

3 Complete the sentences. Use the passive form of the verbs in the box.

> discover employ remember grow not wash teach
> invent make

1 Tea _____ in India.
2 'When _____ television _____ ?' 'In 1926.'
3 This plate is dirty. It _____.
4 Tim Berners-Lee _____ in the future for inventing the worldwide web.
5 Penicillin _____ in 1927.
6 Ferrari cars _____ in Italy.
7 My dad _____ by Sony since 2003.
8 The inventor Thomas Edison _____ at home by his mother.

Parts of a car

Check the meaning of the words in the box and match them with (1–12) in the picture.

> ~~bonnet~~ bumper door handle front grille headlight
> indicator rear window tyre wheel windscreen
> windscreen wiper wing mirror

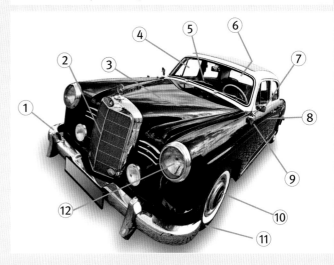

1 _____
2 _____
3 bonnet
4 _____
5 _____
6 _____
7 _____
8 _____
9 _____
10 _____

I CAN ...

Read the statements. Think about your progress and tick (✓) one of the boxes.

★ I need more practice.   ★★ I sometimes find this difficult.   ★★★ No problem!

	★	★★	★★★
I can understand a text about explorers.			
I can describe the different stages of a process.			
I can talk about inventions and why they're important.			
I can use different forms of the passive.			
I can write an article giving my opinion.			

●●●○○ Workbook: Self check pages 82–83

Kidnapped

by Robert Louis Stevenson

When I woke up in darkness, my head was hurting badly, and I was unable to move my hands or feet. I could hear the sailors' shouts and the sound of the wind and the waves. The whole world seemed to go up, up, up, and then down again. I felt very ill, and at first could not understand what was happening. After a while I realized that I must be somewhere inside the ship, which was moving very fast through the water. 'I've been kidnapped!' I thought angrily. It was clear that my uncle and the captain had planned it together. I began to feel frightened and hopeless, as I lay there in the dark.

Some hours later, a light shone in my face. Mr Riach, one of the ship's officers, stood looking down at me. He washed the cut on my head, gave me some water, and told me kindly to go to sleep. The next time he came, I was feeling very hot and ill. He had brought Captain Hoseason with him.

'Now, sir, see for yourself,' said Mr Riach. 'The lad's seriously ill. We must take him out of this unhealthy hole at once.'

'That's none of your business,' answered the captain. 'Ye're paid to do your job, not worry about the boy. He's staying down here.'

'I'm only paid to be an officer on this ship,' replied Mr Riach sharply. He looked hard at the captain. 'I'm not paid, like you, to kidnap and murder—'

Hoseason turned on him angrily. 'What did ye say?' he cried. 'What do ye mean?'

'You understand,' said Mr Riach, looking calmly at him.

'You should know me by now, Mr Riach. I'm a hard man. But if ye say the lad will die—'

'Aye, he will!' said Mr Riach.

'Well, sir, put him where ye like!'

So I was carried up into the sunlight a few minutes later, and put in a cabin where some of the sailors were sleeping. It was a wonderful feeling to see the daylight and to be able to talk to people again. I lay in the cabin for several days, and after a while began to feel better.

---

1 *Kidnapped* is set in Scotland. Match Scottish words 1–3 with definitions a–c. Then read the text and check.

1 lad	a you
2 ye	b yes
3 aye	c boy

2 🎧 (3.13) Read the text and answer the questions.
The story is narrated by the main character, David.
David is a young man who has been kidnapped by his uncle.

1 Why couldn't David see where he was when he first woke up?
2 Who did he think had organized his kidnap?
3 Why did Mr Riach take Captain Hoseason to see David?
4 What would happen if they didn't move David?
5 Where did they move David to?

3 Answer the questions. Look at the text, and use your own words and ideas.

1 Why do you think David couldn't move his hands or feet?
2 When do you think he got the cut on his head?
3 What qualities did Mr Riach possess?
4 What do you think the captain was going to do with David?

4 The ship was sailing near some Scottish islands when a huge wave knocked David and some of the sailors into the sea. Write a short paragraph about what you think happened to David.

Sherlock Holmes

READ

1 Look at the picture. Do you know the detective on the right? Describe him. Was he a real character or was he fictional?

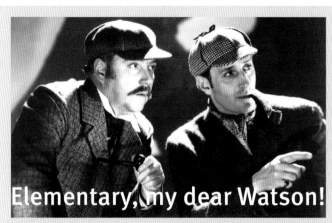

Elementary, my dear Watson!

Detective stories are the most popular type of stories in the world. But who is the most famous fictional detective? Without a doubt, it is Sherlock Holmes.

The author of the Sherlock Holmes stories was Arthur Conan Doyle. He was born in Scotland in 1859 and studied medicine at Edinburgh University. After leaving university he moved to the south of England and worked as a doctor, but in his spare time he started to write detective stories.

The hero of the stories is a private detective called Sherlock Holmes, who lives at 221b Baker Street in London. There is now a museum at that address. (See http://www.sherlock-holmes.co.uk.) Holmes is tall and thin, with a long, sharp face. He usually wears a deerstalker hat, smokes a pipe or cigarettes, and carries a magnifying glass. He is an extremely intelligent man who always thinks logically about the crimes he is trying to solve. He is also a brilliant violinist. However, he has a dark side to his character: he is a lonely and rather sad man who is easily bored with everyday life. He often gets depressed and sometimes spends all day in bed. He is not married and says that he doesn't understand women. Holmes' assistant, and only friend, is Dr Watson. Watson describes him in one of the stories as 'a brain without a heart' and 'more a machine than a man'.

In 1895, after Conan Doyle had written 25 stories about Holmes, he got bored with his detective and decided that Holmes would die in the next story. At the end of the story called *The Final Problem*, Holmes fights Professor Moriarty, his greatest enemy, by a huge waterfall in Switzerland. They both die when they fall into the waterfall. But the Holmes stories were already incredibly popular and his fans were very upset. Conan Doyle had to bring his character back to life. He continued to write Sherlock Holmes stories for another 25 years. In the end, he wrote four novels and 56 short stories about the great detective.

2 Read the text. Which one of the descriptions of Holmes is not completely accurate?

1 A very intelligent man who didn't have many friends and didn't understand women.
2 A sad and lonely man who easily got depressed and sometimes spent all day in bed.
3 A brilliant logical thinker who lived with his assistant Dr Watson and never got married.
4 An intelligent, funny, friendly man who smoked a pipe and played the violin brilliantly.

3 Are the sentences true or false?

1 Arthur Conan Doyle was Scottish.
2 By 1895 Conan Doyle had written all his Sherlock Holmes stories.
3 Conan Doyle wrote the Sherlock Holmes stories in Scotland.
4 Holmes dies at the end of *The Final Problem*.
5 Conan Doyle started to write about Holmes again because his fans were very unhappy.
6 In total, Conan Doyle wrote 25 stories and four novels about Holmes.

LISTEN

1 🎧 (3.14) Listen to part one of a Sherlock Holmes story called *The Speckled Band*. Put the events of Helen Stoner's life in the correct order.

☐ Helen's mother marries Doctor Roylott.
☐ Doctor Roylott murders a servant.
☐ The family returns to England.
☐ Helen's father dies.
☐ Helen's mother dies.
☐ Somebody burgles their house in India.
☐ Doctor Roylott goes to prison.
☐ Helen's twin sister, Julia, dies in her bedroom.

2 🎧 (3.15) Listen to part two of the story. Answer the questions.

1 How did Julia Stoner die?
2 What happens to Doctor Roylott?

SPEAK AND WRITE

1 Ask and answer the questions.

1 Have you seen any Sherlock Holmes films or read any of the stories? If so, did you enjoy them?
2 How many books, films or TV shows about crime and detectives can you name?
3 How do crime stories usually begin? How do they usually end?
4 Do you enjoy reading or watching crime stories? Why? / Why not?

2 Write an article about a book you really like.

Present simple

We form the present simple like this:

Affirmative	
I play	we play
you play	you play
he / she / it plays	they play

Spelling: 3rd person singular (he / she / it)

We add -s to the end of most verbs.

| + -s | start → starts | play → plays |

We add -es if the verb ends in -ch, -ss, -sh or -o.

| + -es | teach → teaches | miss → misses |
| | do → does | go → goes |

If the verb ends in a consonant + -y, we change -y to i and add -es.

| -y → -ies | study → studies | carry → carries |

Negative	
Full form	**Short form**
I do not play	I don't play
you do not play	you don't play
he / she / it does not play	he / she / it doesn't play
you do not play	you don't play
we do not play	we don't play
they do not play	they don't play
Question	**Short answer**
Do I play ...?	Yes, I do. / No, I don't.
Do you play ...?	Yes, you do. / No, you don't.
Does he / she / it play ...?	Yes, she does. / No, she doesn't.
Do we / you / they play ...?	Yes, we / you / they do.
	No, we / you / they don't.

We use the present simple:
- for something that always happens or happens regularly (e.g. every week, often, sometimes).
  Sally cycles to school every day.
- for facts.
  Cows eat grass.
- with certain verbs that are not used in continuous tenses, e.g. *believe, hate, like, love, need, know, prefer, want.*
  I like this book. (NOT ~~I'm liking~~ this book. ✗)

Present continuous

We form the present continuous like this:
- the correct form of *be* + the *-ing* form of the main verb.
  Daniel is eating.
  The class aren't listening.
  Are you playing?

Spelling: verb + -ing form

We add -ing to the end of most verbs.
    play + -ing → playing
    study + -ing → studying

If the verb ends in a consonant + -e, we usually drop the -e and add -ing.

| -e → -ing | write → writing |
| | make → making |

If the verb ends in a short, stressed vowel + a consonant, we double the consonant.

-m → -mming	swim → swimming
-g → -gging	jog → jogging
-p → -pping	tap → tapping
-t → -tting	cut → cutting

We use the present continuous:
- for something that is happening now.
  Look! It's raining.
- for something that is happening temporarily, not necessarily at the moment of speaking.
  My mum's learning English in the evenings.
- for arrangements in the future.
  We're playing tennis tomorrow.

We don't use the present continuous:
- with certain verbs, e.g. *believe, hate, like, love, need, know, prefer, want.*
  I like this book. (NOT ~~I'm liking~~ this book. ✗)

Verb + infinitive or -ing form

When we put two verbs together, the second verb is usually in the infinitive or the *-ing* form.

I **want to go** home. (infinitive)

John **suggested playing** chess. (-ing form)

British teenagers **like to watch** TV. / British teenagers **like watching** TV. (infinitive or -ing form)

Below is a list of verbs that are followed by the infinitive, the *-ing* form, or both.

verb + infinitive		verb + -ing form		Verb + infinitive or -ing form
agree	offer	avoid	finish	begin
decide	prepare	can't help	imagine	continue
expect	pretend	can't stand	keep	hate
fail	promise	don't mind	practise	like
hope	refuse	enjoy	spend time	love
manage	seem	fancy	suggest	prefer
mean	want	feel like		start

Present simple and present continuous

1 Make the affirmative statements negative. Make the negative statements affirmative.

1 I wear a suit at school.
   I don't wear a suit at school.

2 He doesn't like weddings.

3 She plays volleyball after school.

4 We live in London.

5 My uncle works in a factory.

6 I want a sandwich.

2 Complete the questions.

1 What _____ at school?
   She wears a tracksuit.

2 Where _____ swimming?
   He goes swimming at the sports centre.

3 Why _____ computer games?
   They play computer games because they enjoy them.

4 When _____ in the morning?
   He gets up at 7:30.

5 How _____ to work?
   He goes by bus.

3 Write sentences using the present continuous.

1 they / wear / tracksuits
   They're wearing tracksuits.

2 she / chat / to her friend

3 I / not have / a shower

4 we / not win / the match

5 he / run / really badly

6 you / not listen / to me

4 Look at the picture. Ask and answer the questions using the present continuous.

1 she / wear / a hat?
   Is she wearing a hat?
   No, she isn't.

2 she / standing up?

3 she / smile?

4 she / eat / a pizza?

5 she / wear / jeans?

6 she / hold / a mobile phone?

5 Complete the pairs of sentences with the present simple or the present continuous form of the verbs in brackets.

1 a She always _____ (wear) a white top for work.
   b I _____ (wear) new shoes. Do you like them?

2 a We _____ (go) skiing next month.
   b They _____ (go) skiing every winter.

3 a I _____ (love) this cake. What is it?
   b I _____ (enjoy) this cake. What is it?

4 a Light _____ (travel) faster than sound.
   b That car _____ (travel) very fast. Be careful!

5 a My dad often _____ (sing) in the car.
   b My brother _____ (sing). What a terrible noise!

6 a I _____ (not believe) him. It's a lie!
   b He _____ (not tell) the truth. It's a lie!

Verb + infinitive or *-ing* form

6 Match the two halves of the sentences.

1 When he was four, he began …   a to pay for his lessons.
2 His mother agreed …   b practising every day.
3 He imagined …   c to study music at university.
4 He hoped …   d to learn the piano.
5 He didn't mind …   e becoming a famous pianist.

7 Complete the sentences with the infinitive or *-ing* form of the verbs in brackets.

1 He's pretending _____ (be) angry.

2 I can't help _____ (feel) nervous.

3 She doesn't enjoy _____ (wear) formal clothes.

4 Have you finished _____ (eat)?

5 I didn't expect _____ (pass) the exam.

6 Do you want _____ (watch) television?

7 I don't feel like _____ (go) home.

8 We decided _____ (have) lunch in a café.

9 Do you fancy _____ (play) tennis tomorrow?

10 I promise _____ (tell) you the truth.

Past simple

The affirmative form of the past simple is the same for all persons, singular and plural (*I*, *you*, *he*, *we*, etc.).
I watched a football match last night.
She watched TV.
They watched a DVD.

Spelling: past simple (affirmative) form of regular verbs

We form the past simple (affirmative) form of regular verbs by adding -*ed* to the verb.

| + -*ed* | work → worked | play → played |

If the verb ends in -*e*, we add -*d*.

| + -*d* | phone → phoned | move → moved |

If the verb ends in a consonant + -*y*, we change -*y* to *i* and add -*ed*.

| -*y* → -*ied* | study → studied | cry → cried |

If the verb ends in a short stressed vowel + a consonant, we double the consonant.

-*p* → -*pped*	drop → dropped
-*n* → -*nned*	plan → planned
-*t* → -*tted*	regret → regretted

Some verbs have irregular past simple (affirmative) forms. There are no spelling rules for these forms: you need to learn them by heart. See the list of irregular verbs on page 124.

Irregular verbs behave in the same way as regular verbs in negative sentences and questions.

In negative sentences and questions we use *did* / *didn't* + the infinitive without *to* (NOT the past simple form) for regular and irregular verbs. The forms are the same for all persons, singular and plural (*I*, *you*, *he*, *we*, etc.).

Negative	Interrogative
I didn't watch.	Did I watch?
he / she / it didn't watch	Did he / she / it watch?
we / you / they didn't watch	Did we / you / they watch?
Short form and full form	**Short answer**
didn't = did not	Yes, I did. / No, I didn't.

The past simple forms of *be* are *was* or *were*.

Affirmative	Negative	Interrogative
I **was** sad	I **wasn't** sad	**Was** I sad?
you **were** sad	you **weren't** sad	**Were** you sad?
he / she / it **was** sad	he / she / it **wasn't** sad	**Was** he / she / it sad?
we / you / they **were** sad	we / you / they **weren't** sad	**Were** we / you / they sad?

We use the past simple:
• for a completed action or event at a definite point in the past.
We played volleyball last Saturday.
• for actions or events that happened one after another.
Joanna got up, had a shower, got dressed and left the house.
• with certain verbs that are not used in continuous tenses, e.g. *believe, hate, like, love, need, know, prefer, want*.
The police officer believed his story. (NOT *The police officer was believing his story.* ✗)

Past continuous

We form the past continuous like this:
• *was* or *were* + the -*ing* form of the main verb
Elizabeth was eating   The children weren't listening.
Were you playing?
We use the past continuous:
• to describe an action lasting for some time or serving as the background to other events.
It was raining.   Some children were playing rugby.
We don't use the past continuous:
• with certain verbs, e.g. *believe, hate, like, love, need, know, prefer, want*.
Tim needed a new car. (NOT *Tim was needing a new car.* ✗)

We often use the past continuous and the past simple in the same sentence. The past continuous describes a background action or event in the past; the past simple describes a shorter action or event that happened during the longer action, or interrupted it.

It was raining when the accident happened.
My friends were watching TV when the fire started.

Past simple

1 Write the past simple form of the regular verbs.

1 compete _____
2 finish _____
3 chat _____
4 cheer _____
5 miss _____
6 carry _____
7 hate _____
8 stop _____

2 Complete the sentences with the past simple affirmative form of the verbs in brackets. Some are regular and some are irregular.

1 I _____ (know) all the answers to the quiz.
2 My sister _____ (win) the tournament.
3 Our team _____ (score) a goal in the first half.
4 I _____ (like) that film.
5 We _____ (leave) home in the morning.
6 You _____ (teach) me how to play chess.
7 They _____ (enjoy) watching the match last night.
8 I _____ (prefer) going to primary school.

3 Make the sentences in exercise 2 negative.

4 Complete the dialogue with past simple questions and short answers.

Jake What [1]_____ (you / do) last night?
Sue I went to the cinema.
Jake What [2]_____ (you / see)?
Sue The new Italian film.
Jake [3]_____ (you / enjoy) it?
Sue Yes, [4]_____. It was great.
Jake [5]_____ (your sister / go) with you?
Sue No, [6]_____.

5 Complete the text messages with *was*, *wasn't*, *were* and *weren't*.

You [1]_____ at home this morning. Where [2]_____ you?

I [3]_____ at the beach.

Really? But it [4]_____ sunny. It [5]_____ cold!

I know. It [6]_____ my surfing lesson.

Past simple and past continuous

6 Complete the text with the past continuous form of the verbs in brackets.

At 9.30 p.m., we arrived at Mike's house. Mike [1]_____ (stand) in the kitchen. He [2]_____ (eat) a pizza. We said hello, but he [3]_____ (not listen). James and Callum [4]_____ (chat) in the hall. Ed [5]_____ (sit) on the stairs. He [6]_____ (hold) his head in his hands. His shoulders [7]_____ (shake) but he [8]_____ (not cry). He [9]_____ (laugh)!

7 Complete the dialogue with the past continuous form of the verbs in brackets.

Policeman What [1]_____ (you / do) at 8 o'clock yesterday evening?
Man I [2]_____ (watch) TV?
Policeman Really? What [3]_____ (you / watch)?
Man A film.
Policeman What was it called?
Man Er ... I can't remember. I [4]_____ (not pay) attention.
Policeman I see. And why is your jacket wet?
Man I [5]_____ (wear) it this morning when I went out.
Policeman But it [6]_____ (not rain) this morning!

8 Complete the sentences with the past simple or past continuous form of the verbs in brackets.

1 The goalkeeper _____ (catch) the ball and _____ (throw) it to the defender.
2 My dad _____ (get) home while I _____ (watch) an ice hockey match on TV.
3 The referee _____ (stop) the match because it _____ (snow).
4 The motorcyclist _____ (put on) his helmet and _____ (get on) the motorbike.
5 She _____ (break) her leg while she _____ (ski).
6 The Los Angeles Lakers _____ (score) 30 points in the last 10 minutes, but they _____ (not win) the game.
7 It _____ (not rain) so we _____ (play) volleyball in the park.
8 Maria _____ (surf) when she _____ (see) a shark near the beach.

Quantifiers
some and *any*
We usually use *some* in affirmative sentences and *any* in negative sentences and questions.
There are some traffic lights at the end of the road.
There's some pasta on the table.

The boy doesn't want any biscuits.
They haven't got any money.

Are there any cinemas in your town?
Do you need any help?

We usually use some when we offer or ask for something.
Would you like some tea?
Can I borrow some money?

a little, a few
We use *a little* with uncountable nouns. We use *a few* with countable nouns.
Julia ate a little rice.
Mike ate a few chips.

much, many and *a lot of*
We use *much*, *many* and *a lot of* to talk about quantity. We use *much* with uncountable nouns. We use *many* with countable nouns.
French people don't drink much tea.
Are there many pedestrian crossings in the town centre?

We use *a lot of* (or *lots of*) with countable and uncountable nouns.
Bill Gates has got a lot of / lots of money.
There are a lot of / lots of roadworks in London.

We often use *much* and *many* in negative sentences and questions. We don't often use them in affirmative sentences.
We didn't eat much food. or We didn't eat a lot of food.
Were there many people at the party? or Were there a lot of people at the party?
Charlotte's got a lot of money. (NOT Charlotte's got ~~much~~ money. ✗)

Articles
Indefinite article
We use *a* before singular countable nouns when we talk about something for the first time.
We use *the* when we talk about something again.
I've got a cat and a dog. The cat's called Joe and the dog's called Sally.
I had a pizza and a coffee. The pizza was great but the coffee was awful.

We use *a* when we say what somebody or something is.
Liverpool is a city in England.
Bob is a taxi driver.
Mozart was a great composer.

We use *a* when we say what somebody or something is like.
France is a beautiful country.
That's a nice dress. Where did you buy it?
He's a good-looking young man.

Definite article
We use *the* when it is clear what we are talking about.
Mum's in the kitchen. (the kitchen in our house)
The station is near the park. (There's only one station and one park in our town.)
The man in the yellow jacket is my uncle. (We know which man – he's wearing a yellow jacket.)

We use *the* when there is only one of something.
the sun, the Red Sea, the sky, the moon, the world

Zero article
We don't use *the* when we are making generalizations.
I don't like classical music.
Fiona never drinks tea or coffee.

GRAMMAR BUILDER 3

Quantity: *some*, *any*, *much*, *many*, etc.

1 Complete the sentences with *some* or *any*.

1 I need _____ fresh air.
2 There isn't _____ traffic on the road.
3 Are there _____ fields near your school?
4 Have you got _____ homework?
5 I'm going out with _____ friends.
6 We haven't got _____ pets.

2 Complete the sentences with *a little* or *a few*.

1 'Would you like some pasta?' 'Just _____. I'm not very hungry.'
2 I went to the cinema with _____ friends last night.
3 I spent _____ time chatting with my uncle.
4 She bought _____ books in town.
5 I only recognized _____ people at the wedding.
6 She isn't a vegetarian, but she only eats _____ meat.

3 Complete the sentences with *much* or *many*.

1 There aren't _____ street lamps in my street.
2 Hurry up! We haven't got _____ time.
3 Has she got _____ friends at school?
4 Do you listen to _____ radio programmes?
5 He doesn't speak _____ Arabic.
6 There aren't _____ cottages in the village.

4 Complete the sentences with *a lot of* and words from the box.

countries	homework	goals	money	old people
traffic				

1 She's always buying expensive jewellery. She's got
_____.
2 Sorry I'm late. There was _____ on the roads.
3 Did Chelsea score _____ in the match?
4 There are _____ in the town.
5 English is spoken in _____.
6 I can't go out tonight. Our teacher gave us
_____.

Articles

5 Complete the sentences with *a* or *the*.

1 My dad's got _____ BMW and my mum's got _____ Volkswagen. _____ BMW is much faster than _____ Volkswagen.
2 I met _____ girl and _____ boy at the sports centre. _____ girl was from France, and _____ boy was from Spain.
3 She lives in _____ flat in the centre of town. _____ flat is very small.
4 There was _____ cinema and _____ theatre in our town, but _____ cinema closed last year.
5 There's _____ bus at 10 or _____ train at 11. _____ bus arrives at 12, _____ train arrives at 11.30.
6 'I'd like _____ pizza and _____ piece of chocolate cake.' 'Would you like chips with _____ pizza?'
7 I bought _____ book about birds and _____ book about fish. _____ book about birds was OK, but _____ book about fish was boring.

6 Complete each pair of sentences with *a* and *the*.

1 a There's _____ clothes shop near the post office.
  b I love _____ clothes shop between the bank and the chemist's.
2 a Shut _____ door, please.
  b My bedroom has got _____ blue door.
3 a I like this song. Who's _____ singer?
  b I think Om Kalthoum was _____ great singer.
4 a Sandra's _____ lovely girl.
  b Who's _____ girl with long dark hair?
5 a Look. There's _____ cat in that tree.
  b 'Which cat is yours?' '_____ black one.'
6 a Dad's watching television in _____ living room.
  b I'd like a house with _____ big living room.

7 Add *the* to the sentences.

1 I saw President on TV last night.
2 I'd like to travel round world.
3 It was cold but sun was shining.
4 If you see an accident, you should phone police.
5 My brother wants to join army.
6 It's too cold to swim in sea.
7 Moon came out from behind the clouds.
8 Paris is capital of France.

8 Choose the correct answer.

1 I hate **cold coffee** / **the cold coffee**.
2 'Where's **coffee** / **the coffee**?' 'It's in the cupboard.'
3 She loves **cats** / **the cats**.
4 I'm going to take **children** / **the children** for a walk.
5 I'm not very interested in **sport** / **the sport**.
6 My favourite sport is **football** / **the football**.
7 Where are **books** / **the books** that I bought yesterday?
8 We went swimming in the sea. **Water** / **The water** was really warm.

Comparative adjectives

Spelling
We add *-er* to short (one-syllable and some two-syllable) adjectives.

   + -er   long → longer

If the short adjective ends in *-e*, we add *-r*.

   + -r   wide → wider

If the short adjective ends in a short vowel + a single consonant, we double the consonant and add *-er*.

   -t → *-tter*   hot → hotter

If the adjective ends in *-y*, we take out the *-y* and add *-ier*.

   -y → *-ier*   friendly → friendlier

If the adjective is long (two syllables or more), we use the word *more*.

   gripping → more gripping

Some adjectives have irregular comparative forms.

   good → better
   bad → worse
   far → further

than

We use *than* to compare two things or people.
Basketball is more entertaining than football.

We usually use the object pronoun (*me, you, her, him, us, them*) after *than*.
You're taller than me. (NOT ~~You're taller than I~~. ✗)
but You're taller than I am. ✓

Superlative adjectives

Spelling
We put *the* in front of short (one-syllable and some two-syllable) adjectives and add *-est*.

   + -est   long → the longest

If the short adjective ends in *-e*, we add *-st*.

   + -st   wide → the widest

If the short adjective ends in a short vowel + a single consonant, we double the consonant and add *-est*.

   -t → *-ttest*   hot → the hottest

If the adjective ends in *-y*, we take out the *-y* and add *-iest*.

   -y → *-iest*   friendly → the friendliest

If the adjective is long (two syllables or more), we use the word *most*.

   gripping → the most gripping

Some adjectives have irregular superlative forms.

   good → the best
   bad → the worst
   far → the furthest

less and the least

less and *the least* have the opposite meaning to *more* and *the most*.
Maths is less difficult than English.
What's the least interesting subject that you study?

(not) as ... as

We use *(not) as ... as* to compare two people or things.

not as ... as means *less ... than*.
Orlando is not as old as Brian. Brian was born in 1998, Orlando in 1999.

as ... as means *equally*.
Alice is as tall as Tina. Alice and Tina are both 170 centimetres.

We usually use the object pronoun after *(not) as ... as*. The subject pronoun sounds very formal.
Sarah's as intelligent as him. (NOT Sarah's as intelligent as ~~he~~. ✗)
but Sarah's as intelligent as he is. ✓

too and enough

too comes before an adjective.
enough comes after an adjective.
This jacket is too small for him.
This jacket isn't big enough for him.

enough comes before a noun.
He can't buy it. He hasn't got enough money.

GRAMMAR BUILDER 4

Comparative and superlative adjectives

1 Write the comparative forms of the adjectives.

1 large _____
2 tall _____
3 thin _____
4 early _____
5 good _____
6 easy _____
7 hot _____
8 bad _____

2 Complete the sentences with comparative adjectives from exercise 1.

1 'Is Dave _____ than George?' 'Yes, he's 1m 85.'
2 This jacket is too small. Have you got a _____ one?
3 It isn't very warm today. It was much _____ yesterday.
4 Exams are _____ if you revise a lot.
5 Oh, dear, it's raining. We can't play tennis unless the weather gets _____.
6 I don't like his latest books. I prefer his _____ novels.
7 This pizza is too thick. I prefer _____ ones.
8 Mr Jones is a _____ teacher than Mr Smith. Mr Smith explains things more carefully.

3 Complete the sentences with the comparative form of the adjectives in brackets and *than*.

1 Do you think Maths is _____ English? (difficult)
2 Science fiction films are _____ comedies. (boring)
3 Real Madrid are a _____ football team _____ Liverpool. (successful)
4 Maria is _____ Joanna. (confident)
5 Historical dramas are _____ than war films. (entertaining)
6 Is football _____ ice hockey? (exciting)

4 Write sentences with superlative adjectives.

1 chimpanzees / funny / animals / in the world
Chimpanzees are the funniest animals in the world.

2 Mark / tall / boy / in the class
3 Russia / large / country / in the world
4 Crime stories / popular stories / in the world
5 Germany / has got / big / population / in Europe
6 who / hard-working / student / in the class?
7 *Titanic* / moving / film / I've ever seen

(not) as ... as, too, enough

5 Write sentences with *as ... as* and the adjective in brackets.

1 The French cookbook and the Italian cookbook both cost £15. (expensive)
The French cookbook is as expensive as the Italian cookbook.

2 Diana was born in 1996. Mike was born in 1996 too. (old)
3 Cathy and Joe both got top marks in the exam. (intelligent)
4 The BMW and the Mercedes both have a top speed of 200 km/h. (fast)
5 I'm very tired. You're very tired too. (tired)
6 I go swimming twice a week. You go swimming twice a week too. (often)

6 Rewrite the sentences with *not as ... as*.

1 Arnold is taller than Sylvester.
Sylvester isn't as tall as Arnold.

2 Disaster films are more gripping than science fiction films.
3 Jane is funnier than Ellen.
4 The acting in *Gladiator* was better than the acting in *Troy*.
5 The sports centre in the town is bigger than the sports centre in the village.
6 I'm more interested in history than you.

7 Complete the sentences with *too* and an adjective from the box.

boring cold expensive sweet tired untidy

1 It's _____ in here to have the window open. Can you close it, please?
2 That blouse is _____. It's £40.
3 I can't drink this tea. It's _____.
4 That film is _____ to watch from beginning to end.
5 I'm not going to stay up and watch the film with you. I'm _____.
6 I can't find anything in my room. It's _____.

8 Complete the sentences with *enough* and a noun or adjective from the box.

exercise funny old people time television

1 I haven't got _____ to finish my homework.
2 I didn't enjoy the comedy. It wasn't _____.
3 He doesn't do _____ to stay healthy.
4 We can't play football. There aren't _____.
5 I'm not _____ to drive a car.
6 Go to bed. You've watched _____.

Present perfect

We form the present perfect like this:

Affirmative	
I've finished	we've finished
you've finished	you've finished
he / she / it's finished	they've finished

Short form and full form	
I've = I have	
she's = she has	

Negative	
I haven't finished	we haven't finished
you haven't finished	you haven't finished
he / she / it hasn't finished	they haven't finished

Short form and full form	
haven't = have not	
hasn't = has not	

Interrogative	
Have I finished ...?	Have we finished ...?
Have you finished ...?	Have you finished ...?
Has he / she / it finished ...?	Have they finished ...?

Short answer	
Yes, I have. / No, I haven't.	
Yes, she has. / No, she hasn't.	

We form the present perfect with the present tense of the auxiliary verb *have* and the past participle.
Pete has finished his homework.

The past participle of regular verbs is the same as the past simple.
played   phoned   studied   dropped

Sometimes irregular verbs have the same past participle as the past simple form, sometimes they are different.
buy – bought – bought
see – saw – seen

See the list of irregular verbs on page 124.

We use the present perfect:
- to talk about recent events.
  Pete has passed all his exams.
- to talk about experiences.
  I've eaten fish and chips in England.
- to talk about an event or situation that began in the past and continues up to now. We use *for* with a period of time and *since* with a point in time.
  My dad has worked for IBM for 10 years.
  I've had this camera since May.
- to talk about actions that have an effect on the present.
  I haven't finished my homework, so I can't go out.

We use both *been* and *gone* as the past participles of the verb *go*. We use *been* when somebody has returned.
John has been shopping. (He went shopping but he is here now.)
We use *gone* when somebody hasn't returned.
John has gone shopping. (He went shopping and he is still at the shops.)

We use *How long ...?* and the present perfect to ask how long a situation has continued up to the present.
'How long have you lived in Canada?' 'Since 2001.'

Present perfect and past simple

We use both the past simple and the present perfect to talk about finished actions.

We use the past simple to talk about completed events at a definite time in the past. The events have no connection with the present.
I visited Dubai last year.

We use the present perfect to talk about past events that have a connection with the present.

We use the present perfect to talk about past events that have a connection with the present.
Have you ever been to Ireland?
Yes, I have. I went last year.

We often use the past simple when we ask for or give more details following a *Have you ever ...?* question.
Have you ever been to Egypt?
Yes, I have. I went Cairo last year.

Have you ever been skiing?
Yes, I have.
Where did you go?
I went to Switzerland.

GRAMMAR BUILDER 5

Present perfect

1 Complete the phone conversation with the present perfect form of the verbs in brackets or short answers.

Steve   Hello, Steve speaking.
Dave   Hi, Steve. It's Dave. I'm phoning from London.
Steve   Hi, Dave! It's great to hear from you. So, you ¹_____ (find) your mobile!
Dave   Actually, no. I ²_____ (buy) a new one, but my number ³_____ (not change).
Steve   Well, it's great to hear from you. We ⁴_____ (not speak) for ages. ⁵_____ (you / find) somewhere to live yet?
Dave   No, I ⁶_____, but I ⁷_____ (just / look) at a beautiful flat near the Thames.
Steve   Are you going to live there?
Dave   I ⁸_____ (not decide) yet. I can't really afford it!
Steve   ⁹_____ (you / start) work?
Dave   Yes, I ¹⁰_____. I ¹¹_____ (give) about twenty lessons, but the school ¹²_____ (not pay) me yet!

2 What have or haven't you done today? Write an affirmative and a negative sentence in the present perfect for each verb in the box.

eat	drink	hear	see	speak	be	go

3 Choose *for* or *since*.

1 My grandparents have been married **for** / **since** 40 years.
2 It hasn't snowed here **for** / **since** 1998.
3 He's had a job **for** / **since** last summer.
4 They've been engaged **for** / **since** twelve years.
5 I've been friends with Britney **for** / **since** I was 12 years old.
6 You haven't phoned me **for** / **since** ages.

4 Write questions with *How long...?* and answers with *for* or *since*.

1 I'm a teacher. I started teaching last year.
   How long have you been a teacher?
   Since last year. / For a year.

2 We live near the coast. We moved there three years ago.
3 She's married. She got married two years ago.
4 I know Mary. We first met last December.
5 My cousin works in a factory. He started working there in 2005.
6 I play the piano. I had my first lesson in 2001.
7 I've got a passport. I got it three years ago.

Present perfect and past simple

5 Complete the conversations with the verbs in the boxes. Use the past simple or present perfect form.

go	stay	visit

Mary   ¹_____ you _____ Vienna?
Fiona   Yes, I ²_____ there last year.
Mary   Where ³_____ you _____?
Fiona   At my uncle's house.

not be	give	open	receive	say	write

Mary   ⁴_____ you _____ a present that you didn't like?
Fiona   Yes, my aunt ⁵_____ me a yellow sweatshirt for my birthday.
Mary   What ⁶_____ you _____ to her?
Fiona   Nothing. She ⁷_____ there when I ⁸_____ it. But I ⁹_____ her a nice thank-you letter.

6 Write questions with *Have you ever ...?* Write true answers about yourself. If the answer is yes, add more details in the past simple.

1 go / snowboarding
   Have you ever been snowboarding?
   No, I haven't.
   Yes, I have. I went snowboarding in Switzerland last winter.

2 go / to France or Germany
3 swim / in the sea
4 break / a bone
5 play / a computer game
6 borrow / money from a friend
7 visit / a museum

7 Some of the sentences are incorrect. Rewrite them using the correct tense.

1 I've been to London yesterday.
   I went to London yesterday.

2 She's written three emails last night.
3 Last summer we saw some beautiful lakes in Italy.
4 Have you ever met anyone famous?
5 Last year my parents have given me a bicycle.
6 I lived in London since last year.
7 'Did you buy any presents yet?' 'No, not yet.'
8 'Have you ever been snorkelling?' 'Yes, I've been snorkelling last summer.'

GRAMMAR REFERENCE 6

will

We use *will* to talk about the future. We form sentences with *will* like this:

> *will* + infinitive without *to*
> I will go.

The form of *will* is the same for all persons (*I, you, he, she*, etc.).

Affirmative
I'll see you later.
She'll be angry.
(full form = will)
Negative
I won't tell anybody.
They won't listen to you.
(full form = will not)
Interrogative
Will you be at home?
Will it work?
Short answer
Yes, I will.
No, it won't.

We use *will*:

- to make factual statements about the future.
  > There will be a solar eclipse in 2026.
- to make predictions, especially when they are based on our own thoughts or beliefs.
  > I think you'll do well in your exams.
  > I don't think Egypt will win the next African Cup.
- to make offers.
  > I'll carry your bags.
  > I'll lend you my phone.
- to make promises.
  > I'll always help you.
- to make instant decisions (decisions that we make while we are speaking).
  > Look! There's Tommy. I'll go and say hello.

going to

We use *going to* to talk about the future. We form sentences with *going to* like this:

- present simple of *be* + *going to* + infinitive without *to*
  > I'm going to study law at university.
  > Roger Federer isn't going to win the match.
  > Are you going to be at home this weekend?
  > Yes, I am. / No, I'm not.

We use *going to*:

- to make predictions, especially when they are based on what we can see.
  > Look at that man! He's going to jump in the river!
- to talk about our intentions.
  > I'm going to invite her to my barbecue.

We use both *will* and *going to* to make predictions and to talk about our decisions. However, we use them in a slightly different way.

We use	*will*	*going to*
predictions	based on our own knowledge and opinions: Rooney will score. He always scores in important games.	based on the situation and what we can see: Rooney's got the ball! He's going to score!
decisions	instant decisions that we make while speaking Show me the menu. Hmm. I'll have chicken.	intentions – things that we have already decided: I'm going to have chicken tonight. I bought it this morning.

Zero conditional

We use the zero conditional to talk about a result which follows a particular action. We use the present simple to describe the action and the present simple to describe the result.
> If you press this button, the light comes on.

The *if* clause can come before or after the main clause. If it comes after, we don't use a comma.
> If you heat ice, it melts.
> Ice melts if you heat it.

will and going to

1 Write predictions about technology in ten years' time. Use *I think* … or *I don't think* … and the phrases in the box.

> all children / have a mobile phone
> camcorders / be very small
> digital cameras / be very expensive
> cars / need petrol
> houses / use solar energy
> watches / include calculators

I think all children will have a mobile phone.

2 Think of offers or promises for the problems in the box. Use *I'll* ….

> I can't do my homework.
> I need to call my mum, but I haven't got my mobile phone.
> I want to watch this film, but my DVD player is broken.
> I'm going to miss my favourite TV programme tonight.

3 Work in pairs. Student A: describe a problem from exercise 2. Student B: Offer or promise to do something.

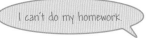

I can't do my homework.

I'll ask my sister to help you.

4 Match the pairs of sentences.

1 'What would you like to eat, sir?'
2 'Have you got Sam's number?'
3 'These pens are 90p each.'
4 'The shower isn't working.'
5 'We're leaving now.'

a 'I'm not sure. I'll look in my phonebook.'
b 'I'll go with you.'
c 'I'll have the pasta, please.'
d 'I'll have a bath.'
e 'I'll take three.'

5 Write predictions about the pictures with *going to*. Use the verbs in the box to help you.

> chase   crash   fall off   fall over   frighten   scream   steal

6 Write down three things you intend to do this weekend and three things you don't intend to do. Use *I'm (not) going to* … .

I'm not going to do any homework.

Zero conditional / may, might, could

7 Match the two halves of the sentences.

1 If you press this button,
2 If you can't say anything nice,
3 I'm here
4 If I drink coffee in the evening,
5 It doesn't matter
6 If you say 'sit',

a if you need me.
b if you break that calculator – it was cheap.
c I never sleep well.
d the lights come on.
e my dog sits down.
f don't say anything at all.

8 Complete the text with *may*, *might* and *could* and the verbs in the box. There is one negative form.

> become   do   happen   prefer   share   want

Sales of CDs are declining because of illegal file sharing, and film companies are worried that the same thing [1]_____ with DVDs. As downloads become faster, more and more people [2]_____ films over the internet rather than buying them. Buying DVDs [3]_____ a thing of the past. The music industry now encourages legal downloads from websites like the iTunes Music Store. The film industry [4]_____ something similar. However, if they try to charge too much for film downloads, people [5]_____ to pay. They [6]_____ to download them illegally, using one of the many file-sharing programs.

must and mustn't

The form of *must* or *mustn't* is the same for all persons (*I*, *you*, *he*, etc.).

Affirmative
I must go home.
You must tell the truth.

Negative
You mustn't tell anybody.
They mustn't be late.
(full form = must not)

Interrogative*
Must you leave so early?

Short answer
Yes, I must.

* We don't often make questions with *must*. It is more common to use *Do you have to ...?*

We use *must* + **infinitive without *to*** to say that something is necessary, and it is very important to do it.
In some Asian countries, you must eat with your right hand.
You must be quiet in the school library.
We use *mustn't* + **infinitive without *to*** to say that something is prohibited, and it is very important not to do it.
We mustn't be late for school.
You mustn't use a mobile phone in the cinema.
We often use *must* or *mustn't* to express rules and laws.
In the UK, you must be 17 to drive a car.
You mustn't smoke on airplanes.

needn't

We use *needn't* + **infinitive without *to*** to say that something is not necessary but isn't against the rules.
You needn't bring a towel. There are towels at the swimming pool.
(But you can bring one if you want.)
You needn't take sandwiches as lunch is provided.
(But you can bring them if you want.)

First conditional

We use the first conditional to predict the result of a future action. We use the present simple to describe the action and ***will*** + **infinitive without *to*** to describe the result.
If you go to bed late, you'll be tired tomorrow.
    (action)   (result)
If I miss the bus, I'll take a taxi.
  (action)   (result)

The *if* clause can come before or after the main clause. If it comes after, we don't use a comma.
If you drink too much coffee, you won't sleep well.
You won't sleep well if you drink too much coffee.

must, mustn't and needn't

1 Match the pairs of sentences.

1 You mustn't eat those mushrooms.
2 You must drive on the left.
3 You mustn't swim here.
4 You must pay for those books.
5 You mustn't worry about your exams.
6 You must try on that top.

a You're in England!
b You don't want to buy the wrong size.
c They're poisonous.
d They'll be fine.
e They aren't free.
f The river is dangerous.

2 What do the signs mean? Complete the sentences with *must* or *mustn't*.

 1 You mustn't turn left.

 2 You _____ stop here.

 3 You _____ smoke.

 4 You _____ switch off your mobile phone.

 5 You _____ be eighteen to see this film.

 6 You _____ dive here.

 7 You _____ wear a hard hat.

 8 You _____ turn right.

3 Rewrite the sentences, using *needn't*.

1 It isn't necessary for you to buy her a present.
You needn't buy her a present.
2 It isn't necessary for us to arrive on time.
3 It isn't necessary for them to phone me.
4 It isn't necessary for him to wear a suit.
5 It isn't necessary for her to cook dinner for me.
6 It isn't necessary for you to wait for me.

First conditional

4 Match the two halves of the sentences.

1 If I don't go to bed soon, …
2 I won't pass my exam …
3 My brother will help me …
4 If you go to the cinema, …
5 We won't have a barbecue …
6 Will your brother be angry …

a … will you invite me?
b … I'll be tired tomorrow.
c … if we use his computer?
d … if my homework is too difficult.
e … if it rains tomorrow.
f … if I don't study hard.

5 Complete the first conditional sentences with the present simple form of the words in brackets.

1 If he _____ (eat) too much, he won't sleep well.
2 I'll feed his cat while he's away if he _____ (ask) me.
3 We won't get home before it's dark if we _____ (leave) after 5.30 p.m.
4 If you _____ (work) harder, you'll do better at school.
5 If it _____ (snow) next month, we'll go skiing.
6 She'll be angry if he _____ (not come) to her party.

6 Complete the first conditional sentences with the *will* form of the words in brackets.

1 If you give me your number, I _____ (call) you tomorrow.
2 They _____ (not buy) a new car if it costs too much.
3 If you don't tell your parents where you are, they _____ (be) worried.
4 You _____ (have) a great time if you come.
5 What _____ you _____ (do) if it rains tomorrow?
6 If we can't find a hotel, where _____ we _____ ? (sleep)

Second conditional

We use the second conditional to talk about situations that are unlikely or unreal. It can refer to the present or the future.

We use the past tense to describe the unlikely, unreal or imaginary action or situation, and *would* + infinitive without *to* to describe the result.

If I had a lot of money, I'd travel around the world.

The *if* clause can come before or after the main clause. If it comes after, we don't use a comma.

If I lived in the country, I'd have a horse.
I'd have a horse if I lived in the country.

I wish ...

We use *wish* + past simple or past continuous to say that we want something to be different from how it is now.
The present situation: Alison has brown eyes.
Wish: Alison wishes she had blue eyes.
The present situation: It's cold. I am wearing a jacket.
Wish: I wish I was wearing a coat.

After *if* and *wish* we sometimes use *were* rather than *was* with *I / he / she / it*. *were* is more formal than *was*.

If I were you I would get some advice.
I wish I were able to attend.

Second conditional

1 Complete the sentences with the past simple form of the verbs in brackets.

1 If I _____ (have) a bicycle, I'd ride to school.
2 If I _____ (owe) money to my parents, I'd pay them back.
3 He'd write more often if he _____ (have) more time.
4 If I _____ (know) the answer, I'd tell you.
5 If we _____ (not live) in the city, I'd get really bored.
6 Would you be angry if I _____ (copy) your homework?
7 You wouldn't be so tired in the mornings if you _____ (not stay up) so late.
8 If Pete _____ (not smoke), he'd be much healthier.

2 Complete the second conditional sentences with the correct form of the verbs in brackets.

1 If they _____ (live) in the city, life _____ (be) easier.
2 I _____ (play) basketball if I _____ (be) taller.
3 If we _____ (have) a DVD player, we _____ (watch) films every evening.
4 You _____ (can) afford that mobile phone if you _____ (not spend) all your money on clothes.
5 What _____ (happen) if you _____ (not go) to school tomorrow?
6 He _____ (not be) very happy if you _____ (not invite) him to the restaurant.
7 If I _____ (find) a credit card, I _____ (take) it to the police.
8 How _____ (you / feel) if you _____ (not pass) your exams?

3 Write second conditional sentences.

1 I don't have a computer, so I don't play computer games.
   If I had a computer, I'd play computer games.
2 Ben has to get up early on Mondays, so he doesn't go out on Sunday evenings.
3 Kate doesn't have a ticket for tennis at Wimbledon, so she isn't going.
4 There isn't a football match on TV this evening, so they're going out.
5 I have a lot of homework, so I'll stay in this evening.
6 We don't have to help with the cooking, so we can watch a DVD.

I wish ...

4 Write the sentences in the correct speech bubbles.

I wish I could buy that jacket.
I wish I lived in the country.
I wish I were taller.
I wish the music wasn't so loud.
I wish we had tickets.
I wish you could talk.

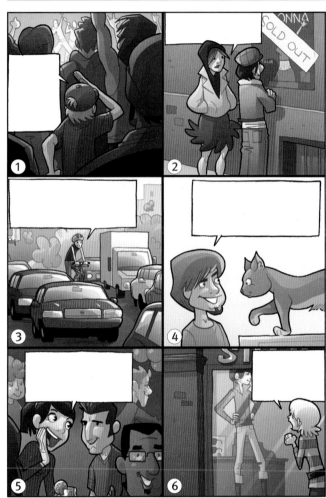

5 Complete the sentences with the correct form of the verbs in brackets.

1 I wish I _____ (not have) so much homework.
2 I wish we _____ (be) in the same class.
3 Jim wishes he _____ (can) speak Japanese.
4 I wish it _____ (not be) winter.
5 Patricia wishes she _____ (not hate) pizza.
6 I'm having a great time in Sydney. I wish you _____ (be) here.
7 I wish I _____ (can) eat bread, but I can't.
8 I wish I _____ (not have to) take an exam at the end of the year.

Past perfect

We form the past perfect like this:

Affirmative
I / you'd gone
he / she / it'd gone
we / you / they'd gone

Short form and full form
'd = had

Negative
I / you hadn't gone
he / she / it hadn't gone
we / you / they hadn't gone

Short form and full form
hadn't = had not

Interrogative
Had I / you gone ...?
Had he / she / it gone ...?
Had we / you / they gone ...?

Short answer
Yes, I had. / No, I hadn't.
Yes, she had. / No, she hadn't.

The past participle of regular verbs is the same as the past simple.

finished   phoned   studied   chatted

Sometimes irregular verbs have the same past participle as the past simple form, sometimes they are different.

go – went – been / gone
buy – bought – bought
see – saw – seen

For a list of irregular verbs see page 124.

We use the past perfect to talk about an event in the past which happened before another event in the past.

Time line

the robbers left the bank   the police arrived   now

When the police arrived, the robbers had left the bank.

Reported speech

When we report somebody else's words, the tense of the verb usually changes.

Direct speech	Reported speech
Present simple →	Past simple
'I don't like dogs,' Ben said.	Ben said (that) he didn't like dogs.
'My dad is at work,' Becky said.	Becky said that her dad was at work.
Present continuous →	Past continuous
'He's wearing a blue top,' Michelle said.	Michelle said (that) he was wearing a blue top.
Past simple →	Past perfect
'We moved to London in 2000,' Phil said.	Phil said (that) they had moved to London in 2000.

It is not necessary to use *that* in reported speech.

The pronouns sometimes change, depending on the context.

'My name's Jill,' she said.
She said that **her** name was Jill.

'We went to the cinema,' Mark said.
Mark said that **they** had gone to the cinema.

'I'll meet you after school,' Becky said.
Becky said **she**'d meet **me** after school.

GRAMMAR BUILDER 9

Past perfect

1 Complete the sentences with the past perfect form of the verbs in brackets.

1 I didn't watch the film because I _____ (see) it.
2 She felt ill because she _____ (eat) too much.
3 We couldn't drive to Liverpool because our car _____ (break down).
4 He _____ (not finish) his homework so he couldn't go out.
5 'Why was he so hungry?' 'Because he _____ (not have) lunch.'
6 I _____ (buy) the tickets before I heard you were ill.
7 She couldn't go out because she _____ (promise) to help her mum with the housework.
8 Last year I went to Beijing. I _____ (not visit) China before.
9 After I _____ (write) the letter, I posted it.
10 When dad _____ (do) the gardening, he watched TV.

2 Write one sentence, using the past simple and the past perfect. Start with *When*.

1 Joe went out. I arrived home.
   When I arrived home, Joe had gone out.
2 I went to bed. Paul phoned.
3 The shoplifter ran away. The police arrived.
4 Mum cooked dinner. Dad got home.
5 We finished our homework. We watched TV.
6 The film started. We arrived at the cinema.
7 It started to rain. We left the beach.
8 The train left. We got to the station.

Reported speech

3 Complete the sentences in reported speech. Use the past simple, past continuous or past perfect.

1 'I like pizza,' said Fred.
   Fred said that he liked pizza.
2 'A shoplifter stole three DVDs,' said the shop assistant.
   The shop assistant said that a shoplifter _____ three DVDs.
3 'That fraud is cheating people,' the man said.
   The man said that a fraud _____ people.
4 'It's getting dark,' said Jess.
   Jess said that it _____ dark.
5 'Some vandals smashed the shop window,' she said.
   She said that some vandals _____ the shop window.
6 'The burglar is in the police car,' said the police officer.
   The police officer said that the burglar _____ in the police car.
7 'Two men robbed the bank,' the bank manager said.
   The bank manager said that two men _____ the bank.
8 'Every day joyriders steal ten cars in the city,' said the police officer.
   The police officer said that every day joyriders _____ ten cars in the city.

4 Complete the sentences with the correct pronoun.

1 'I'm going home,' said Cathy.
   Cathy said that _____ was going home.
2 'We live in Birmingham,' she said.
   She said that _____ lived in Birmingham.
3 'I like watching TV in my bedroom,' he said.
   He said that _____ liked watching TV in _____ bedroom.
4 'You're late!' she said to me.
   She said to _____ that _____ was late.
5 'She never phones me,' said Elizabeth.
   Elizabeth said that _____ never phoned _____.

5 Rewrite what Fiona says using reported speech.

1 I'm hungry. | *Fiona said that she was hungry.*
2 I didn't have any breakfast. _____
3 I want a banana. _____
4 I'm going out. _____
5 My friend is meeting me at the cinema. _____
6 My friend's name is Helen. _____
7 I first met her last year. _____
8 We're going to see a French film. _____

6 Rewrite the sentences in direct speech.

1 He said that it wasn't raining.
   'It isn't raining,' he said.
2 She said that last month joyriders had stolen her car.
3 He said that he needed a holiday.
4 You said that you were going to Tom's party this evening.
5 He said that he'd seen the robbers leaving the bank.
6 She said that I was greedy.
7 You said that you'd had lunch.
8 He said that he was feeling ill.

GRAMMAR REFERENCE 10

The passive (present simple)

We form the present simple passive like this:
- present simple of *be* + past participle of the main verb.

Affirmative
This newspaper is published daily.
These grapes are grown in Italy.
Negative
This cheese isn't made in France.
Cars aren't used on the island of Tresco.
Interrogative
Is your bicycle serviced regularly?
Are your clothes washed by hand?
Short answer
Yes, it is. / No, it isn't.
Yes, they are. / No, they aren't.

We use the passive when we want to focus on the action, not on who performs it, or when we don't know who performs it.
We often use the present simple passive to describe a process.
First, the bottles are washed. Then they're sorted into different colours. Next, they ..., etc.

When we want to say who performed the action, we use *by*.
My exams are marked by the teachers.

The passive (other tenses)

We form other tenses of the passive like this:
- correct tense of *be* + past participle of the main verb.

Tense	Example
past simple	*This house **was built** in 1850.*
	*My friends **were robbed** in Mexico last year.*
present perfect	*Our car **has been stolen**!*
	*His books **have been read** by millions.*
will (future simple)	*His first novel **will be published** next year.*
	*The pyramids **will be closed** next week.*

The passive (present simple)

1 Complete the sentences with the present simple passive form of the verbs in brackets.

1 Rice _____ (grow) in China.
2 Helmets _____ (wear) by ice hockey players.
3 Spanish _____ (speak) in Mexico.
4 Coffee _____ (drink) in most countries of the world.
5 English _____ (teach) in schools in Jordan.
6 Noodles _____ (eat) in China.

2 Complete the text with the present simple passive form of the verbs in brackets.

Magazine Interviews

First, the person [1]_____ (contact) by the magazine.
If the person agrees to the interview, a reporter
[2]_____ (send) to their house. The person
[3]_____ (interview) and lots of photographs
[4]_____ (take). Then the article [5]_____ (write) –
it's always a very kind one – and money
[6]_____ (pay) to the person interviewed!

3 Complete the sentences with the present simple passive form of the verbs in the box.

eat	grow	make	sell	send	speak	visit

1 Tea _____ in India.
2 Newspapers and magazines _____ in a newsagent's.
3 English _____ in Australia and New Zealand.
4 The best chocolate _____ in Belgium and Switzerland.
5 In the UK too many criminals _____ to prison.
6 Every year, 38 billion burgers _____ in the USA.
7 Every year Paris _____ by 24 million tourists.

4 Rewrite the sentences in the passive.

1 They recycle a lot of paper and cardboard in Britain.
2 They don't sell books in this shop.
3 They don't speak English in Germany.
4 They use recycled paper in newspapers.
5 They don't grow oranges in Antartica.
6 They don't drink tap water in some countries.

The passive (other tenses)

5 Complete the sentences with the past simple passive form of the verbs in brackets.

1 This DVD player _____ (make) in Korea.
2 *Hamlet* _____ (write) by Shakespeare.
3 Jeans _____ (invent) in the USA.
4 Shakespeare's plays _____ (perform) for the first time about 400 years ago.
5 John Lennon _____ (murder) in New York in 1980.
6 Pluto _____ (discover) in 1930.

6 Rewrite the sentences in the passive. Use *by* if necessary to say who has done the action.

1 Somebody has stolen my camera.
2 Somebody has vandalized the bus stop.
3 Shoplifters have taken the new DVDs.
4 Somebody has burgled their house.
5 They've murdered three people.
6 The police have interviewed three suspects.

7 Complete the advertisement with the passive form of *will*.

Car Valet Service!

Your car [1]_____ (collect) from your home.
It [2]_____ (clean) by hand, and the doors and
windows [3]_____ (polish). Any rubbish [4]_____
(take) out of the car and the seats [5]_____ (hoover).
The car [6]_____ (return) to you the same day!

Nouns

appearance 🔑 /əˈpɪərəns/
apron /ˈeɪprən/
argument 🔑 /ˈɑːgjumənt/
attitude 🔑 /ˈætɪtjuːd/
brand 🔑 /brænd/
behaviour 🔑 /bɪˈheɪvjə(r)/
boss 🔑 /bɒs/
brand 🔑 /brænd/
bungee jump /ˈbʌndʒi ˌdʒʌmp/
chef /ʃef/
coach 🔑 /kəʊtʃ/
company 🔑 /ˈkʌmpəni/
confidence 🔑 /ˈkɒnfɪdəns/
decision 🔑 /dɪˈsɪʒn/
design 🔑 /dɪˈzaɪn/
diver /ˈdaɪvə(r)/
dress code 🔑 /ˈdres ˌkəʊd/
expert 🔑 /ˈekspɜːt/
fault 🔑 /ˈfɔːlt/
interview 🔑 /ˈɪntəvjuː/
judge 🔑 /dʒʌdʒ/
jumpsuit /ˈdʒʌmpsuːt/
keyboard 🔑 /ˈkiːbɔːd/
label 🔑 /ˈleɪbl/
logo /ˈləʊgəʊ/
mechanic /məˈkænɪk/
nurse 🔑 /nɜːs/
occasion 🔑 /əˈkeɪʒn/
office worker 🔑 /ˈɒfɪs ˌwɜːkə(r)/
overalls 🔑 /ˈəʊvərɔːlz/
packaging 🔑 /ˈpækɪdʒɪŋ/
personality 🔑 /pɜːsəˈnæləti/
physician /fɪˈzɪʃn/
pilot 🔑 /ˈpaɪlət/
profession 🔑 /prəˈfeʃn/
slogan /ˈsləʊgən/
staff 🔑 /stɑːf/
stereotype /ˈsteriəʊtaɪp/
suit 🔑 /suːt/
text message /ˈtekst ˌmesɪdʒ/
theatre group 🔑 /ˈθɪətə ˌgruːp/
tie 🔑 /taɪ/
tracksuit /ˈtræksuːt/
uniform 🔑 /ˈjuːnɪfɔːm/
weather conditions 🔑 /ˈweðə kənˌdɪʃnz/
web design 🔑 /ˈweb dɪˌzaɪn/
wetsuit /ˈwetsuːt/
white coat 🔑 /ˌwaɪt ˈkəʊt/
wig and gown /ˌwɪg ən ˈgaʊn/

Verbs

attend 🔑 /əˈtend/
avoid 🔑 /əˈvɔɪd/
chat 🔑 /tʃæt/
dress 🔑 /dres/
expect 🔑 /ɪkˈspekt/
fancy (doing sth) 🔑 /ˌfænsi ˈ(duːɪŋ ...)/
invest 🔑 /ɪnˈvest/
judge 🔑 /dʒʌdʒ/
make (a decision) 🔑 /ˌmeɪk (ə dɪˈsɪʒn)/
pretend 🔑 /prɪˈtend/
refuse 🔑 /rɪˈfjuːz/
text 🔑 /tekst/
wear 🔑 /weə(r)/

Adjectives

ambitious /æmˈbɪʃəs/
amusing 🔑 /əˈmjuːzɪŋ/
assertive /əˈsɜːtɪv/
bad-mannered /ˌbæd ˈmænəd/
casual /ˈkæʒuəl/
certain 🔑 /ˈsɜːtn/
compulsory /kəmˈpʌlsəri/
considerate /kənˈsɪdərət/
earnest /ˈɜːnɪst/
fashionable 🔑 /ˈfæʃnəbl/
fearless /ˈfɪələs/
friendly 🔑 /ˈfrendli/
generous 🔑 /ˈdʒenərəs/
hard-working 🔑 /ˌhɑːd ˈwɜːkɪŋ/
impatient 🔑 /ɪmˈpeɪʃnt/
informal 🔑 /ɪnˈfɔːml/
intolerant /ɪnˈtɒlərənt/
keen on sth/sb 🔑 /ˈkiːn ˌɒn .../
lazy 🔑 /ˈleɪzi/
mean 🔑 /miːn/
nervous 🔑 /ˈnɜːvəs/
optimistic /ɒptɪˈmɪstɪk/
patient 🔑 /ˈpeɪʃnt/
pessimistic /pesɪˈmɪstɪk/
phobic /ˈfəʊbɪk/
popular 🔑 /ˈpɒpjələ(r)/
quiet 🔑 /ˈkwaɪət/
respectable /rɪˈspektəbl/
rude 🔑 /ruːd/
shy 🔑 /ʃaɪ/
talkative /ˈtɔːkətɪv/
thoughtless /ˈθɔːtləs/
timid /ˈtɪmɪd/
tolerant /ˈtɒlərənt/
torn 🔑 /tɔːn/
unfriendly 🔑 /ʌnˈfrendli/
well mannered /ˌwel ˈmænəd/

Adverbs

furthermore /ˌfɜːðəˈmɔː(r)/
quite 🔑 /kwaɪt/
not at all 🔑 /ˌnɒt ət ˈɔːl/
really 🔑 /ˈriːəli/
slightly 🔑 /ˈslaɪtli/
very 🔑 /ˈveri/

Expressions and idioms

afraid of heights 🔑 /əˌfreɪd əv ˈhaɪts/
don't fancy sth 🔑 /ˌdəʊnt ˈfænsi .../
don't mind sth 🔑 /ˌdəʊnt ˈmaɪnd .../
make new friends 🔑 /ˌmeɪk ˌnjuː ˈfrendz/
can't help sth 🔑 /ˌkɑːnt ˈhelp .../
can't stand sth 🔑 /ˌkɑːnt ˈstænd .../

Determiner

a little 🔑 /ə ˈlɪtl/

🔑 a keyword of the **Oxford 3000™ list**, denoting words which should receive priority in vocabulary study because of their importance and usefulness.

/i/ happy	/æ/ flag	/ɜː/ her	/ʊ/ look	/ʌ/ mum	/ɔɪ/ noisy	/ɪə/ here
/ɪ/ it	/ɑː/ art	/ɒ/ not	/uː/ you	/eɪ/ day	/aʊ/ how	/eə/ wear
/iː/ he	/e/ egg	/ɔː/ four	/ə/ sugar	/aɪ/ why	/əʊ/ go	/ʊə/ tourist

Nouns

athletics /æθ'letɪks/
badminton /'bædmɪntən/
ball sport 🔑 /'bɔːl ˌspɔːt/
baseball /'beɪsbɔːl/
basketball /'bɑːskɪtbɔːl/
career 🔑 /kə'rɪə(r)/
champion /'tʃæmpiən/
cheer /tʃɪə(r)/
cycling 🔑 /'saɪklɪŋ/
danger 🔑 /'deɪndʒə(r)/
dead heat /ˌded 'hiːt/
football 🔑 /'fʊtbɔːl/
football team 🔑 /'fʊtbɔːl ˌtiːm/
freestyle /'friːstaɪl/
golf /gɒlf/
gymnastics /dʒɪm'næstɪks/
hurdles /'hɜːdlz/
ice hockey /'aɪs ˌhɒki/
judo /'dʒuːdəʊ/
karate /kə'rɑːti/
long jump 🔑 /'lɒŋ ˌdʒʌmp/
racial discrimination /ˌreɪʃl dɪskrɪmɪ'neɪʃn/
referee /refə'riː/
rugby /'rʌgbi/
school trip 🔑 /ˌskuːl 'trɪp/
second half 🔑 /'sekənd ˌhɑːf/
shore /ʃɔː(r)/
spectator /spek'teɪtə(r)/
sponsor /'spɒnsə(r)/
sports commentary /'spɔːts ˌkɒməntri/
sports commentator /'spɔːts ˌkɒmənteɪtə(r)/
sports fan 🔑 /'spɔːts ˌfæn/
sportsperson /'spɔːtspɜːsn/
surfboard /'sɜːfbɔːd/
surfer /'sɜːfə(r)/
surfing /'sɜːfɪŋ/
swimming 🔑 /'swɪmɪŋ/
table tennis /'teɪbl ˌtenɪs/
team sport 🔑 /'tiːm ˌspɔːt/
tennis /'tenɪs/
volleyball /'vɒlibɔːl/
water sport 🔑 /'wɔːtə ˌspɔːt/
weightlifting /'weɪtlɪftɪŋ/
world champion /ˌwɜːld 'tʃæmpiən/
wound 🔑 /wuːnd/

Verbs

arrive 🔑 /ə'raɪv/
attack 🔑 /ə'tæk/
battle 🔑 /'bætl/
cheat 🔑 /tʃiːt/
compete 🔑 /kəm'piːt/
delay 🔑 /dɪ'leɪ/
finish last 🔑 /ˌfɪnɪʃ 'lɑːst/
go surfing 🔑 /ˌgəʊ 'sɜːfɪŋ/
grip /grɪp/
head (for) 🔑 /'hed ˌfɔː(r), fə(r)/
keep 🔑 /kiːp/
prepare (for) sth 🔑 /prɪ'peə (fə) .../
recuperate /rɪ'kuːpəreɪt/
rush 🔑 /rʌʃ/
save 🔑 /seɪv/
shake 🔑 /ʃeɪk/
sink 🔑 /sɪŋk/
start 🔑 /stɑːt/
stay 🔑 /steɪ/
steer a boat 🔑 /ˌstɪər ə 'bəʊt/
stop 🔑 /stɒp/

Adjectives

dangerous 🔑 /'deɪndʒərəs/
destined /'destɪnd/
outstanding 🔑 /aʊt'stændɪŋ/
professional 🔑 /prə'feʃənl/
sharp 🔑 /ʃɑːp/
talented /'tæləntɪd/

Adverbs

face down 🔑 /ˌfeɪs 'daʊn/
unfortunately 🔑 /ʌn'fɔːtʃənətli/

Expressions and idioms

backwards and forwards 🔑 /'bækwədz ən 'fɔːwədz/
become professional 🔑 /bɪˌkʌm prə'feʃə nl/
catch fire 🔑 /ˌkætʃ 'faɪə(r)/
earliest success 🔑 /ˌɜːliəst sək'ses/
get ready to do sth 🔑 /ˌget ˌredi tə 'duː .../
greatest achievement 🔑 /ˌgreɪtɪst ə'tʃiːvmə nt/
it was clear that 🔑 /ˌɪt wəz 'klɪə ðət/
miss an easy shot 🔑 /ˌmɪs ən ˌiːzi 'ʃɒt/
play a joke 🔑 /ˌpleɪ ə 'dʒəʊk/
play along with 🔑 /ˌpleɪ ə'lɒŋ wɪð/
play back 🔑 /ˌpleɪ 'bæk/
play for time 🔑 /ˌpleɪ fə 'taɪm/
play it cool 🔑 /ˌpleɪ ɪt 'kuːl/
play the fool /ˌpleɪ ðə 'fuːl/
play with fire 🔑 /ˌpleɪ wɪð 'faɪə(r)/
play your cards right 🔑 /ˌpleɪ jə 'kɑːdz ˌraɪt/
set a world record 🔑 /ˌset ə ˌwɜːld 'rekɔːd/
survival instinct /sə'vaɪvl ˌɪnstɪŋkt/
take place 🔑 /ˌteɪk 'pleɪs/
treat sb badly 🔑 /ˌtriːt ... 'bædli/

Phrasal verbs

send off 🔑 /ˌsend 'ɒf/
set in 🔑 /ˌset 'ɪn/
set off 🔑 /ˌset 'ɒf/
set on sb 🔑 /'set ˌɒn .../
set sb down 🔑 /ˌset ... 'daʊn/
set sth aside 🔑 /ˌset ... ə'saɪd/
set sth back 🔑 /ˌset ... 'bæk/

Prepositions

across 🔑 /ə'krɒs/
along 🔑 /ə'lɒŋ/
into 🔑 /'ɪntuː, 'ɪntə/
through 🔑 /θruː/
towards 🔑 /tə'wɔːdz/
up 🔑 /ʌp/

Literature Corner

gold rush (n) 🔑 /'gəʊld rʌʃ/
growl (v) /graʊl/
prospector (n) /prə'spektə(r)/
rope (n) 🔑 /rəʊp/

/p/ pen	/d/ dog	/tʃ/ beach	/v/ very	/s/ speak	/ʒ/ television	/n/ now	/r/ radio
/b/ big	/k/ can	/dʒ/ job	/θ/ think	/z/ zoo	/h/ house	/ŋ/ sing	/j/ yes
/t/ two	/g/ good	/f/ food	/ð/ then	/ʃ/ she	/m/ meat	/l/ late	/w/ we

Nouns

advertisement 🔑 /əd'vɜːtɪsmənt/
appointment 🔑 /ə'pɔɪntmənt/
block 🔑 /blɒk/
bus stop 🔑 /'bʌs ˌstɒp/
clerk 🔑 /klɑːk/
commuter /kə'mjuːtə(r)/
cottage /'kɒtɪdʒ/
deer /dɪə(r)/
dust 🔑 /dʌst/
emigrant /'emɪɡrənt/
field 🔑 /fiːld/
footpath /'fʊtpɑːθ/
gate 🔑 /ɡeɪt/
globetrotter /'ɡləʊbtrɒtə(r)/
harbour /'hɑːbə(r)/
harm 🔑 /hɑːm/
hedge /hedʒ/
hill 🔑 /hɪl/
immigrant /'ɪmɪɡrənt/
inhabitant /ɪn'hæbɪtənt/
junk /dʒʌŋk/
lane 🔑 /leɪn/
leaflet /'liːflət/
mayor 🔑 /'meə(r)/
memory 🔑 /'meməri/
neighbourhood 🔑 /'neɪbəhʊd/
nomad /'nəʊmæd/
paperwork /'peɪpəwɜːk/
pavement /'peɪvmənt/
pedestrian /pə'destriən/
pedestrian crossing /pəˌdestriən 'krɒsɪŋ/
pilgrim /'pɪlɡrɪm/
pollution 🔑 /pə'luːʃn/
postbox /'pəʊstbɒks/
railway 🔑 /'reɪlweɪ/
refugee /refjuː'dʒiː/
region 🔑 /'riːdʒən/
resort 🔑 /rɪ'zɔːt/
road sign 🔑 /'rəʊd ˌsaɪn/
roadworks /'rəʊdwɜːks/
rubbish bin 🔑 /'rʌbɪʃ ˌbɪn/
rural landscape 🔑 /ˌrʊərəl 'lændskeɪp/
sandy beach /ˌsændi 'biːtʃ/
scenery /'siːnəri/
side 🔑 /saɪd/
storey /'stɔːri/
story 🔑 /'stɔːri/
stream 🔑 /striːm/
street lamp /'striːt ˌlæmp/
suburbs /'sʌbɜːbz/
tourist attraction 🔑 /'tʊərɪst əˌtrækʃn/
traffic 🔑 /'træfɪk/
traffic lights /'træfɪk ˌlaɪts/
treasurer /'treʒərə(r)/
urban landscape 🔑 /ˌɜːbən 'lændskeɪp/

valley 🔑 /'væli/
wood 🔑 /wʊd/

Verbs

abandon 🔑 /ə'bændən/
attract 🔑 /ə'trækt/
blow 🔑 /bləʊ/
brake /breɪk/
break 🔑 /breɪk/
compete with sth 🔑 /kəm'piːt ˌwɪð .../
die 🔑 /daɪ/
dye /daɪ/
found 🔑 /faʊnd/
groan 🔑 /ɡrəʊn/
grow 🔑 /ɡrəʊ/
marvel (at) /'mɑːvl (ət)/
migrate /maɪ'ɡreɪt/
move away (from) 🔑 /ˌmuːv ə'weɪ (frəm)/
rust /rʌst/
sigh /saɪ/
spend time 🔑 /ˌspend 'taɪm/
surround 🔑 /sə'raʊnd/
take the train (to) 🔑 /'teɪk ðə ˌtreɪn (tə)/
thrive /θraɪv/
wander (through) 🔑 /'wɒndə (ˌθruː)/

Adjectives

abandoned 🔑 /ə'bændənd/
atmospheric /ˌætməs'ferɪk/
connected with 🔑 /kə'nektɪd ˌwɪð/
cosmopolitan /ˌkɒzmə'pɒlɪtən/
dear 🔑 /dɪə(r)/
dyed /daɪd/
enormous 🔑 /ɪ'nɔːməs/
fascinating /'fæsɪneɪtɪŋ/
historic /hɪ'stɒrɪk/
ideal 🔑 /aɪ'diːəl/
industrialized /ɪn'dʌstriəlaɪzd/
informative /ɪn'fɔːmətɪv/
local 🔑 /'ləʊkl/
peaceful 🔑 /'piːsfl/
rural 🔑 /'rʊərəl/
rusting /'rʌstɪŋ/
stunning /'stʌnɪŋ/
talkative /'tɔːkətɪv/
thriving /'θraɪvɪŋ/
tiny 🔑 /'taɪni/
urban 🔑 /'ɜːbən/
well known 🔑 /'wel ˌnəʊn/

Adverbs

originally 🔑 /ə'rɪdʒənəli/

Expressions and idioms

bad impression 🔑 /ˌbæd ɪm'preʃn/
be in charge of sth/sb 🔑 /ˌbiː ɪn 'tʃɑːdʒ əv .../
do a job 🔑 /ˌduː ə 'dʒɒb/
do badly 🔑 /ˌduː 'bædli/
do harm (to) 🔑 /ˌduː 'hɑːm (tə)/
do maths 🔑 /ˌduː 'mæθs/
do well 🔑 /ˌduː 'wel/
don't miss ... 🔑 /'dəʊnt ˌmɪs .../
from place to place 🔑 /frəm ˌpleɪs tə 'pleɪs/
I'm sure ... 🔑 /ˌaɪm 'ʃʊə(r) .../
in ruins 🔑 /ˌɪn 'ruːɪnz/
make a bad impression 🔑 /ˌmeɪk ə ˌbæd ɪm'preʃn/
make a living 🔑 /ˌmeɪk ə 'lɪvɪŋ/
make a mistake 🔑 /ˌmeɪk ə mɪ'steɪk/
make an appointment 🔑 /ˌmeɪk ən ə'pɔɪntmənt/
make money 🔑 /ˌmeɪk 'mʌni/
natural disaster 🔑 /ˌnætʃrəl dɪ'zɑːstə(r)/
take a trip (to) 🔑 /ˌteɪk ə 'trɪp (tə)/
take care of oneself 🔑 /ˌteɪk 'keər əv (...)ˌself/
That's enough! 🔑 /ˌðæts ɪ'nʌf/
vast stretches (of) 🔑 /ˌvɑːst ˌstretʃɪz əv/
we can't miss ... 🔑 /ˌwiː 'kɑːnt ˌmɪs .../

Phrasal verbs

live by 🔑 /'lɪv ˌbaɪ/

Prepositions

across 🔑 /ə'krɒs/
along 🔑 /ə'lɒŋ/
over 🔑 /'əʊvə(r)/
past 🔑 /pɑːst/
through 🔑 /θruː/

/i/ happy	/æ/ flag	/ɜː/ her	/ʊ/ look	/ʌ/ mum	/ɔɪ/ noisy	/ɪə/ here
/ɪ/ it	/ɑː/ art	/ɒ/ not	/uː/ you	/eɪ/ day	/aʊ/ how	/eə/ wear
/iː/ he	/e/ egg	/ɔː/ four	/ə/ sugar	/aɪ/ why	/əʊ/ go	/ʊə/ tourist

Nouns

armed forces 🔑 /ˌɑːmd ˈfɔːsɪz/
attempt 🔑 /əˈtempt/
award 🔑 /əˈwɔːd/
bravery /ˈbreɪvəri/
business empire 🔑 /ˈbɪznəs ˌempaɪə(r)/
charity worker 🔑 /ˈtʃærəti ˌwɜːkə(r)/
chatroom /ˈtʃætruːm/
civilian /səˈvɪliən/
courage 🔑 /ˈkʌrɪdʒ/
cowardice /ˈkaʊədɪs/
education 🔑 /ˌedʒuˈkeɪʃn/
entrepreneur /ˌɒntrəprəˈnɜː(r)/
fighting spirit 🔑 /ˈfaɪtɪŋ ˌspɪrɪt/
first language 🔑 /ˌfɜːst ˈlæŋgwɪdʒ/
generosity 🔑 /ˌdʒenəˈrɒsəti/
goal-scoring record /ˈgəʊl ˌskɔːrɪŋ ˌrekɔːd/
heroism /ˈherəʊɪzəm/
inspiration /ˌɪnspəˈreɪʃn/
intelligence 🔑 /ɪnˈtelɪdʒəns/
lawyer 🔑 /ˈlɔːjə(r)/
leadership /ˈliːdəʃɪp/
loyalty /ˈlɔɪəlti/
meanness /ˈmiːnnəs/
modesty /ˈmɒdəsti/
news programme 🔑 /ˈnjuːz ˌprəʊgræm/
novelist /ˈnɒvəlɪst/
patience 🔑 /ˈpeɪʃns/
performance 🔑 /pəˈfɔːməns/
perseverance /ˌpɜːsɪˈvɪərəns/
personal acquaintance /ˌpɜːsənl əˈkweɪntəns/
physique /fɪˈziːk/
positive quality 🔑 /ˈpɒzətɪv ˌkwɒləti/
recipient /rɪˈsɪpiənt/
rescue services 🔑 /ˈreskjuː ˌsɜːvɪsɪz/
role model 🔑 /ˈrəʊl ˌmɒdl/
sensation /senˈseɪʃn/
sense of humour 🔑 /ˌsens əv ˈhjuːmə(r)/
water level 🔑 /ˈwɔːtə ˌlevl/
whirlpool /ˈwɜːlpuːl/
wisdom /ˈwɪzdəm/

Verbs

betray /bɪˈtreɪ/
book sth online /ˌbʊk ... ɒnˈlaɪn/
crawl /krɔːl/
identify (with) 🔑 /aɪˈdentɪfaɪ (ˌwɪð)/
inspire /ɪnˈspaɪə(r)/
investigate 🔑 /ɪnˈvestɪgeɪt/
manage to 🔑 /ˈmænɪdʒ tə/
regain /rɪˈgeɪn/
rescue (from) 🔑 /ˈreskjuː (frəm)/

Adjectives

admirable /ˈædmərəbl/
agonizing /ˈægənaɪzɪŋ/
annoyed 🔑 /əˈnɔɪd/
annoying 🔑 /əˈnɔɪɪŋ/
astounded /əˈstaʊndɪd/
astounding /əˈstaʊndɪŋ/
bewildered /bɪˈwɪldəd/
bewildering /bɪˈwɪldərɪŋ/
bored 🔑 /bɔːd/
boring 🔑 /ˈbɔːrɪŋ/
countless /ˈkaʊntləs/
coveted /ˈkʌvətɪd/
dazed /deɪzd/
determined 🔑 /dɪˈtɜːmɪnd/
disappointed 🔑 /ˌdɪsəˈpɔɪntɪd/
disappointing 🔑 /ˌdɪsəˈpɔɪntɪŋ/
distressed /dɪˈstrest/
dreadful /ˈdredfl/
embarrassed 🔑 /ɪmˈbærəst/
embarrassing 🔑 /ɪmˈbærəsɪŋ/
exceptional /ɪkˈsepʃənl/
exhausted /ɪgˈzɔːstɪd/
exhausting /ɪgˈzɔːstɪŋ/
frightened 🔑 /ˈfraɪtnd/
frightening 🔑 /ˈfraɪtnɪŋ/
gripping /ˈgrɪpɪŋ/
hardworking /ˌhɑːdˈwɜːkɪŋ/
heroic /həˈrəʊɪk/
horrific /həˈrɪfɪk/
horrified /ˈhɒrɪfaɪd/
impoverished /ɪmˈpɒvərɪʃt/
imprisoned /ɪmˈprɪznd/
inspiring /ɪnˈspaɪərɪŋ/
intense /ɪnˈtens/
moving 🔑 /ˈmuːvɪŋ/
old enough 🔑 /ˌəʊld ɪˈnʌf/
old-fashioned 🔑 /ˌəʊld ˈfæʃnd/
overseas /ˌəʊvəˈsiːz/
mesmerized /ˈmezməraɪzd/
mesmerizing /ˈmezməraɪzɪŋ/
panic-stricken /ˈpænɪk ˌstrɪkən/
searing /ˈsɪərɪŋ/
spectacular /spekˈtækjələ(r)/
stressful /ˈstresfl/
surprised 🔑 /səˈpraɪzd/
surprising 🔑 /səˈpraɪzɪŋ/
talented /ˈtæləntɪd/
terrified /ˈterɪfaɪd/
thought-provoking /ˈθɔːt prəˌvəʊkɪŋ/
thrilled /θrɪld/
thrilling /ˈθrɪlɪŋ/
unconscious 🔑 /ʌnˈkɒnʃəs/
unique 🔑 /juˈniːk/
well-known 🔑 /ˌwel ˈnəʊn/

Adverbs

certainly 🔑 /ˈsɜːtnli/
in the end ... 🔑 /ˌɪn ði ˈend/

Expressions and idioms

best-known work 🔑 /ˌbest ˌnəʊn ˈwɜːk/
biggest asset /ˌbɪgɪst ˈæset/
lose one's temper /ˌluːz (...) ˈtempə(r)/
perform an act (of) 🔑 /pəˈfɔːm ən ˌækt (əv)/
uncommon bravery /ʌnˌkɒmən ˈbreɪvəri/
wait one's turn 🔑 /ˌweɪt ... ˈtɜːn/

Phrasal verbs

burst into (flames) 🔑 /ˌbɜːst ɪntə ˈfleɪmz/
end up with 🔑 /ˌend ˈʌp ˌwɪð/
give up 🔑 /ˌgɪv ˈʌp/
look up to sb 🔑 /ˌlʊk ˈʌp tə .../
stand by (sb) 🔑 /ˌstænd ˈbaɪ/

Prepositions

at the back of 🔑 /ət ðə ˈbæk əv/
at the front of 🔑 /ət ðə ˈfrʌnt əv/
in the face of 🔑 /ˌɪn ðə ˈfeɪs əv/

Literature corner

prison (n) 🔑 /ˈprɪzn/
spy (n) /spaɪ/
station master (n) 🔑 /ˈsteɪʃn ˌmɑːstə(r)/
tea time (n) /ˈtiːtaɪm/
train driver (n) 🔑 /ˈtreɪn draɪvə(r)/
waiting room (n) 🔑 /ˈweɪtɪŋ ruːm/

/p/ pen	/d/ dog	/tʃ/ beach	/v/ very	/s/ speak	/ʒ/ television	/n/ now	/r/ radio
/b/ big	/k/ can	/dʒ/ job	/θ/ think	/z/ zoo	/h/ house	/ŋ/ sing	/j/ yes
/t/ two	/g/ good	/f/ food	/ð/ then	/ʃ/ she	/m/ meat	/l/ late	/w/ we

Nouns

arch /ɑːtʃ/
audience ☞0 /ˈɔːdiəns/
ballroom /ˈbɔːlruːm/
beam /biːm/
boardroom /ˈbɔːdruːm/
building ☞0 /ˈbɪldɪŋ/
cash till ☞0 /ˈkæʃ ˌtɪl/
castle ☞0 /ˈkɑːsl/
cathedral /kəˈθiːdrəl/
charity shop ☞0 /ˈtʃærəti ˌʃɒp/
clothes rail ☞0 /ˈkləʊðz ˌreɪl/
column ☞0 /ˈkɒləm/
concert hall ☞0 /ˈkɒnsət ˌhɔːl/
congregation /ˌkɒŋɡrɪˈɡeɪʃn/
congress hall ☞0 /ˈkɒŋɡres hɔːl/
construction ☞0 /kənˈstrʌkʃn/
corner shop /ˈkɔːnə ˌʃɒp/
delicatessen /ˌdelɪkəˈtesən/
department store /dɪˈpɑːtmənt ˌstɔː(r)/
diner /ˈdaɪnə(r)/
dome /dəʊm/
earthquake /ˈɜːθkweɪk/
educational facilities ☞0 /ˌedʒuˌkeɪʃənl fəˈsɪlətiz/
exhibition ☞0 /ˌeksɪˈbɪʃə/
fan ☞0 /fæn/
food counter ☞0 /ˈfuːd ˌkaʊntə(r)/
generation ☞0 /ˌdʒenəˈreɪʃn/
gift ☞0 /ɡɪft/
government building ☞0 /ˈɡʌvnmənt ˌbɪldɪŋ/
grounds ☞0 /ɡraʊndz/
guest ☞0 /ɡest/
hardware store /ˈhɑːdweə ˌstɔː(r)/
headquarters /ˌhedˈkwɔːtəz/
housekeeper /ˈhaʊskiːpə(r)/
label ☞0 /ˈleɪbl/
landlord /ˈlændlɔːd/
landmark /ˈlændmɑːk/
leisure facilities /ˈleʒə fəˌsɪlətiz/
lighthouse /ˈlaɪthaʊs/
mate ☞0 /meɪt/
minaret /ˌmɪnəˈret/
monument /ˈmɒnjumənt/
museum ☞0 /mjuˈziːəm/
newsagent's /ˈnjuːzeɪdʒənts/
oilfield /ˈɔɪlfiːld/
opera house /ˈɒpərə ˌhaʊs/
palace ☞0 /ˈpæləs/
parade /pəˈreɪd/
price tag /ˈpraɪs ˌtæɡ/
property ☞0 /ˈprɒpəti/
retail /ˈriːteɪl/
shop window ☞0 /ˌʃɒp ˈwɪndəʊ/
skyline /ˈskaɪlaɪn/

skyscraper /ˈskaɪskreɪpə(r)/
spectator /spekˈteɪtə(r)/
stadium /ˈsteɪdiəm/
step ☞0 /step/
storey /ˈstɔːri/
structure ☞0 /ˈstrʌktʃə(r)/
temple /ˈtempl/
terrace /ˈterəs/
thank-you letter ☞0 /ˈθæŋk juː ˌletə(r)/
tile /taɪl/
top floor ☞0 /ˌtɒp ˈflɔː(r)/
tourist attraction ☞0 /ˈtʊərɪst əˌtrækʃn/
tower ☞0 /ˈtaʊə(r)/
variety of ☞0 /vəˈraɪəti əv/
visitor ☞0 /ˈvɪzɪtə(r)/
window shopping ☞0 /ˈwɪndəʊ ʃɒpɪŋ/
woodland /ˈwʊdlənd/

Verbs

belong (to) ☞0 /bɪˈlɒŋ tə/
browse /braʊz/
celebrate (with) ☞0 /ˈselɪbreɪt (ˌwɪð)/
dominate ☞0 /ˈdɒmɪneɪt/
go with sth ☞0 /ˈɡəʊ ˌwɪð .../
host ☞0 /həʊst/
last ☞0 /lɑːst/
queue up /kjuː ʌp/
reside /rɪˈzaɪd/
ship ☞0 /ʃɪp/
walk (through) ☞0 /ˌwɔːk (ˈθruː)/
warn ☞0 /wɔːn/

Adjectives

ancient ☞0 /ˈeɪnʃənt/
former ☞0 /ˈfɔːmə(r)/
gorgeous /ˈɡɔːdʒəs/
huge ☞0 /hjuːdʒ/
informal ☞0 /ɪnˈfɔːml/
monumental /ˌmɒnjuˈmentl/
spectacular /spekˈtækjələ(r)/

Adverbs

in the past ☞0 /ˌɪn ðə ˈpɑːst/
since then ☞0 /ˌsɪns ˈðen/

Expressions and idioms

Great idea! ☞0 /ˈɡreɪt aɪˌdɪə/
I reckon ... ☞0 /aɪ ˈrekən/
impressive sight ☞0 /ɪmˌpresɪv ˈsaɪt/
latest adventure film ☞0 /ˌleɪtɪst ədˈventʃə ˌfɪlm/
open to the public ☞0 /ˌəʊpən tə ðə ˈpʌblɪk/
send a text message ☞0 /ˌsend ə ˈtekst ˌmesɪdʒ/
special occasion ☞0 /ˌspeʃl əˈkeɪʒn/
spend a fortune on ☞0 /ˌspend ə ˈfɔːtʃuːn ˌɒn/
the colour goes with ... ☞0 /ðə ˈkʌlə ˌɡəʊz ˌwɪð .../

Phrasal verbs

try on ☞0 /ˌtraɪ ˈɒn/

Prepositions

against ☞0 /əˈɡenst/

/i/ happy	/æ/ flag	/ɜː/ her	/ʊ/ look	/ʌ/ mum	/ɔɪ/ noisy	/ɪə/ here
/ɪ/ it	/ɑː/ art	/ɒ/ not	/uː/ you	/eɪ/ day	/aʊ/ how	/eə/ wear
/iː/ he	/e/ egg	/ɔː/ four	/ə/ sugar	/aɪ/ why	/əʊ/ go	/ʊə/ tourist

Nouns

adding machine   /ˈædɪŋ məˌʃiːn/
business 🔑   /ˈbɪznəs/
calculator   /ˈkælkjəleɪtə(r)/
camcorder   /ˈkæmkɔːdə(r)/
casualty   /ˈkæʒuəlti/
CCTV camera   /ˌsiː ˌsiː ˌtiː ˈviː ˌkæmərə/
CD player 🔑   /ˌsiː ˈdiː ˌpleɪə(r)/
cine camera   /ˈsɪni ˌkæmərə/
crystal radio   /ˌkrɪstl ˈreɪdiəʊ/
DAB radio   /ˌdiː aɪ ˈbiː ˈreɪdiəʊ/
device 🔑   /dɪˈvaɪs/
diagnosis   /ˌdaɪəɡˈnəʊsɪs/
digital camera   /ˌdɪdʒɪtl ˈkæmərə/
disease 🔑   /dɪˈziːz/
environment 🔑   /ɪnˈvaɪrənmənt/
epidemic   /ˌepɪˈdemɪk/
fault 🔑   /fɔːlt/
future 🔑   /ˈfjuːtʃə(r)/
futurist   /ˈfjuːtʃərɪst/
gadget   /ˈɡædʒɪt/
games console   /ˈɡeɪmz ˌkɒnsəʊl/
gramophone   /ˈɡræməfəʊn/
greengrocer   /ˈɡriːnɡrəʊsə(r)/
head 🔑   /hed/
infection   /ɪnˈfekʃn/
instructions 🔑   /ɪnˈstrʌkʃnz/
manufacturer 🔑   /ˌmænjuˈfæktʃərə(r)/
marble   /ˈmɑːbl/
material 🔑   /məˈtɪəriəl/
medicine 🔑   /ˈmedsn/
mobile phone company 🔑   /ˌməʊbaɪl ˈfəʊn ˌkʌmpəni/
modem   /ˈməʊdem/
muscle 🔑   /ˈmʌsl/
nanotechnology   /ˌnænəʊtekˈnɒlədʒi/
nightmare   /ˈnaɪtmeə(r)/
nuclear weapon 🔑   /ˌnjuːkliə ˈwepən/
organ 🔑   /ˈɔːɡən/
outpatient   /ˈaʊtpeɪʃnt/
patient 🔑   /ˈpeɪʃnt/
Polaroid™ camera   /ˈpəʊlərɔɪd ˈkæmərə/
prediction 🔑   /prɪˈdɪkʃn/
reality 🔑   /riˈæləti/
receipt 🔑   /rɪˈsiːt/
ringtone   /ˈrɪŋtəʊn/
robot   /ˈrəʊbɒt/
satellite navigation system   /ˈsætəlaɪt ˌnævɪˈɡeɪʃn ˌsɪstəm/
science   /ˈsaɪəns/
science fiction   /ˌsaɪəns ˈfɪkʃn/
sign (of) 🔑   /ˈsaɪn (əv)/
signature 🔑   /ˈsɪɡnətʃə(r)/
size 🔑   /saɪz/
skeleton   /ˈskelɪtn/
submarine   /ˌsʌbməˈriːn/

success 🔑   /səkˈses/
supermarket chain 🔑   /ˈsuːpəmɑːkɪt ˌtʃeɪn/
tablet 🔑   /ˈtæblət/
technology 🔑   /tekˈnɒlədʒi/
telegraph   /ˈtelɪɡrɑːf/
telephone 🔑   /ˈtelɪfəʊn/
text messaging 🔑   /ˈtekst ˌmesɪdʒɪŋ/
typewriter   /ˈtaɪpraɪtə(r)/
vehicle 🔑   /ˈviːəkl/
video game 🔑   /ˈvɪdiəʊ ˌɡeɪm/
virus 🔑   /ˈvaɪrəs/
webcam   /ˈwebkæm/
word processor   /ˈwɜːd ˌprəʊsesə(r)/

Verbs

access 🔑   /ˈækses/
charge 🔑   /tʃɑːdʒ/
connect 🔑   /kəˈnekt/
consume 🔑   /kənˈsjuːm/
crash 🔑   /ˈkæ ˌkræʃ/
cure 🔑   /kjʊə(r)/
delete 🔑   /dɪˈliːt/
destroy 🔑   /dɪˈstrɔɪ/
diagnose 🔑   /ˈdaɪəɡnəʊz/
fast forward   /ˌfɑːst ˈfɔːwəd/
get annoyed 🔑   /ˌɡet əˈnɔɪd/
going (to) 🔑   /ˈɡəʊɪŋ (tə)/
inject 🔑   /ɪnˈdʒekt/
measure 🔑   /ˈmeʒə(r)/
pause 🔑   /pɔːz/
predict 🔑   /prɪˈdɪkt/
prescribe   /prɪˈskraɪb/
reboot   /ˌriːˈbuːt/
record 🔑   /ˈrɪˈkɔːd/
repair 🔑   /rɪˈpeə(r)/
replace 🔑   /rɪˈpleɪs/
report 🔑   /rɪˈpɔːt/
reproduce 🔑   /ˌriːprəˈdjuːs/
rewind   /ˌriːˈwaɪnd/
shrink 🔑   /ʃrɪŋk/
unplug 🔑   /ˌʌnˈplʌɡ/

Adjectives

addicted (to)   /əˈdɪktɪd (ˌtuː, tə)/
electronic 🔑   /ɪˌlekˈtrɒnɪk/
entire 🔑   /ɪnˈtaɪə(r)/
environmental 🔑   /ɪnˌvaɪrənˈmentl/
everyday   /ˈevrideɪ/
extreme 🔑   /ɪkˈstriːm/
ferocious   /fəˈrəʊʃəs/
futuristic 🔑   /ˌfjuːtʃəˈrɪstɪc/
infectious 🔑   /ɪnˈfekʃəs/
invisible   /ɪnˈvɪzəbl/
medicinal   /məˈdɪsɪnl/
muscular   /ˈmʌskjələ/
scientific 🔑   /ˌsaɪənˈtɪfɪk/
successful 🔑   /səkˈsesfl/
technological   /ˌteknəˈlɒdʒɪkl/

Adverbs

eventually 🔑   /ɪˈventʃuəli/
properly 🔑   /ˈprɒpəli/
under water 🔑   /ˌʌndə ˈwɔːtə(r)/

Expressions and idioms

everyday life   /ˌevrideɪ ˈlaɪf/
hurry up 🔑   /ˌhʌri ˈʌp/
just a minute 🔑   /ˌdʒʌst ə ˈmɪnɪt/
make the world a better/worse place 🔑   /ˌmeɪk ðə ˌwɜːld ə ˌbetə, ˌwɜːs ˈpleɪs/
period of time 🔑   /ˌpɪəriəd əv ˈtaɪm/
receive treatment (for) 🔑   /rɪˌsiːv ˈtriːtmənt fə(r)/
stay in touch (with) 🔑   /ˌsteɪ ɪn ˈtʌtʃ (ˌwɪð)/
tell a lie 🔑   /ˌtel ə ˈlaɪ/
travel around the world 🔑   /ˌtrævl əˌraʊnd ðə ˈwɜːld/

Phrasal verbs

close down 🔑   /ˌkləʊz ˈdaʊn/
plug (sth) in 🔑   /ˌplʌɡ ˈɪn/
switch (on) 🔑   /ˌswɪtʃ (ˈɒn)/
turn (off) 🔑   /ˌtɜːn (ˈɒf)/

Prepositions

in the middle of 🔑   /ˌɪn ðə ˈmɪdl əv/

Literature Corner

chain (n) 🔑   /tʃeɪn/
container (n) 🔑   /kənˈteɪnə(r)/
continuous (adj) 🔑   /kənˈtɪnjuəs/
engine (n) 🔑   /ˈendʒɪn/
mysterious (adj) 🔑   /mɪˈstɪəriəs/

/p/ pen	/d/ dog	/tʃ/ beach	/v/ very	/s/ speak	/ʒ/ television	/n/ now	/r/ radio
/b/ big	/k/ can	/dʒ/ job	/θ/ think	/z/ zoo	/h/ house	/ŋ/ sing	/j/ yes
/t/ two	/g/ good	/f/ food	/ð/ then	/ʃ/ she	/m/ meat	/l/ late	/w/ we

Nouns

authorities 🔑0 /ɔːˈθɒrətiz/
bad luck 🔑0 /ˌbæd ˈlʌk/
ban 🔑0 /bæn/
bucket /ˈbʌkɪt/
casualties /ˈkæʒuəltiz/
celebration 🔑0 /selɪˈbreɪʃn/
chopstick /ˈtʃɒpstɪk/
compliment /ˈkɒmplɪmənt/
concussion /kənˈkʌʃn/
culture 🔑0 /ˈkʌltʃə(r)/
custom 🔑0 /ˈkʌstəm/
festival 🔑0 /ˈfestɪvl/
flock (of birds) /ˌflɒk (əv ˈbɜːdz)/
gesture /ˈdʒestʃə(r)/
good luck 🔑0 /ˌɡʊd ˈlʌk/
graduation do /ˌɡrædʒuˈeɪʃn ˌduː/
greeting /ˈɡriːtɪŋ/
herd (of cows) /ˌhɜːd (əv ˈkaʊz)/
horn 🔑0 /hɔːn/
index finger /ˈɪndeks ˌfɪŋɡə(r)/
limb /lɪm/
mirror 🔑0 /ˈmɪrə(r)/
pack (of wolves) /ˌpæk (əv ˈwʊlvz)/
participant /pɑːˈtɪsɪpənt/
pride (of lions) /ˌpraɪd (əv ˈlaɪənz)/
protest 🔑0 /ˈprəʊtest/
proverb /ˈprɒvɜːb/
respect 🔑0 /rɪˈspekt/
road accident 🔑0 /ˈrəʊd ˌæksɪdənt/
safety rules 🔑0 /ˈseɪfti ruːlz/
school (of sardines) /ˌskuːl (əv ˈweɪlz)/
sole /səʊl/
spectator /spekˈteɪtə(r)/
superstition /suːpəˈstɪʃn/
tradition 🔑0 /trəˈdɪʃn/
troop (of monkeys) /ˌtruːp (əv ˈmʌŋkiz)/
violence 🔑0 /ˈvaɪələns/

Verbs

accept (an invitation) 🔑0 /əkˌsept (ən ɪnvɪˈteɪʃn)/
allow 🔑0 /əˈlaʊ/
authorize 🔑0 /ˈɔːθəraɪz/
ban 🔑0 /bæn/
beckon /ˈbekən/
bow /baʊ/
boycott /ˈbɔɪkɒt/
censor /ˈsensə(r)/
chase 🔑0 /tʃeɪs/
consist (of) 🔑0 /kənˈsɪst (əv)/
decline (an invitation) 🔑0 /dɪˌklaɪn (ən ɪnvɪˈteɪʃn)/
douse /daʊs/
embrace /ɪmˈbreɪs/
escape (from sth) 🔑0 /ɪˈskeɪp frɒm/
exile /ˈeksaɪl, ˈeɡ-/
fall 🔑0 /fɔːl/
frown /fraʊn/
gesticulate /dʒeˈstɪkjuleɪt/
greet sb /ˈɡriːt .../
leap 🔑0 /liːp/
nod 🔑0 /nɒd/
obey 🔑0 /əˈbeɪ/
pack 🔑0 /pæk/
participate (in) /pɑːˈtɪsɪpeɪt (ˌɪn)/
point at sb/sth 🔑0 /ˈpɔɪnt ət .../
pour 🔑0 /pɔː(r)/
prohibit /prəˈhɪbɪt/
reduce 🔑0 /rɪˈdjuːs/
relieve /rɪˈliːv/
rise 🔑0 /raɪz/
soar /sɔː(r)/
throw 🔑0 /θrəʊ/
tie 🔑0 /taɪ/

Adjectives

broken 🔑0 /ˈbrəʊkən/
concerned about 🔑0 /kənˈsɜːnd əbaʊt/
elderly 🔑0 /ˈeldəli/
embarrassing 🔑0 /ɪmˈbærəsɪŋ/
lucky 🔑0 /ˈlʌki/
offensive 🔑0 /əˈfensɪv/
steep 🔑0 /stiːp/
superstitious /suːpəˈstɪʃəs/
unlucky 🔑0 /ʌnˈlʌki/
unpleasant 🔑0 /ʌnˈpleznt/
violent 🔑0 /ˈvaɪələnt/

Adverbs

exactly 🔑0 /ɪɡˈzæktli/
indoors 🔑0 /ɪnˈdɔːz/
politely 🔑0 /pəˈlaɪtli/

Expressions and idioms

an important part of 🔑0 /ən ɪmˈpɔːtnt ˌpɑːt əv/
be able to make it 🔑0 /ˌbi ˌeɪbl tə ˈmeɪk ˌɪt/
be at risk 🔑0 /ˌbi ət ˈrɪsk/
cross your legs 🔑0 /ˌkrɒs jɔː ˈleɡz/
fold your arms 🔑0 /ˌfəʊld jɔːr ˈɑːmz/
give a reason (for) 🔑0 /ˌɡɪv ə ˈriːzn fə(r)/
hold hands 🔑0 /ˌhəʊld ˈhændz/
it might be a good idea to ... 🔑0 /ˌɪt ˈmaɪt ˌbi ə ˌɡʊd aɪˌdɪə tə .../
it's better to ... 🔑0 /ˌɪts ˈbetə tə .../
it's rude to ... 🔑0 /ˌɪts ˈruːd tə .../
it's too bad 🔑0 /ˌɪts ˈtuː ˌbæd/
lose consciousness /ˌluːz ˈkɒnʃəsnəs/
on safari /ˌɒn səˈfɑːri/
pat sb on the back/head /ˌpæt ... ˌɒn ðə ˈbæk, ˈhed/
raise your hat 🔑0 /ˌreɪz jɔː ˈhæt/
serious injury 🔑0 /ˌsɪəriəs ˈɪndʒəri/
shake hands 🔑0 /ˌʃeɪk ˈhændz/
shake your head 🔑0 /ˌʃeɪk jɔː ˈhed/
take part in sth 🔑0 /ˌteɪk ˈpɑːt ˌɪn .../
wave goodbye 🔑0 /ˌweɪv ɡʊdˈbaɪ/
wear a uniform 🔑0 /ˌweər ə ˈjuːnɪfɔːm/

Phrasal verbs

crowd around sb/sth 🔑0 /ˌkraʊd əˈraʊnd/
run after sb/sth 🔑0 /ˌrʌn ˈɑːftə .../
sign up 🔑0 /ˌsaɪn ˈʌp/

/i/ happy	/æ/ flag	/ɜː/ her	/ʊ/ look	/ʌ/ mum	/ɔɪ/ noisy	/ɪə/ here
/ɪ/ it	/ɑː/ art	/ɒ/ not	/uː/ you	/eɪ/ day	/aʊ/ how	/eə/ wear
/iː/ he	/e/ egg	/ɔː/ four	/ə/ sugar	/aɪ/ why	/əʊ/ go	/ʊə/ tourist

Nouns

action 🔑 /'ækʃn/
active volcano /ˌæktɪv vɒl'keɪnəʊ/
atmosphere 🔑 /'ætməsfɪə(r)/
authority 🔑 /ɔː'θɒrəti/
avalanche /'ævəlɑːnʃ/
catastrophe /kə'tæstrəfi/
century 🔑 /'sentʃəri/
child labour 🔑 /ˌtʃaɪld 'leɪbə(r)/
chunk /tʃʌŋk/
coal 🔑 /kəʊl/
coastline /'kəʊstlaɪn/
confusion 🔑 /kən'fjuːʒn/
creation /kri'eɪʃn/
damage 🔑 /'dæmɪdʒ/
decade 🔑 /'dekeɪd/
destruction 🔑 /dɪ'strʌkʃn/
devastation /devə'steɪʃn/
developing world 🔑 /dɪˌveləpɪŋ 'wɜːld/
disaster 🔑 /dɪ'zɑːstə(r)/
disease 🔑 /dɪ'ziːz/
drought /draʊt/
earthquake /'ɜːθkweɪk/
electricity 🔑 /ɪlek'trɪsəti/
endangered species /ɪnˌdeɪndʒəd 'spiːʃiːz/
energy 🔑 /'enədʒi/
environment 🔑 /ɪn'vaɪrənmənt/
eruption /ɪ'rʌpʃn/
famine /'fæmɪn/
flood 🔑 /flʌd/
fortnight /'fɔːtnaɪt/
gas 🔑 /gæs/
global issue 🔑 /ˌgləʊbl 'ɪʃuː/
global warming 🔑 /ˌgləʊbl 'wɔːmɪŋ/
greenhouse gas /'griːnhaʊs ˌgæs/
havoc /'hævək/
homelessness /'həʊmləsnəs/
hurricane /'hʌrɪkən/
information 🔑 /ɪnfə'meɪʃn/
irrigation /ɪrɪ'geɪʃn/
landslide /'lændslaɪd/
leap year /'liːp ˌjɪə(r)/
millennium /mɪ'leniəm/
oil 🔑 /ɔɪl/
ozone layer /'əʊzəʊn ˌleɪə(r)/
pesticide /'pestɪsaɪd/
petrol 🔑 /'petrəl/
piracy /'paɪrəsi/
pollution 🔑 /pə'luːʃn/
poverty 🔑 /'pɒvəti/
prediction /prɪ'dɪkʃn/
protection 🔑 /prə'tekʃn/
public transport 🔑 /ˌpʌblɪk 'trænspɔːt/
quarter 🔑 /'kwɔːtə(r)/
racism /'reɪsɪzəm/
rubbish 🔑 /'rʌbɪʃ/

solar power /ˌsəʊlə 'paʊə(r)/
terrorism /'terərɪzəm/
thunderstorm /'θʌndəstɔːm/
tidal wave /'taɪdl ˌweɪv/
tornado /tɔː'neɪdəʊ/
tsunami /tsuː'nɑːmi/
ultraviolet light /ˌʌltrə ˌvaɪələt 'laɪt/
volcano /vɒl'keɪnəʊ/
warning 🔑 /'wɔːnɪŋ/
water power 🔑 /'wɔːtə ˌpaʊə(r)/
wave power 🔑 /'weɪv ˌpaʊə(r)/
wind power 🔑 /'wɪnd ˌpaʊə(r)/

Verbs

burn 🔑 /bɜːn/
care (about) 🔑 /'keər (əˌbaʊt)/
collapse 🔑 /kə'læps/
decompose 🔑 /diːkəm'pəʊz/
devastate /'devəsteɪt/
dribble /'drɪbl/
drip /drɪp/
erupt /ɪ'rʌpt/
evacuate /ɪ'vækjueɪt/
explode 🔑 /ɪk'spləʊd/
face 🔑 /feɪs/
fear (that) 🔑 /'fɪə (ðət)/
flatten /'flætn/
found 🔑 /faʊnd/
improve 🔑 /ɪm'pruːv/
invest (in) 🔑 /ɪn'vest (ɪn)/
irrigate /'ɪrɪgeɪt/
look (towards) 🔑 /'lʊk (təˌwɔːdz)/
plunge /plʌndʒ/
pollute /pə'luːt/
prevent 🔑 /prɪ'vent/
produce /prə'djuːs/
record 🔑 /rɪ'kɔːd/
recycle /riː'saɪkl/
reduce 🔑 /rɪ'djuːs/
smash 🔑 /smæʃ/
soak /səʊk/
spill /spɪl/
splash /splæʃ/
squirt /skwɜːt/
unleash /ʌn'liːʃ/
vaccinate /'væksɪneɪt/
water 🔑 /'wɔːtə(r)/

Adjectives

catastrophic /kætə'strɒfɪk/
compulsory /kəm'pʌlsəri/
entire 🔑 /ɪn'taɪə(r)/
illegal 🔑 /ɪ'liːgl/
optional /'ɒpʃənl/
organic /ɔː'gænɪk/
petrol-driven 🔑 /'petrəl ˌdrɪvn/
renewable /rɪ'njuːəbl/
smaller 🔑 /'smɔːlə(r)/
steep 🔑 /stiːp/
unusual 🔑 /ʌn'juːʒuəl/

Adverbs

accidentally 🔑 /æksɪ'dentəli/
at the weekends 🔑 /ət ðə wiːk'endz/
furthermore /fɜːðə'mɔː(r)/
inland /ɪn'lænd/

Expressions and idioms

as I see it … 🔑 /əz ˌaɪ ˌsiː ˌɪt/
express (an) opinion 🔑 /ɪkˌspres (ən) ə'pɪnjən/
I believe that … 🔑 /ˌaɪ bɪ'liːv ðət …/
I think that … 🔑 /ˌaɪ 'θɪŋk ðət …/
I'm convinced that … 🔑 /ˌaɪm kən'vɪnst ðət …/
In my view … 🔑 /ˌɪn 'maɪ ˌvjuː …/
leave sth standing 🔑 /ˌliːv … 'stændɪŋ/
make sure (that) 🔑 /'meɪk ˌʃʊə (ðət)/
rule (the world) 🔑 /ˌruːl (ðə 'wɜːld)/
the arms trade 🔑 /ðiː 'ɑːmz ˌtreɪd/

Phrasal verb

pick up 🔑 /ˌpɪk 'ʌp/

Determiner

the rest (of) 🔑 /ðə 'rest (əv)/

Literature Corner

alarmed (adj) 🔑 /ə'lɑːmd/
branch (n) 🔑 /brɑːntʃ/
hedge (n) /hedʒ/
moor (n) /mɔː(r)/

/p/ pen	/d/ dog	/tʃ/ beach	/v/ very	/s/ speak	/ʒ/ television	/n/ now	/r/ radio
/b/ big	/k/ can	/dʒ/ job	/θ/ think	/z/ zoo	/h/ house	/ŋ/ sing	/j/ yes
/t/ two	/g/ good	/f/ food	/ð/ then	/ʃ/ she	/m/ meat	/l/ late	/w/ we

Nouns

author ☞0 /ˈɔːθə(r)/
backup /ˈbækʌp/
bank robber /ˈbæŋk ˌrɒbə(r)/
burglar /ˈbɜːɡlə(r)/
burglary /ˈbɜːɡləri/
bus shelter ☞0 /ˈbʌs ˌʃeltə(r)/
chaos /ˈkeɪɒs/
clue /kluː/
computer program ☞0 /kəmˈpjuːtə ˌprəʊɡræm/
court ☞0 /kɔːt/
crime scene ☞0 /ˈkraɪm ˌsiːn/
criminal ☞0 /ˈkrɪmɪnl/
detective /dɪˈtektɪv/
file ☞0 /faɪl/
fraud /frɔːd/
fraudster /ˈfrɔːdstə(r)/
halt /hɔːlt/
information technology /ˌɪnfəˌmeɪʃn tekˈnɒlədʒi/
investigation ☞0 /ɪnvestɪˈɡeɪʃn/
joyrider /ˈdʒɔɪraɪdə(r)/
joyriding /ˈdʒɔɪraɪdɪŋ/
murder ☞0 /ˈmɜːdə(r)/
murderer /ˈmɜːdərə(r)/
postal service /ˈpəʊstl ˌsɜːvɪs/
punishment ☞0 /ˈpʌnɪʃmənt/
radio programme ☞0 /ˈreɪdiəʊ ˌprəʊɡræm/
reward ☞0 /rɪˈwɔːd/
robber /ˈrɒbə(r)/
robbery /ˈrɒbəri/
shoplifter /ˈʃɒplɪftə(r)/
shoplifting /ˈʃɒplɪftɪŋ/
software ☞0 /ˈsɒftweə(r)/
theft /θeft/
thief ☞0 /θiːf/
tip-off /ˈtɪp ˌɒf/
trial ☞0 /ˈtraɪəl/
vandal ☞0 /ˈvændl/
vandalism ☞0 /ˈvændəlɪzəm/
witness ☞0 /ˈwɪtnəs/

Verbs

admit ☞0 /ədˈmɪt/
arrest ☞0 /əˈrest/
attach ☞0 /əˈtætʃ/
burgle /ˈbɜːɡl/
charge ☞0 /tʃɑːdʒ/
cheat ☞0 /tʃiːt/
click ☞0 /klɪk/
crash ☞0 /kræʃ/
create problems (for) ☞0 /kriˌeɪt ˈprɒbləmz (fə)/
delete /dɪˈliːt/
infect ☞0 /ɪnˈfekt/
install ☞0 /ɪnˈstɔːl/
murder ☞0 /ˈmɜːdə(r)/
need (to do sth) ☞0 /ˌniːd (tə ˈduː ...)/
protect ☞0 /prəˈtekt/
question sb about ☞0 /ˈkwestʃən ... əˌbaʊt/
realize ☞0 /ˈriːəlaɪz/
release ☞0 /rɪˈliːs/
smash ☞0 /smæʃ/
spread ☞0 /spred/
steal (from) ☞0 /stiːl (frəm)/
take sth out (of) ☞0 /ˌteɪk ... ˈaʊt (əv)/
trace ☞0 /treɪs/
update ☞0 /ʌpˈdeɪt/
vandalize /ˈvændəlaɪz/

Adjectives

astonished /əˈstɒnɪʃt/
brilliant ☞0 /ˈbrɪliənt/
careless ☞0 /ˈkeələs/
delighted ☞0 /dɪˈlaɪtɪd/
enormous ☞0 /ɪˈnɔːməs/
first-class /ˈfɜːst ˌklɑːs/
guilty ☞0 /ˈɡɪlti/
identical /aɪˈdentɪkl/
second-hand /ˈsekənd ˌhænd/
terrible ☞0 /ˈterəbl/
terrific /təˈrɪfɪk/
terrified /ˈterɪfaɪd/
tiny ☞0 /ˈtaɪni/
unknown ☞0 /ʌnˈnəʊn/
vital ☞0 /ˈvaɪtl/

Adverbs

after a while ☞0 /ˌɑːftər ə ˈwaɪl/
as soon as ☞0 /əz ˈsuːn əz/
at first ☞0 /ət ˈfɜːst/
earlier ☞0 /ˈɜːliə(r)/
eventually ☞0 /ɪˈventʃuəli/
in the end ☞0 /ˌɪn ðɪ ˈend/
regularly ☞0 /ˈreɡjələli/

Preposition

within ☞0 /wɪˈðɪn/

Expressions and idioms

a second chance ☞0 /ə ˌsekənd ˈtʃɑːns/
admit guilt (to) /ədˌmɪt ˈɡɪlt (tə)/
admit one's guilt ☞0 /ədˌmɪt ... ˈɡɪlt/
by the time ... ☞0 /ˌbaɪ ðə ˈtaɪm .../
commit a crime ☞0 /kəˌmɪt ə ˈkraɪm/
create havoc /kriˌeɪt ˈhævək/
criminal damage ☞0 /ˌkrɪmɪnl ˈdæmɪdʒ/
find sb guilty (of) ☞0 /ˌfaɪnd ... ˈɡɪlti (əv)/
go joyriding /ˌɡəʊ ˈdʒɔɪraɪdɪŋ/
prison sentence ☞0 /ˈprɪzn ˌsentəns/
rob someone/a bank/shop ☞0 /ˈrɒb ..., ə ˌbæŋk, ʃɒp/
send sb to prison ☞0 /ˌsend ... tə ˈprɪzn/
suspended sentence /səˌspendɪd ˈsentəns/
the following (day) ☞0 /ðə ˌfɒləʊɪŋ (ˈdeɪ)/
the next (day) ☞0 /ðə ˌnekst (ˈdeɪ)/

Phrasal verb

go off ☞0 /ˌɡəʊ ˈɒf/

Conjunction

while ☞0 /waɪl/

/i/ happy	/æ/ flag	/ɜː/ her	/ʊ/ look	/ʌ/ mum	/ɔɪ/ noisy	/ɪə/ here
/ɪ/ it	/ɑː/ art	/ɒ/ not	/uː/ you	/eɪ/ day	/aʊ/ how	/eə/ wear
/iː/ he	/e/ egg	/ɔː/ four	/ə/ sugar	/aɪ/ why	/əʊ/ go	/ʊə/ tourist

Nouns

account /əˈkaʊnt/
achievement /əˈtʃiːvmənt/
algebra /ˈældʒɪbrə/
ambassador /æmˈbæsədə(r)/
antibiotic /ˌæntibaɪˈɒtɪk/
cafeteria /ˌkæfəˈtɪəriə/
caravan /ˈkærəvæn/
cargo /ˈkɑːɡəʊ/
carriage /ˈkærɪdʒ/
character /ˈkærəktə(r)/
civil servant /ˌsɪvl ˈsɜːvənt/
coast /kəʊst/
combustion engine /kəmˈbʌstʃən endʒɪn/
conclusion /kənˈkluːʒn/
contact lens /ˈkɒntækt lenz/
contemporaries /kənˈtemprəriz/
contribution /kɒntrɪˈbjuːʃn/
creator /kriˈeɪtə(r)/
departures board /dɪˈpɑːtʃəz ˌbɔːd/
derrick /ˈderɪk/
destination /destɪˈneɪʃn/
detective /dɪˈtektɪv/
development /dɪˈveləpmənt/
diesel oil /ˈdiːzl ˌɔɪl/
diplomat /ˈdɪpləmæt/
discovery /dɪˈskʌvəri/
dishwasher /ˈdɪʃwɒʃə(r)/
electricity /ɪˌlekˈtrɪsəti/
emergency /ɪˈmɜːdʒənsi/
explorer /ɪkˈsplɔːrə(r)/
founder /ˈfaʊndə(r)/
freezer /ˈfriːzə(r)/
fridge /frɪdʒ/
frozen food /ˌfrəʊzn ˈfuːd/
gaol /dʒeɪl/
gasoline /ˈɡæsəliːn/
geometry /dʒiˈɒmətri/
goods /ɡʊdz/
gravity /ˈɡrævəti/
guard /ɡɑːd/
harbour /ˈhɑːbə(r)/
hardship /ˈhɑːdʃɪp/
hovercraft /ˈhɒvəkrɑːft/
information desk /ˌɪnfəˈmeɪʃn ˌdesk/
invention /ɪnˈvenʃn/
inventor /ɪnˈventə(r)/
kerosene /ˈkerəsiːn/
locomotive /ˌləʊkəˈməʊtɪv/
mathematician /ˌmæθəməˈtɪʃn/
merchant /ˈmɜːtʃənt/
microwave oven /ˈmaɪkrəʊweɪv ˌʌvn/
mobile phone /ˌməʊbaɪl ˈfəʊn/
MP3 player /em piː ˈθriː pleɪə(r)/

novel /ˈnɒvl/
nuclear power /ˌnjuːkliə ˈpaʊə(r)/
oil refinery /ˈɔɪl rɪˌfaɪnəri/
opinion /əˈpɪnjən/
passenger /ˈpæsɪndʒə(r)/
penicillin /penɪˈsɪlɪn/
pilgrimage /ˈpɪlɡrɪmɪdʒ/
pilot /ˈpaɪlət/
pipeline /ˈpaɪplaɪn/
plastics /ˈplæstɪks/
platform /ˈplætfɔːm/
printing press /ˈprɪntɪŋ ˌpres/
reason /ˈriːzn/
route /ruːt/
scholar /ˈskɒlə(r)/
shipwreck /ˈʃɪprek/
sleeping car /ˈsliːpɪŋ ˌkɑː(r)/
solar system /ˈsəʊlə ˌsɪstəm/
source /sɔːs/
space shuttle /speɪs ˈʃʌtl/
spice /spaɪs/
story /ˈstɔːri/
telegram /ˈtelɪɡræm/
telescope /ˈtelɪskəʊp/
theology /θiˈɒlədʒi/
ticket inspector /ˈtɪkɪt ɪnˌspektə(r)/
ticket office /ˈtɪkɪt ˌɒfɪs/
vaccination /væksɪˈneɪʃn/
waiting area /ˈweɪtɪŋ ˌeəriə/
waterwheel /ˈwɔːtəwiːl/
X-ray /ˈeks ˌreɪ/

Verbs

abandon /əˈbændən/
appreciate /əˈpriːʃieɪt/
cause /kɔːz/
combine (with) /kəmˈbaɪn (ˌwɪð)/
create /kriˈeɪt/
depart /dɪˈpɑːt/
develop /dɪˈveləp/
drill /drɪl/
erect /ɪˈrekt/
guide sb/sth in/into /ˈɡaɪd ... ˌɪn, ˌɪntə/
imprison /ɪmˈprɪzn/
locate /ləʊˈkeɪt/
motivate /ˈməʊtɪveɪt/
navigate /ˈnævɪɡeɪt/
object (to) /əbˈdʒekt (tə)/
power /ˈpaʊə(r)/
pump /pʌmp/
reach (a destination) /ˌriːtʃ (ə destɪˈneɪʃn)/
refine /rɪˈfaɪn/
retire /rɪˈtaɪə(r)/
separate /ˈsepəreɪt/

survive /səˈvaɪv/
walk (on) /ˈwɔːk (ˌɒn)/
write (an account of) /ˈraɪt (ən əˌkaʊnt əv)/

Adjectives

additional /əˈdɪʃənl/
available /əˈveɪləbl/
convenient /kənˈviːniənt/
greatest /ˈɡreɪtɪst/
influential /ˌɪnfluˈenʃl/
inspired /ɪnˈspaɪəd/
modern /ˈmɒdn/
pasteurized /ˈpɑːstʃəraɪzd/
significant /sɪɡˈnɪfɪkənt/
wealthy /ˈwelθi/

Adverbs

clearly /ˈklɪəli/
overland /ˌəʊvəˈlænd/
shortly after /ˈʃɔːtli ˌɑːftə(r)/
underground /ˌʌndəˈɡraʊnd/

Expressions and idioms

alternative source (of) /ɔːlˈtɜːnətɪv ˌsɔːs əv/
be impressed by /ˌbi ɪmˈprest ˌbaɪ/
be located in /ˌbi ləʊˈkeɪtɪd ɪn/
become an expert (in) /bɪˌkʌm ən ˈekspɜːt (ˌɪn)/
renewable energy /rɪˌnjuːəbl ˈenədʒi/
without a doubt /wɪˌðaʊt ə ˈdaʊt/

Phrasal verbs

blast off /ˌblɑːst ˈɒf/
check in /ˌtʃek ˈɪn/
check out /ˌtʃek ˈaʊt/
drop sb off /ˌdrɒp ... ˈɒf/
get back /ˌɡet ˈbæk/
get off /ˌɡet ˈɒf/
get on /ˌɡet ˈɒn/
pick sb up /ˌpɪk ... ˈʌp/
set off /ˌset ˈɒf/
touch down /ˌtʌtʃ ˈdaʊn/

Preposition

throughout /θruːˈaʊt/

Literature Corner

aye /aɪ/
cabin (n) /ˈkæbɪn/
kidnap (v) /ˈkɪdnæp/
lad (n) /læd/

/p/ pen	/d/ dog	/tʃ/ beach	/v/ very	/s/ speak	/ʒ/ television	/n/ now	/r/ radio
/b/ big	/k/ can	/dʒ/ job	/θ/ think	/z/ zoo	/h/ house	/ŋ/ sing	/j/ yes
/t/ two	/g/ good	/f/ food	/ð/ then	/ʃ/ she	/m/ meat	/l/ late	/w/ we

IRREGULAR VERB LIST

Base form	Past simple	Past participle
be	was/were	been
become	became	become
begin	began	begun
bend	bent	bent
bite	bit	bitten
blow	blew	blown
break	broke	broken
bring	brought	brought
build	built	built
burn	burnt	burnt
buy	bought	bought
can	could	been able to
catch	caught	caught
choose	chose	chosen
come	came	come
cost	cost	cost
cut	cut	cut
do	did	done
draw	drew	drawn
drink	drank	drunk
drive	drove	driven
eat	ate	eaten
fall	fell	fallen
feel	felt	felt
fight	fought	fought
find	found	found
fly	flew	flown
forget	forgot	forgotten
get	got	got
give	gave	given
go	went	gone
grow	grew	grown
hang	hung	hung
have	had	had
hear	heard	heard
hide	hid	hidden
hit	hit	hit
keep	kept	kept
know	knew	known
lay	laid	laid
lead	led	led
learn	learnt/-ed	learnt/-ed
leave	left	left
lend	lent	lent
lose	lost	lost

Base form	Past simple	Past participle
make	made	made
mean	meant	meant
meet	met	met
overcome	overcame	overcome
pay	paid	paid
put	put	put
read	read	read
ride	rode	rode
ring	rang	rung
rise	rose	risen
run	ran	run
say	said	said
see	saw	seen
sell	sold	sold
send	sent	sent
set	set	set
shake	shook	shaken
shine	shone	shone
shoot	shot	shot
show	showed	shown/-ed
shrink	shrunk	shrunk
shut	shut	shut
sing	sang	sung
sink	sank	sunk
sit	sat	sat
sleep	slept	slept
smell	smelt/-ed	smelt/-ed
speak	spoke	spoken
spell	spelt/-ed	spelt/-ed
spend	spent	spent
spread	spread	spread
spill	spilt/-ed	spilt/-ed
stand	stood	stood
steal	stole	stolen
swim	swam	swum
take	took	taken
teach	taught	taught
tell	told	told
think	thought	thought
throw	threw	thrown
understand	understood	understood
wake	woke	woken
wear	wore	worn
win	won	won
write	wrote	written

OXFORD
UNIVERSITY PRESS

Great Clarendon Street, Oxford OX2 6DP

Oxford University Press is a department of the University of Oxford.
It furthers the University's objective of excellence in research, scholarship,
and education by publishing worldwide in

Oxford New York

Auckland Cape Town Dar es Salaam Hong Kong Karachi
Kuala Lumpur Madrid Melbourne Mexico City Nairobi
New Delhi Shanghai Taipei Toronto

With offices in

Argentina Austria Brazil Chile Czech Republic France Greece
Guatemala Hungary Italy Japan Poland Portugal Singapore
South Korea Switzerland Thailand Turkey Ukraine Vietnam

OXFORD and OXFORD ENGLISH are registered trade marks of
Oxford University Press in the UK and in certain other countries

© Oxford University Press 2010

The moral rights of the author have been asserted

Database right Oxford University Press (maker)

First published 2010

2014 2013 2012 2011 2010

10 9 8 7 6 5 4 3 2 1

ISBN: 978 0 19 445304 2

Printed in China

This book is printed on paper from certified and well-managed sources.

ACKNOWLEDGEMENTS

*The authors and publisher are grateful to those who have given permission to reproduce
the following extracts and adaptations of copyright material:* p.20 Extract from
Oxford Bookworms Library 3: *The Call of the Wild* by Jack London, retold by
Nick Bullard © Oxford University Press 2008. Reproduced by permission;
p.22 Adapted from *Introducing the mayor of Monowi: (population: 1)* by Tim
Reid, 19 February 2005, *The Times* © The Times 19.02.05/nisyndication.com.
Reproduced by permission; p.38 Extract from Oxford Bookworms Library 3:
The Railway Children by Edith Nesbit, retold by John Escott © Oxford University
Press 2008. Reproduced by permission; p.56 Extract from Oxford Bookworms
Library 4: *Gulliver's Travels* by Jonathan Swift, retold by Clare West © Oxford
University Press 2008. Reproduced by permission; p.71 *I Wish I Knew How It
Would Feel To Be Free* (Billy Taylor and Dick Dallas) © 1964 Duane Music Inc.
Assigned to Westminster Music Ltd. of Suite 2.07, Plaza 535 King's Road,
London, SW10 0SZ. International Copyright secured. All rights reserved.
Used by permission; p.74 Extract from Oxford Bookworms Library 4: *The
Thirty-Nine Steps* by John Buchan, retold by Nick Bullard © Oxford University
Press 2008. Reproduced by permission; p.92 Extract from Oxford Bookworms
Library 3: *Kidnapped* by Robert Louis Stevenson, retold by Clare West © Oxford
University Press 2008. Reproduced by permission.

Sources: p.30 www.wikipedia.com

*The publisher would like to thank the following for permission to reproduce
photographs:* AA World Travel Photography p.27; Alamy pp.4 (Businessman/
RMT), 4 (Mechanic/Ingram Publishing (Superstock Limited)), 4 (Girl in
school uniform/Gaertner), 28 (Medieval city wall, York/Graham Oliver),
32 (Flooded town/blickwinkel), 32 (Exhausted woman/allOver photography),
32 (Stressed man/Dellnesco), 37 (Mountaineering/Philippe Roy), 37 (London
Marathon/bobhdeering sport), 37 (Lifeguard/Charles Stirling), 44 (Shopping
for clothes/Ace Stock Limited), 44 (Shop/Mr Standfast), 44 (Newsagent/
Photofusion Picture Library), 60 (Lion pride/uwesMASAIMARA), 57 (Ethan,
Cindy), 79 (dj), 83 (Truncheon/Friedrich Saurer), 83 (Policeman wearing riot
gear/RTimages), 83 (Police officer/Joe Fox), 88 (Johann Gutenberg's printing
press Mainz Germany 1450s/North Wind Picture Archives), 88 (Freezer/Mark
Philips), 88 (Falling apple/Steve Hynes), 89 (Maths/Steven May), 90 (Garbage
landfill/David Ball), 91 (Mercedes car/WoodyStock); Apple p.48 (laptop);

Arnos Design pp.39 (road sign), 48 (Mini), 57 (text message), 63 (mirror),
75 (bag), 89 (Wikipedia); Aquarius Library p.35 (Everyone's Hero poster/
IDT Entertainment); Brunswick Films Ltd p.17; Camera Press p.21; Casio
p.48 (Baby-G watch); Collections p.39 (village); Corbis pp.12, 16 (Tiger
Woods), 20 (Prospectors in tent settlement/Museum of History and Industry),
34 (Mahatma Gandhi/Bettmann), 34 (President Anwar Sadat of Egypt/Kevin
Fleming), 34 (Naguib Mahfouz/epa), 39 (teens), 40 (Warsaw), 41, 44 (baker's),
51 (Map reading/Philippe Chevreuil), 52 (Edison Standard Phonograph/
Bettmann), 57 (Darren), 59 (Pamplona), 63 (magpie, Salamanca), 70 (Monsoon
floods, India/John Henry Claude Wilson/Robert Harding World Imagery),
80 (burglar), 84 (Marco Polo by Giovanni Antonio da Varese/The Gallery
Collection), 85 (Portrait of Vasco da Gama/Stefano Bianchetti), 88 (Internal
combustion engine/Frank Cruz/Monsoon/Photolibrary), 111; European
Youth Eco Parliament p.75 (logo); Getty pp.8 (Woman with rose under her
nose/Stuart O'Sullivan), 8 (Man wearing black shirt/Dougal Waters), 8 (Boy
lazing on sofa/Ann Summa), 8 (Businesswoman/LWA), 15 (Moussambani,
Rafter), 16 (Footballer), 33 (Footballer Amr Zaki/AFP), 61 (Family dinner/
Jon Riley), 95 (Teenage girl talking on phone/Rebecca Emery); iStockphoto
pp.5 (Nurse/Chris Schmidt), 45 (Machu Picchu/Amy Harris), 64 (College
graduate/Sean Locke), 68 (Hurricane/Chieh Cheng), 68 (Dry lake/Miguel
Angelo Silva), 68 (Tornado/Sean Martin), 68 (Earthquake/Rui Pestana),
68 (Avalanche/Lorenzo Puricelli), 68 (Lightning/Clint Spencer), 72 (Woman
contemplating/James Steidl), 79 (car), Images 83 (Police helmet/Marianna
Bettini), 83 (Handcuffs/James Brey), 83 (Flashlight), 84 (Treasure map
background), 88 (Power Station), 88 (Medicine capsules/Denis Dryashkin),
88 (Telescope/Mark Evans); Ron Morris/2bangkok.com p.58 (Thailand);
Muslim Heritage Images p.85 (Artistic impression of Ibn Battuta/Ali Amro);
Oxford University Press pp.8 (Businesswoman/Photodisc), 8 (Businesswoman/
Photodisc), 9 (both), 10 (both), 40 (Statue of Liberty), 53 (girl), 57 (girl
texting, Paula), 67, 69 (Earth), 70 (panda), 88 (Putting in contact lenses/
Good Shoot), 88 (X-ray/Photodisc), 88 (Milk/Mark Mason), 97 (Eating pizza/
Photodisc), 105 (Girl using laptop/Corbis); Panos Pictures p.70 (poverty, child
labour); Photolibrary pp.5 (Military uniform/Photodisc), 32 (Surprised girl/
Image Source), 32 (Bored student/Banana Stock), 37 (Surgeon/Silverstock/
Digital Vision), 37 (Man on construction site/Image100), 61 (Shoes at
restaurant entrance, Kyoto/Glow Images), 87 (Nodding donkey/Digital
Vision); Popperfoto p.15 (football); PunchStock p.52 (Adding machine/
Brand X Pictures); Delia & Kathy Purviance p.22 (bottom); Rex Features
pp.13, 16 (Roger Federer/C Petch/Newspix), 36 (*The Old Man and the Sea* –
Spencer Tracy/Everett Collection), 37 (Paramedic/Image Source), 59 (cheese
rolling), 69 (Darryl Hannah), 70 (homeless), 113; Science and Society Picture
Library p.52 (Bain's chemical telegraph, 1850/Science Museum); Science
Photo Library pp.48 (satellite, robot, CCTV), 52 (1930s movie camera),
52 (Crystal radio set/Sheila Terry), 70 (pollution), 75 (crop spraying, power
station), 80 (shoplifter, rubber), 93; TRH Pictures p.48 (rocket); Dan Tuffs
p.22 (top two).

Illustrations by: Jonas Bergstrand/CIA p.21; Rachel Birkett p.38; Claude
Bordeleau pp.7, 17, 19, 51, 62, 71, 81, 86, 100, 105, 109; Paul Daviz p.82;
Neil Gower p.84; Jean-Luc Guerin/Comillus pp.26, 27; Nick Harris p.56; Andy
Lackow p.25; David Oakley/Arnos Design pp.53, 107; ODI pp.49, 78; ODI pp.6,
30, 42, 66, 87; William Rowsell p.92; Stephen Strong p.77; Ron Tiner p.74.